WATERCOLOUR
THE NATURAL WORLD

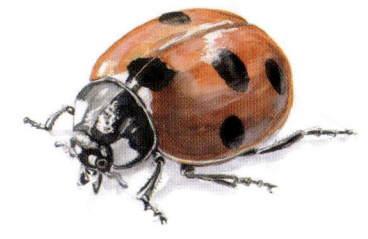

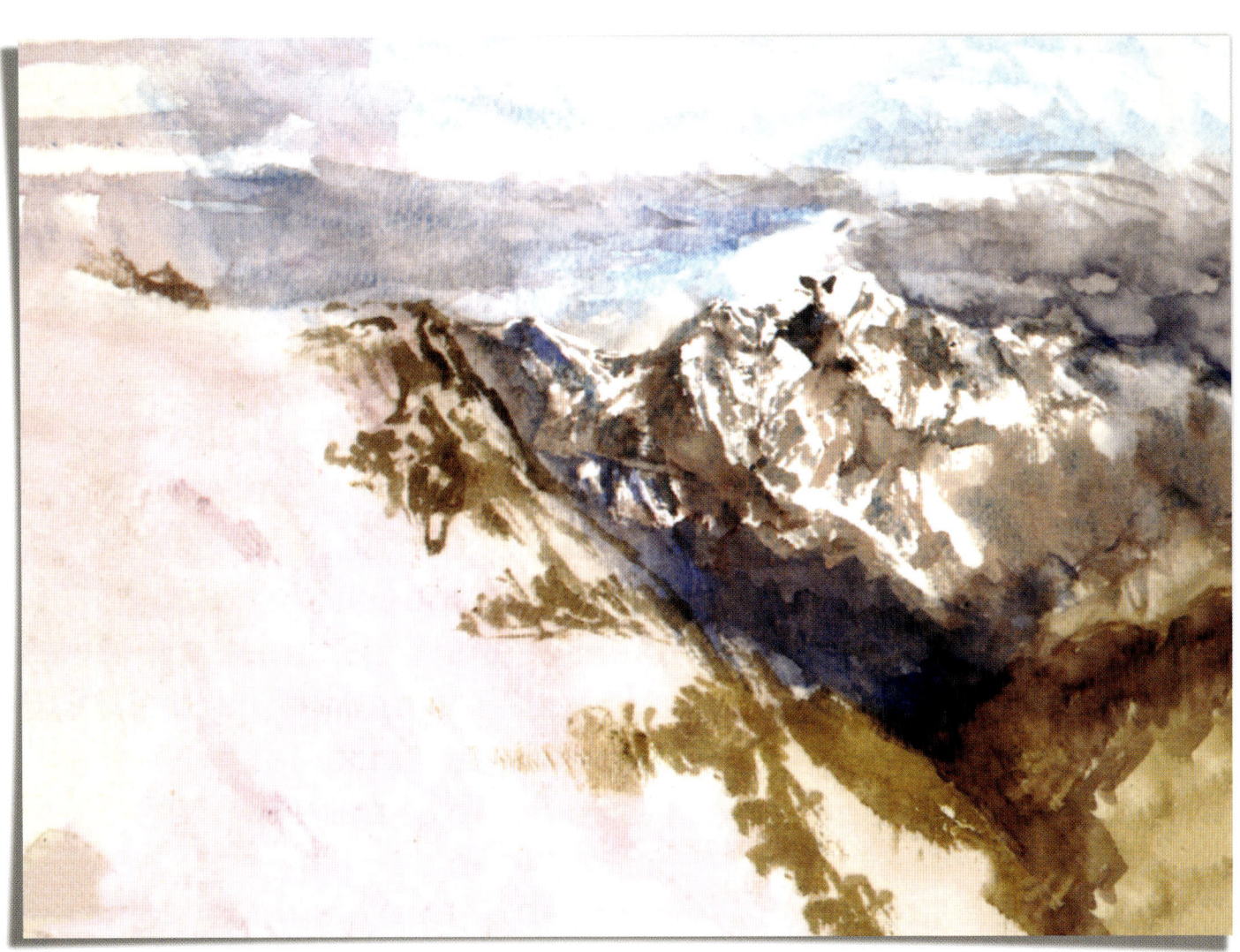

▲ **The Valley of Eagle River, Chugach Mountain Range, Alaska**

When spring comes to Alaska, the snow melts, revealing the scarred craggy rock face beneath and creating mighty churning rivers. In this sketch, I wanted to capture the retreating snow on the jagged rock surface. For economy and speed, I simply left white gaps and sketched the shadows of the ridges and gullies. The rocky texture of the cliffs is created by a dry brush dragged over the surface of the watercolour paper, as I try to capture the rusty-looking sharp shale.

WATERCOLOUR
THE NATURAL WORLD

TIM POND

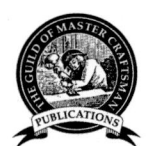

Contents

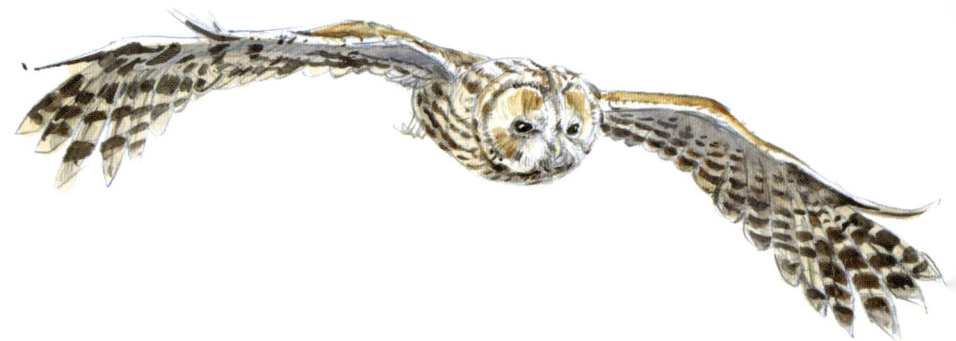

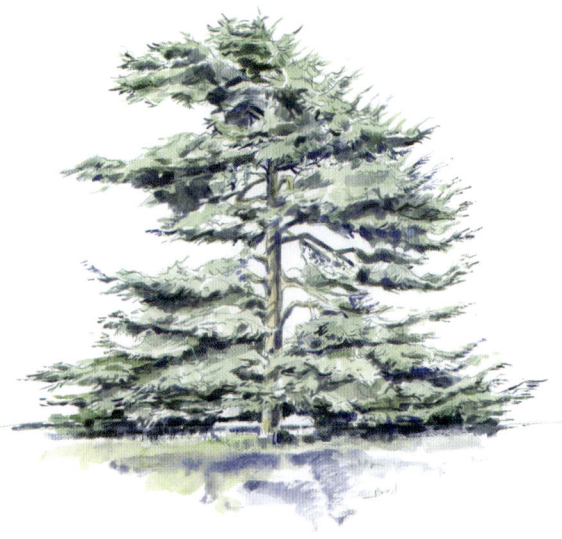
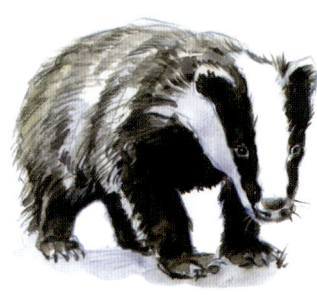
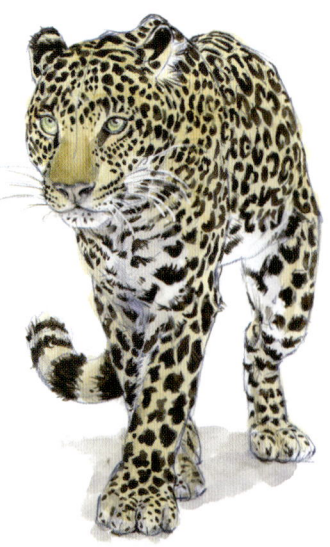

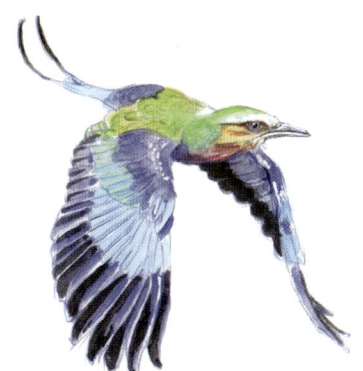

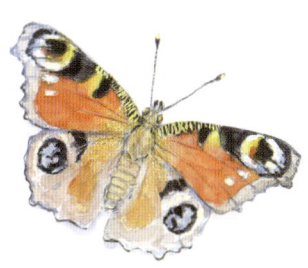

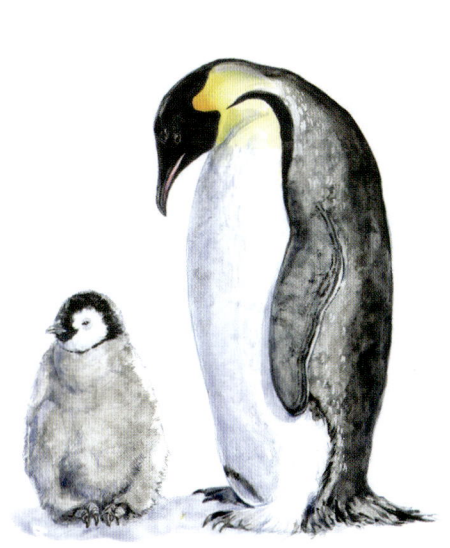

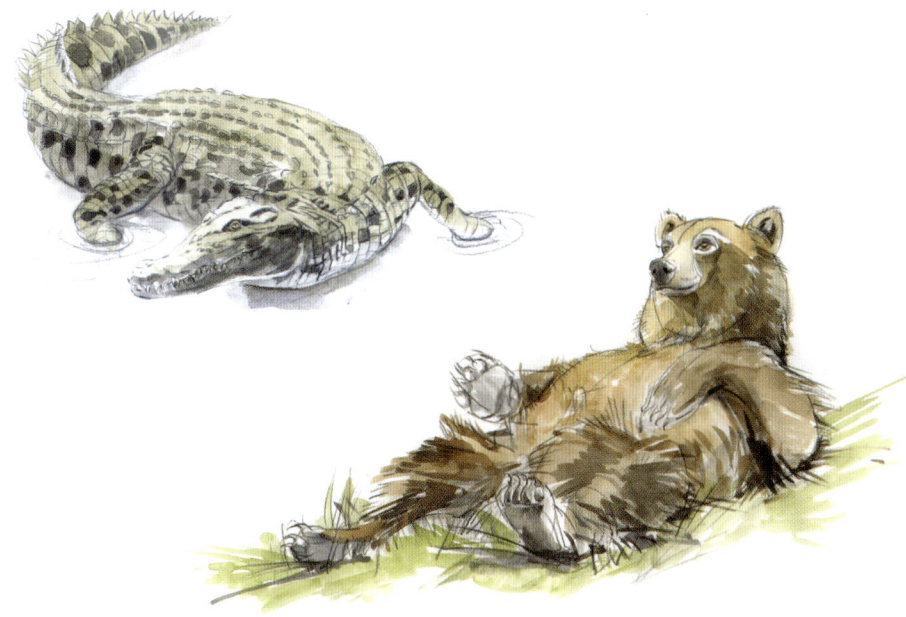

Introduction

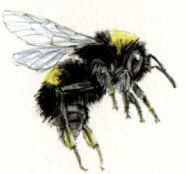

Although often viewed as an activity reserved for those with an innate talent, watercolour is a flexible medium that anyone can learn.

In this book, I want to take you on a journey from pole to pole to discover a wide range of habitats, from pristine frozen wilderness areas and coniferous forests to dense tropical rainforests. I will introduce you to many of the plant and animal species that have made these locations their home. I will also explain some of the adaptations that nature has evolved to survive bitter fierce winters or sweltering rainforest temperatures.

Over the years, I have been fortunate enough to visit many of these places, either in my capacity as an expedition artist or on holiday. When I have not travelled to a specific habitat, then visits to the local botanical gardens, aquarium and natural history museum have sufficed; these places of fascination and wonder are to be celebrated, and I encourage you to explore those that are near to you.

There is pleasure in watercolour painting, which comes from overlaying translucent washes that glow with a unique, vibrant luminosity as light passes through the paint and is reflected on the paper beneath. So get ready to take yourself outside into nature, go on a rambling walk with a sketchbook in hand and explore watercolour in the field.

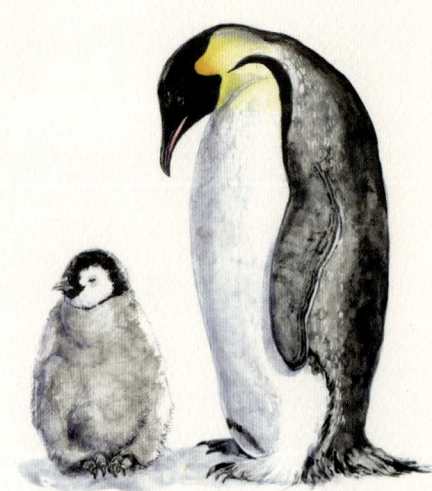

▶ **Emperor penguins**
Emperor penguins have adapted to one of the harshest and most uncompromising habitats in the world, Antarctica. This is a land of barren mountains buried beneath a 2 mile (3km) thick ice cap where freezing winds which can reach up to 200mph (320km/h) and create the equivalent of a sand storm lifting up snow and ice and creating massive white blizzards.

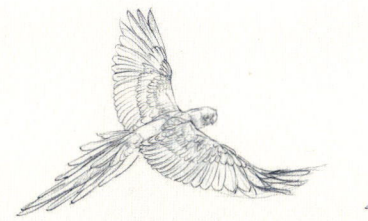 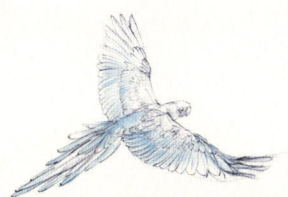 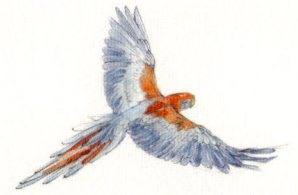 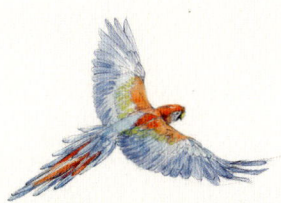

▲ **Macaw in flight**
The liveliness and immediacy of watercolour makes it ideal for capturing the movement of animals. Particles of pigments floating around in the water are in themselves a kinetic medium full of spontaneity and happy accidents.

Why I use watercolour

I began using watercolour in my early twenties when I took part in an expedition in Alaska as an artist. In those conditions, working in oil would have proved impractical, not only because of all the cumbersome equipment I would have had to carry but also because of the lengthy drying time that oils require – any image I created would have quickly become a smeared abstract painting. Watercolour, on the other hand, is an incredibly accessible and portable medium to use. The lightness and simplicity of the materials required – a paint tin, water, paper and a few brushes – meant my art kit could be carried without weighing me down as I travelled through this wild and rugged land. Importantly, too, watercolour paint dries quickly, and its qualities lend themselves to capturing the landscape.

Some of the artwork in this book comes from this incredible adventure, when I explored spectacular landscapes and attempted to capture the ever-changing light and moods in sketchbooks stored in waterproof zipped bags to protect them from the torrents of rain and flurries of snow. Looking at these paintings brings back so many memories, including melting snow over a camp stove to give me water to paint with, as I hurried to capture a glimpse of a blue-white mountain peak while the mist momentarily cleared; and the sound of howling wolves as we kayaked, swept along by the tide, through the myriad gullies of the Prince William Sound, our paddles effortlessly touching the water.

Watercolour has an incredible immediacy that focuses the artist's attention while building up transparent washes. This medium can be used in a great variety of ways to create images that can range from lively impressions of landscapes to detailed botanical studies.

Observing nature and capturing it in watercolour helps everyone to think, feel and understand. The final painting can capture a moment in time and create an indelible memory as you transfer the scene in front of you to the page; perhaps how the sun felt on your cheek or how spots of rain stained your pages when a shower passed overhead... Watercolour painting solidifies the moment, making it more memorable than any photo. To paint in harmony with nature is one of this book's guiding principles, aiming to engender in the reader a connection with nature and to enhance their powers of observation and curiosity.

This book intends to put all plants and animals on an equal footing, as subjects worthy of equal attention in the life room. One of the lessons Charles Darwin taught us some two hundred years ago is that we all depend on each other. All the world's plants and animals play a crucial role in creating the healthy earth on which we also depend. If we want to preserve a species of animal, we need to maintain the whole community of plants and animals that support it. Never has it been more critical for us to develop a compassionate regard for nature. Animals and plants, who have pioneered and adapted to these places, play a vital role in maintaining our habitat's health and even the air we breathe. Watercolour painting is a fantastic way of spending time among nature and developing a healthy respect for its remarkable variety.

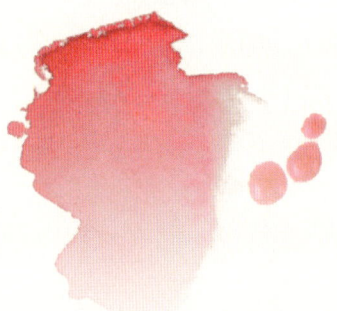

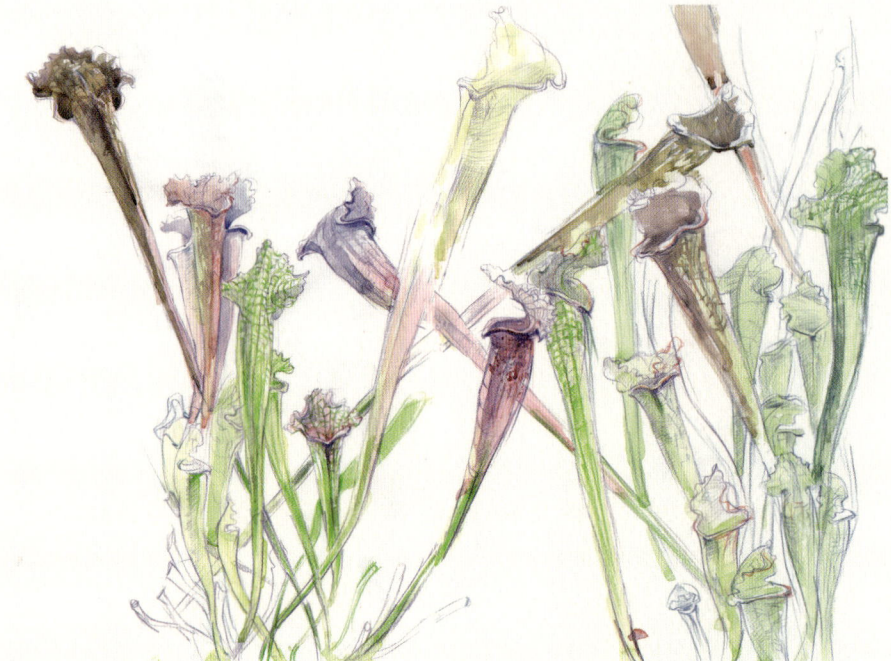

▶ **Pitcher plants**

Pitcher plants have evolved extraordinary leaves that have a more sinister purpose than those of most other plants. Pitcher plants grow in nutrient-poor soil, so they have to find sustenance' in other ways. The leaf grows to create a well of death that attracts flies with the colour and scent of rotting flesh. The lip of the leaf well is so slippery that it is difficult for the fly to grip, and many of them fall to their doom into the digestive juices at the bottom.

How to use this book

The impulse to paint is as natural as talking. Our caveman ancestors began creating animal depictions over 45,000 years ago using the most basic of raw materials. The way we develop as an artist is a very personal journey, often influenced by other artists' work that inspires us along the way. There is no single road in art education, and I believe it is all the better for it. Some students might be more drawn to abstraction or pattern, while others are to Impressionism or Realism. Whichever style attracts us, it is essential to remember that we can learn from the entirety of the history of art. Even in representational art, every brush mark is an abstract equivalent of what the artist is seeing.

I have endeavoured to ensure that every page in this book is packed with handy tips, techniques and critical concepts to speed up your progress at getting the landscape, rock, plant or animal in front of you down on paper. There are also suggested activities to participate in as an individual or part of a social group to create an entertaining afternoon.

For me, learning about the natural world goes hand in hand with developing the skills to capture it. I believe an understanding of a subject helps foster sympathy for it. The more we know, the more we care. So I have tried to include enough information to turn anyone into a budding natural historian, learning many new discoveries myself as I wrote this book. I always encourage my students to see themselves as part of a much broader branching tree of life – as being part of nature rather than separate from it. The act of drawing and painting can bring us all closer to nature and connect with the natural world, which has been proven to have beneficial psychological effects.

Don't feel that you need to read this book from front to back. Once you have the necessary tools and materials (see pages 10–15) and have familiarized yourself with the basic techniques (see pages 16–33), you can start anywhere. The tutorials, which you can dip in and out of, are built upon experiences I have found useful and conducted with my students. Anyone with practice and perseverance can be rewarded with the satisfying feeling of creating a successful sketch, an incremental step in the right direction, whatever your ability.

This book is for all abilities, whether you are entirely new to watercolour painting or an experienced professional, there is always something new to learn. Follow the guidance, but never treat it as gospel or be rigid with the direction. Experiment with your own ideas and techniques and, importantly, have fun!

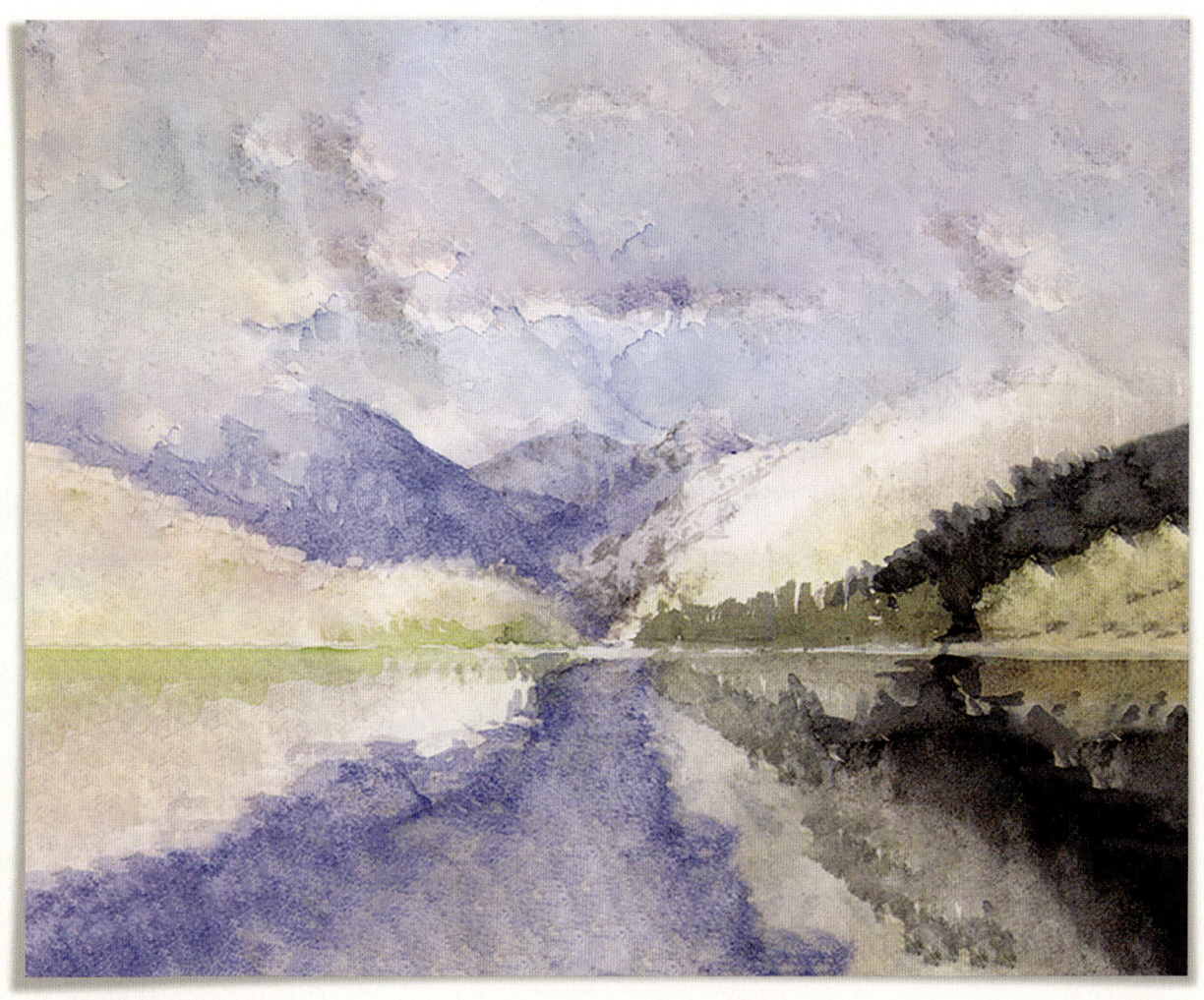

▲ Lake reflections
Prince William Sound, Alaska, USA.

*All around us, the natural world is living,
breathing and growing. We are a small part of
a bigger picture and can feel part of this world
by observing the natural world's beauty.*

Tools and Materials

At its heart, watercolour is a brush, water, pigment and paper. From this, manufacturers have invented a dazzling array of choices. I recommend experimenting, without paying out for very expensive brushes, and over time you will get to know what suits your style of work best.

Paper

I use watercolour paper and thick cartridge paper to paint on. Typically, I use the less expensive cartridge paper when I'm creating study sheets (see page 30) and the more expensive watercolour paper for artwork that I plan to keep long-term.

Watercolour paper

Traditionally, the highest quality watercolour papers are made from cotton fibres. The term 100% rag is used to denote pure cotton fibre content. Others have the addition of wood pulp. Artist-quality watercolour paper is made on a moulding machine, which provides all the appeal of handmade paper. The best papers are acid-free, preventing degradation and creating archival properties.

There are three main surface textures. HP stands for 'hot pressed' and is the smoothest paper suitable for high-detail work, such as natural history illustrations. CP stands for 'cold pressed' and is also commonly known as NOT – as in 'not hot pressed'. It is a slightly textured surface and popular because it is suitable for most types of work. ROUGH is precisely what its name suggests and is suitable when a heavily textured paper will enhance the final work, such as an atmospheric seascape.

The thickness of watercolour paper is indicated by its weight, measured either in pounds per ream (lb) or in grams per square metre (gsm). The standard machine weights are 90lb (190gsm), 140lb (300gsm), 260lb (356gsm) and 300lb (638gsm).

Mid-tone paper

Mid-tone paper is great to experiment with and can be an excellent option for painting animals that have a mottled coat, such as an African hunting dog. You can plunge into the darker values of the pelt with transparent watercolour, then add White Gouache to create the lighter colours. It can also help enhance the white plumage of a duck by creating contrast with the background. I've had good results with Canson Mi-Teintes pastel paper, which comes in a wide range of pretty hues and responds similarly to 90lb (190gsm) cold-pressed watercolour paper. To prevent the paper from buckling, I use less water than when working on watercolour paper. The paper has two distinct surfaces: one side has a fine grain which I prefer, and the other is honeycomb textured.

Sketchbook

Picking a sketchbook is a personal choice. I recommend having several and selecting the one that seems most suitable on the day – I find this is typically a question of portability. I always use hardback sketchbooks, as the cover makes a strong drawing board to rest on. I suggest experimenting with both watercolour and cartridge sketchbooks. Most cartridge sketchbooks feature 27lb (100gsm) medium-grain paper and are available in either spiral or hardbound covers. I find this is thick enough to take watercolour without buckling. I avoid spiral-bound books, as the pages rub together and smudge the artwork. I prefer the paper of my sketchbook to have a bit of a tooth rather than being smooth. My favourite sketchbook, whether watercolour or cartridge, is 11¾ x 16½in (A3 portrait) which can open to 16½ x 23⅜in (A2 size) and create plenty of working space.

▶ **Bringing out contrast**
You can really bring out the contrast of an animal's pelt by sketching on a mid-tone-value paper with White Gouache.

Stretching watercolour paper

When creating a painting I wish to keep, I usually stretch the paper first. This prevents buckling and the ridges that make valleys of stronger pigment. Instead, the surface remains flat and taut. I sometimes even stretch paper with just a sketch on it by dampening the underside of the paper, allowing me to lay down flat washes of watercolour that don't 'pool'. There are only a few rules that you will need to follow to ensure a successful stretch. Very thick paper – above 140lb (300gsm) – doesn't need to be stretched, while thinner papers will buckle when they become damp. Stretching paper involves damping the fibres and then attaching the paper to a rigid surface with gum strip. When the paper dries, it shrinks and becomes taut.

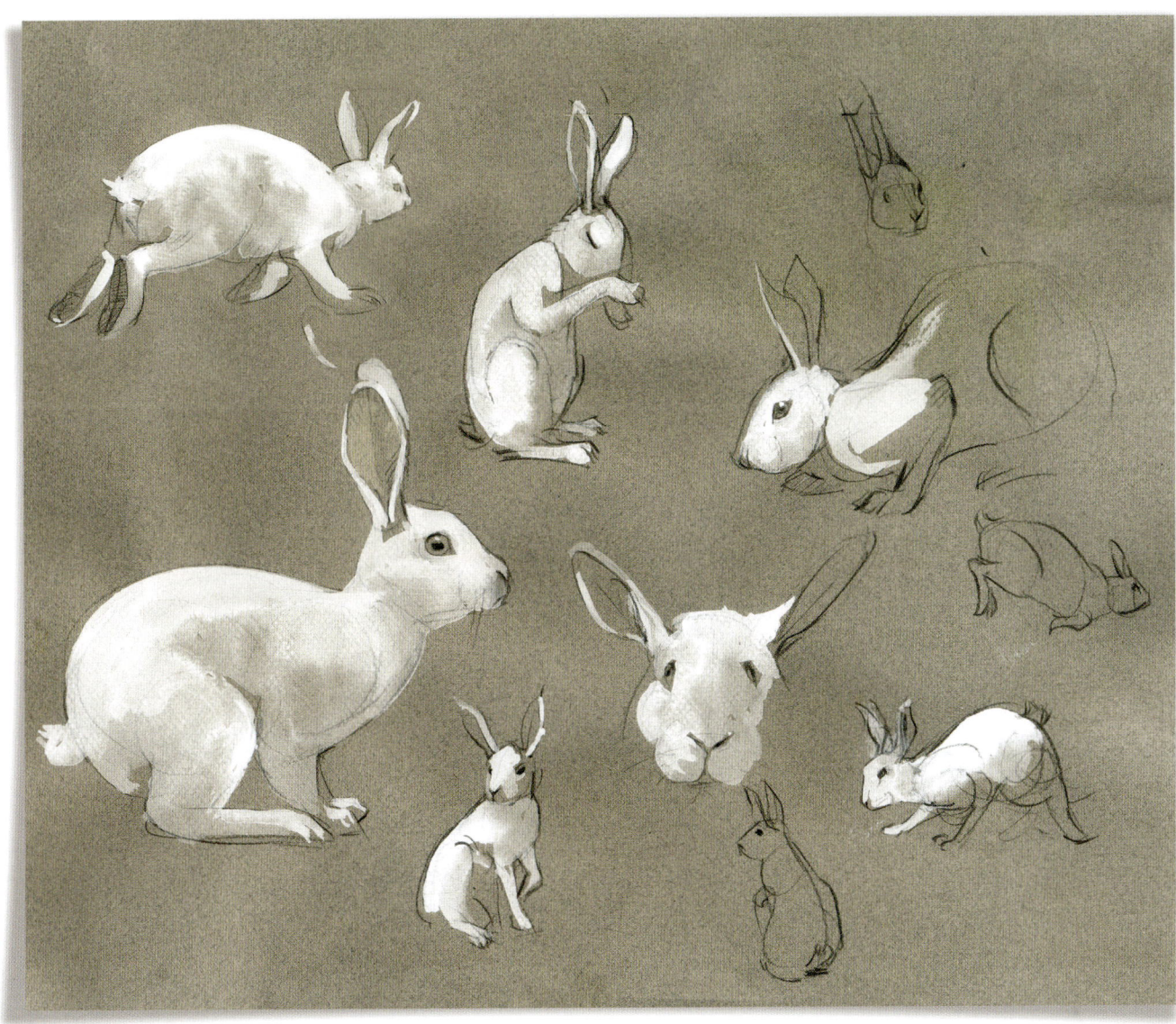

Soaking the paper

Each paper is different. A thinner paper can just be lightly dampened on one side, whereas a thicker paper, higher than 54lb (203gsm), might need to be fully submerged to get the fibres thoroughly sodden. Don't over soak the paper, as you may remove the sizing on the surface and make your paper too absorbent, like blotting paper. I recommend giving the paper a quick dip in a large water bath or wiping it with a large, soft sponge.

Taping down

Next, wet a wooden drawing board thoroughly on one side, ensuring it is at least 1½in (4cm) bigger than your paper to give the gum strip space to adhere to the wood. Take the wet paper

and place one of the short edges at the lip of the board. Bow the paper so that it bends in a smooth curve and lay the paper down on the board, trying to avoid large air pockets. Small air pockets are to be expected and won't affect the overall stretch. If your paper does not land flat, lift it up and try again. Smooth the paper gently with a soft, clean sponge, being careful not to damage the surface of the paper, lifting off puddles of water. It is best to work with a reasonably wide gum strip, around 2in (5cm), and ensure it has 50/50 contact with the paper and board. Wet the tape by either running it under a tap or rubbing it with a wet sponge. Be careful not to over soak the tape, as this will cause it to lose some of its adherence. Then, leave it to dry for a few hours and your paper should be wonderfully taut and an excellent surface to work on.

Drawing board and gummed tape

These are essential for stretching your paper (see box on pages 10—11) to avoid cockling, which is where the sheet wrinkles and forms ridges. A drawing board also creates a satisfyingly firm surface to work on at home or in the field – for this purpose, you can use bulldog clips rather than gummed tape to hold your paper in place.

Easel

A telescopic easel is fairly simple to make, and you will find they are far easier to use than the traditional artist's easel because they allow the board to change from an angled sketching position to flat, enabling you to apply watercolour with the simple turn of a handle. I created mine from a second-hand photography tripod. I started by drawing a cross from corner to corner on a light drawing board to find the exact centre. I then drilled a hole and glued the quick release plate to the board permanently.

Lightweight stool

When I go sketching, I always take a lightweight stool, as sometimes there is no convenient place to rest a sketchbook.

Pencils for sketching

I use a B pencil or softer for an initial sketch. I recommend using a Faber Castell Polychromos colouring pencil in a dark blue or green, sharpened to a fine point. Note that colouring pencils do not erase but leave an attractive sketchy quality.

Dip pen and ink for sketching

If you would like to use ink instead of pencil for your initial sketches, I recommend a medium elastic drawing nib, such as a Gillot 303 nib, and a quality Indian ink. The 303 nib can produce fine hair-like to medium-thick lines, depending on the pressure placed upon it.

Watercolour pencils

Otherwise known as water-soluble pencils, watercolour pencils are a highly versatile art medium. They can be used dry like standard colouring pencils or with water. In wet application, the artist first lays down the dry pigment, then follows up with a water-loaded paintbrush to disperse the colour into a wash. This technique can also blend colours together. I like to work with them alongside brush watercolour (see pages 14—15 for information on watercolour paints).

Eraser

A kneadable putty eraser can erase graphite pencil once an illustration is complete. They work by absorbing colour rather than wearing it away. They are soft and less abrasive than standard erasers, so they won't damage the paper surface.

Brushes

Watercolour brushes need to be able to lay down watercolour paint (see pages 26—27) gently and smoothly and hold a lot of water. They are specially made to allow the artist to control the flow of the colour from the brush onto the paper.

There are several types of watercolour brush and it's worth experimenting with them. A mop brush can hold a lot of water and allows for easy coverage. A fan brush is good for creating fur textures. Rigger brushes are the longest and thinnest round watercolour brush, with a long, tapering point that is made for drawing and excellent for continuous fine lines. It is one of my favourite brushes. Chisel brushes have shortened hairs and a square shape. They can be used dynamically at an angle to create sharp lines (particularly good for branches, twigs and grasses) or they can be used flat to make a stubby mark or fill in a shape. The brushes I use most are round brushes, as they are so versatile. With pressure, they allow medium coverage and return to their shape by lifting off, allowing the tip to create detail. They are ideal for drawing with the brush rather than filling in, creating exciting, dynamic, fluid brushwork.

Size of brush

The size of a brush is denoted by a number. Larger brushes have larger numbers and vice versa. I recommend the following for starting out in round brushes: small (around size 3), medium (5—6) and large (12). Mix and match, collect over time and find your own personal favourites.

Palette

You will need a palette on which to mix your watercolour paints (see pages 24—25). Some ceramic palettes have an angled recessed well, which is helpful to squeeze some of the liquid out of the tip of the brush. I use old white china plates in the studio and a plastic repurposed tray in the field.

Jar of water

When sketching in the field I take an old plastic soup pot to fill with water, so as to avoid the risk of breakages.

Sponge

A small natural sponge is a handy tool for lifting out paint and clearing up puddles.

Granulation medium

Winsor & Newton Granulation Medium is an exciting addition to your materials. It separates the pigment from the water in mixed watercolour paint so that you can see the tiny grains of pigment. I like to use it to create texture in my paintings, from the speckled wings of a dead leaf butterfly to capturing the multitude of feathers on a penguin's coat.

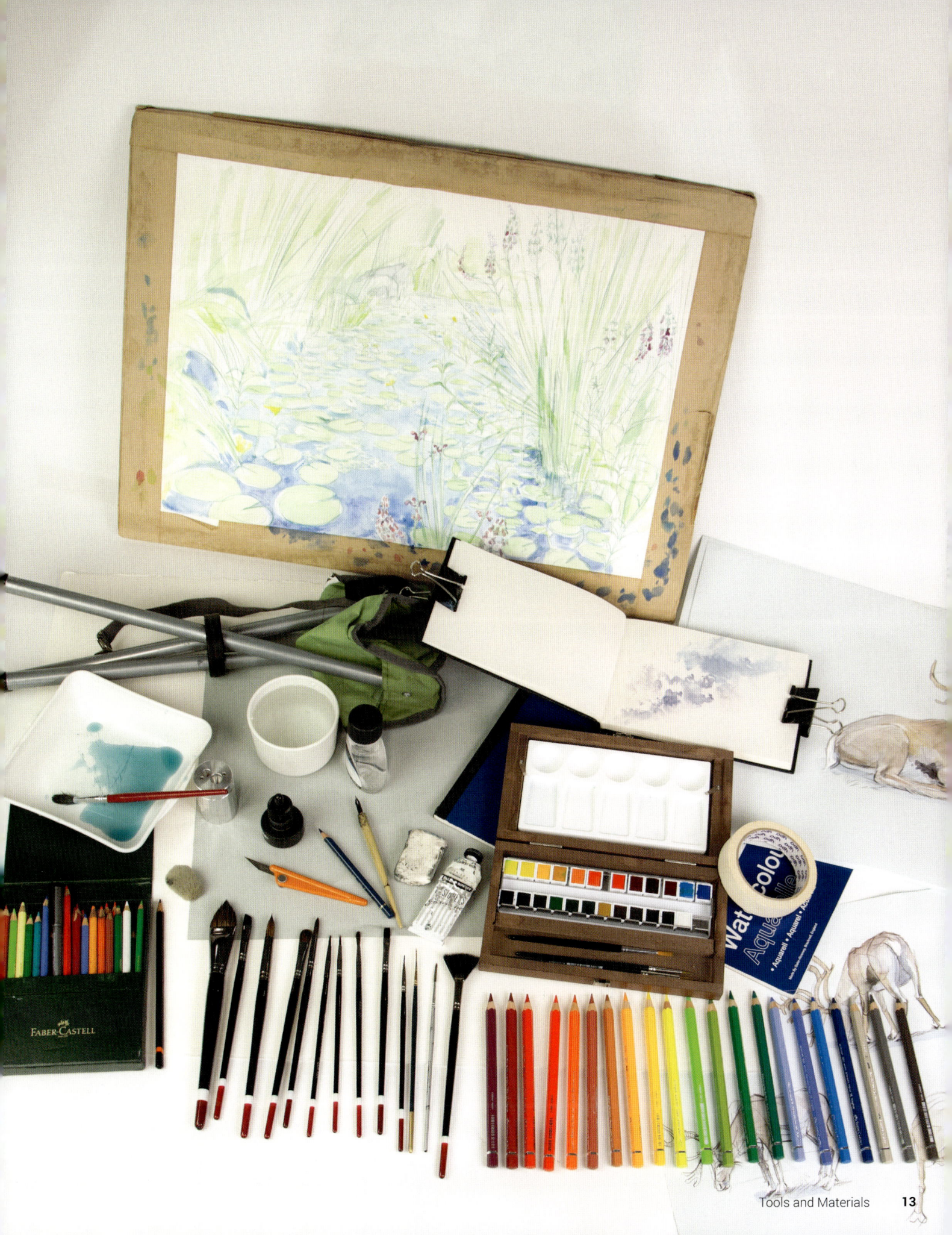

Watercolour paints

Watercolour paint is a pigment with a binder, which is usually Gum Arabic (although my paints of preference, Sennelier, are bound with honey), that can be applied to watercolour paper or a thick cartridge paper. As water evaporates from the paper and the binder, it fixes the pigment to the support. Light passes through this thin translucent layer of paint and reflects off the paper's white or off-white surface, giving it a luminosity that can be truly magical. I am continually surprised at how watercolours created centuries ago can look as if they were painted yesterday.

Watercolours come in two grades: student and professional. Professional-, or artist-quality, watercolour paint is typically made with better-quality pigment with a longer permanence. It gives the artist a greater range and brilliance of colour.

I recommend using a 24 half-pan travel set in a metal tin for durability. Travel sets are suitable for anyone from a beginner to an experienced artist and can be modified to personal taste and new colour discoveries. Not having to take tops on and off tubes of paint means that you can dive straight in, too. A 24-paint set means that you won't have too few colours, which would result in spending a lot of time mixing (not ideal if you're working out of doors or from wildlife and want to get your subject down on paper quickly); a larger, 64-pan palette, while giving incredible versatility in colour, creates the risk of a lack of coherence creeping in.

Gouache

Gouache is an opaque watercolour. It can be used heavily diluted or applied thickly. When applied thickly, the paper and any preliminary drawings will not show through nearly as much as other watercolours. The versatility of gouache's ability to cover up an area that might need reworking can be most welcome. It also gives the option to paint light on dark and, when mixed with Gum Arabic or an acrylic medium, can take on the painterly qualities of oil paint.

Tip

Palettes are laid out chromatically to allow for easy navigation. If you are working with tubes, it is a good idea to follow this layout roughly, too. Over time it will become second nature where to go for a specific colour.

▶ White Gouache

If you use white as I do, I recommend swapping the Chinese White for a tube of permanent White Gouache. It has far better coverage and is much more effective.

Always remember to change your water regularly to keep your colours bright. Try to keep your pans clean, too – especially the light yellows.

▲ Metal paint tin
Having a paint tin made of metal means it can take the knocks when travelling.

Colours you should know

There is a massive array of different pigments out there. Here are some of the ones I consider to be important for painting nature.

Cool colours

Greens

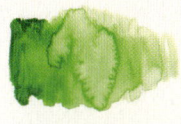

Sap Green
A vibrant mid-range green with a yellow undertone that is excellent for foliage.

Hooker's Green
Created by the nineteenth-century English botanist and botanical illustrator William J Hooker.

Viridian Green
A transparent, emerald green that can be overpowering.

Blues

Cerulean Blue
Cerulean Blue was invented in 1805. Its name derives from the Latin Caeruleum meaning 'sky-blue pigment', which is what it is perfect for.

Cobalt Blue
I consider this to be a primary, clean blue. It was discovered in 1802 by the French chemist Louis Thénard.

French Ultramarine
This warm, purplish blue is the most used colour of my palette. It is fantastic for creating shadow colours.

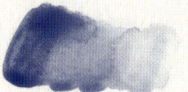

Prussian Blue
A potent greenish-blue pigment that Van Gogh used in the swirling sky of *The Starry Night* painting, 1889.

Warm colours

Yellows

Lemon Yellow
A cool, acidic yellow, suitable for sharp yellows and mixing bright greens. Be careful to keep colours near this end of the spectrum clean in your palette.

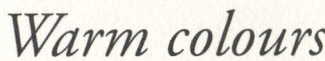

Cadmium Yellow Orange (Deep)
A warm yellow, like the colour of an egg yolk.

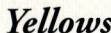

Yellow Ochre
A warm golden-yellow colour. Originally made from natural iron oxides found in the earth, it is one of the oldest pigments used by mankind.

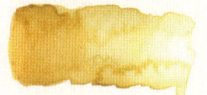

Raw Sienna
A rich orange-brown pigment that can be found in prehistoric cave art. It is named after Siena, Italy, where the pigment was sourced during the Renaissance.

Purple and reds

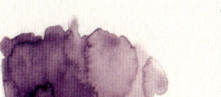

Cobalt Violet
A delicate, semi-transparent purple pigment enjoyed by Monet.

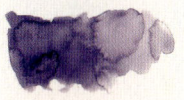

Winsor Violet
A vibrant purple pigment introduced in the 1960s by Winsor & Newton.

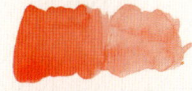

Cadmium Red
I consider this to be a primary red.

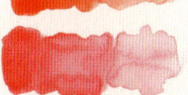

Alizarin Crimson
This blue-red mixes well with French Ultramarine to create violet.

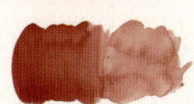

Alizarin Red Brown
A warm, rich red used throughout history, primarily for dyeing textiles.

Neutrals

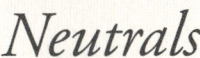

Ivory Black
A fantastic sooty colour that is great for smoky greys when mixed with blue.

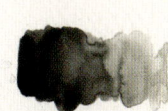

Payne's Grey
A dark blue-grey. Eighteenth-century watercolourist William Payne created the mixture as an alternative to black.

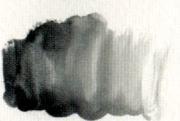

Terre Verte
A soft, neutral, emerald-green colour. It was also known as Verona Green because it was mined near Verona, Italy.

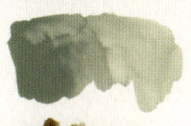

Raw Umber
A rich, cool brown pigment made by the clays found in the earth.

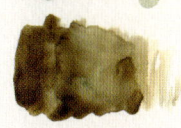

Burnt Umber
A rich dark-brown pigment, named after Umbria, a region in Italy where it was mined.

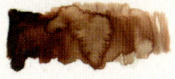

White Gouache
A white body colour with far greater covering ability than the watercolour white.

Fundamentals of Form

Being able to suggest form gives a shape a sense of dimension and weight, of being an object in the world. Throughout this book, you will see that I have included 'widgets' and 'gizmos'. These are neat little tricks that will rapidly speed up your sketching skills. They offer combinations of simple forms that are easy to remember and provide a quick-start guide. They create a framework to build on and will ensure that your artwork doesn't look too flat.

Widgets

I have coined the word 'widget' to mean 'combining any three-dimensional form'. Widgets are powerful enabling tools to carry around with you in your head and can particularly help when an animal is moving. It is worthwhile creating your own widgets before embarking on any study to understand the fundamentals of form. Ask yourself, how can I break down what I am looking at into the five primary forms of the sphere, cube, pyramid, cylinder and cone?

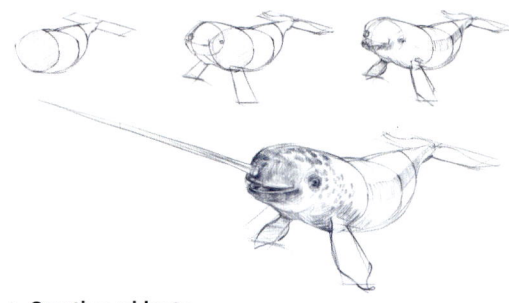

▲ Creating widgets
Dissect and combine simple forms to create widgets.

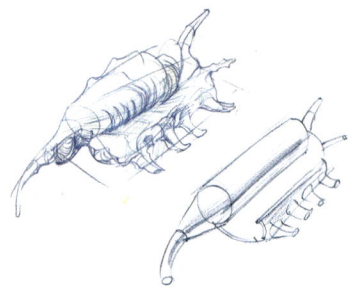

▲ Seashell widget
This seashell is fundamentally a tube with a cone attached at one end with an opening lip. On the opening lip are protective pyramid-shaped spikes.

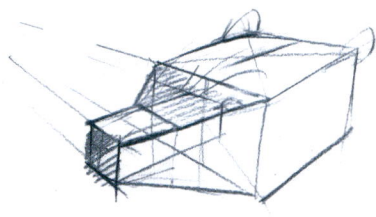

▲ Polar bear head widget
Reduced to its bare essentials, a polar bear head can be visualized as a brain box with an attached muzzle.

a tube helps line up the eyes   **bilateral line of symmetry**

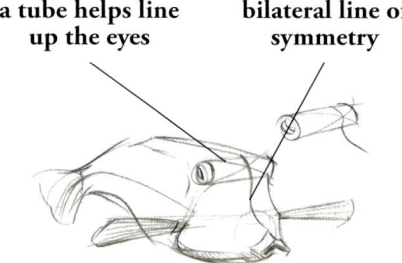

▲ Fish widget
I always prefer to draw animals that are alive. Breaking fish down into their primary forms is a game-changer in being able to sketch them swimming towards and away from you.

Gizmos

I have coined the word 'gizmo' to mean 'flat versions of the widget'. These neat little devices also aid understanding of the form.

▶ Kite gizmo
Kite gizmos are a good starting point for sketching the forehead of a horse and all hoofed mammals, such as the goat shown here.

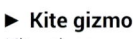

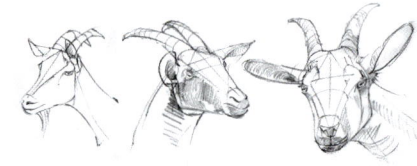

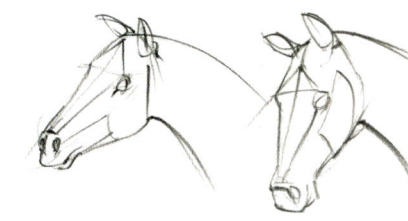

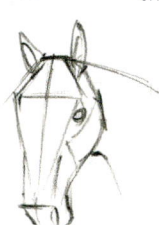

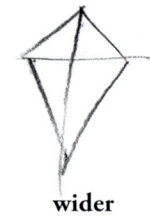

▲ Dog paw gizmo
By drawing a pentagon, finding the line of symmetry, and placing a cross through the centre, there's a clear understanding that the two front claws are in front of a dog's paw.

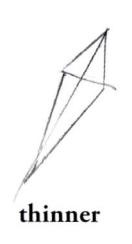

thinner   **wider**

Work nose to tail

When looking at form, it is important to break your subject down into manageable body parts. Start out by creating a side view, then challenge yourself to capture more dynamic poses.

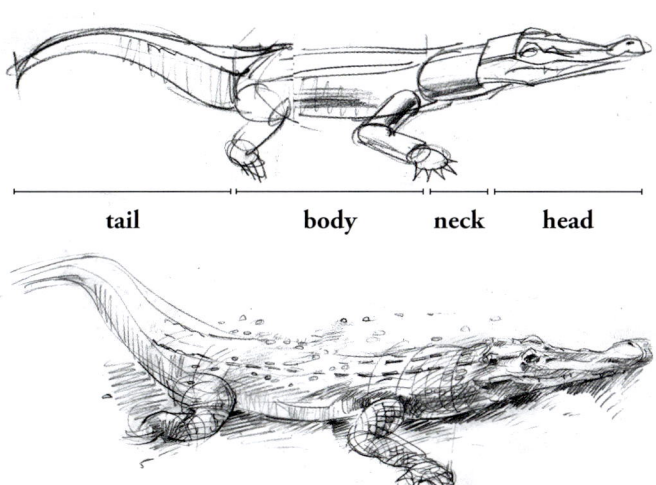

tail | body | neck | head

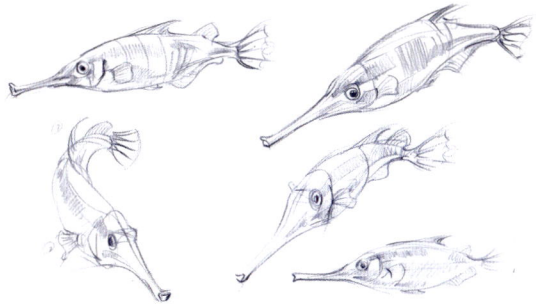

▲ **Viewing from all angles**
Draw a new subject a lot and from all sorts of angles, investigating it thoroughly. It will start to become more familiar, enabling you to capture more ambitious poses.

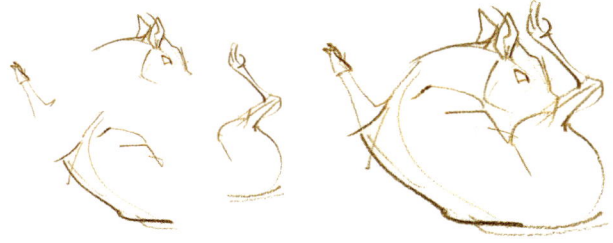

▲ **Philippine crocodile**
Zoological Society of London, London Zoo, UK.

Abstract shapes

Forget your preconceptions about the shape of the subject. In the quick sketches of a mara preening (see right) I have broken apart the drawing to show that combining a set of abstract shapes together becomes readable as an animal, a bit like a jigsaw puzzle.

Irregular and organic forms

Nature's forms are not always based on regular geometric shapes. Rocks, plants and animals can have all sorts of lumps, bumps and imperfections that make them even more interesting to draw and paint. In his book *The Elements of Drawings*, John Ruskin says, 'For all drawing depends, primarily, on your power of representing Roundness'. And goes on to say that 'For Nature is made up of roundness; not the roundness of perfect globes, but variously curved surfaces. Boughs are rounded, leaves are rounded, clouds are rounded, cheeks are rounded...' To practise portraying roundness, he advocates drawing a pebble, and this is something you can do, too.

▶ **Shadow of form**
This is created when part of an object lies on the opposite side from the light source. The shadow of form tends to have a softer edge than the cast shadow because the light reaches around the surface, so practise graduating your tone from dark to light.

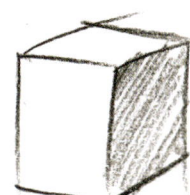

Shadows

Shadows helps create the illusion of form. The three types of shadow to be aware of are described below and right.

▶ **Core shadow**
The core shadow is a dark band of shadow, created by light reflected onto an object from the surface it sits on.

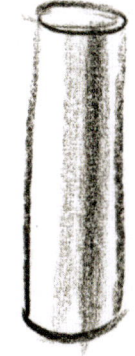

▶ **Cast shadow**
The cast shadow brings drama to a study and stops the object from floating on the page. Painting shadows requires thought about the light source, and cast shadows are no exception, so pinpoint it in your mind or even draw an arrow on your page. How dark the cast shadow is will depend on the strength of the light source and the tonal value of the surface that the object is sitting on.

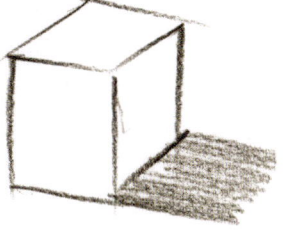

Depth and Perspective

When we pick up a piece of paper we can see that it is flat. Turn the sheet around, and there is nothing behind it. However, as artists we need to be able to create the illusion that the piece of paper is not flat at all but a window through which we can visualize the three-dimensional world. There are a few tricks that we can learn to help us with this, including linear perspective and atmospheric perspective, foreshortening, overlapping lines, tone and colour.

Linear perspective

This is a method of using lines to create the illusion of space on a two-dimensional surface. In perspective drawing, as in real life, objects appear smaller the further they are away from the viewer until they vanish from sight. You can have one, two or three vanishing points.

A good understanding of perspective will inform your broader practice, whether watercolour-sketching landscapes or animals.

One-point perspective

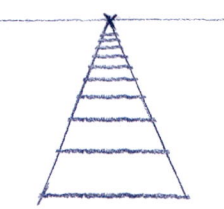

▲ A fundamental rule of perspective is that lines that are parallel to each other will converge to a single vanishing point. One-point perspective is a drawing technique that shows how things appear to get smaller the further away they are, converging towards a single vanishing point on the horizon line. Imagine standing on a railway line and picture how the two railway lines converge to a single point.

Two-point perspective

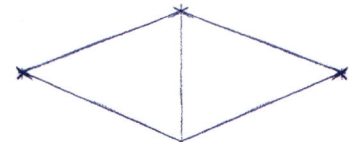

▲ If we take two railway lines and turn them on their side, we have two-point perspective.

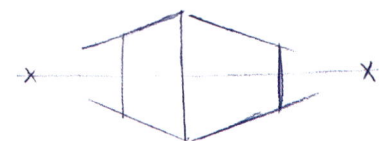

▲ We can draw two more vertical lines to create a short and long side. Ensure that you keep your verticals straight and 90 degrees to the horizontal.

Three-point perspective

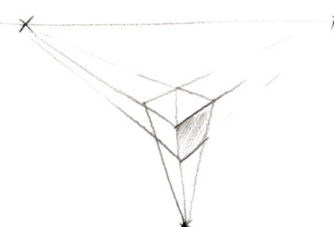

▲ In three-point perspective, the vertical lines converge at a vanishing point. It is typically used in computer games and films to create a feeling of vertigo.

To create a natural feeling of perspective, the vanishing points will often be off the page and wide apart. Imagine the position of these vanishing points before you start sketching.

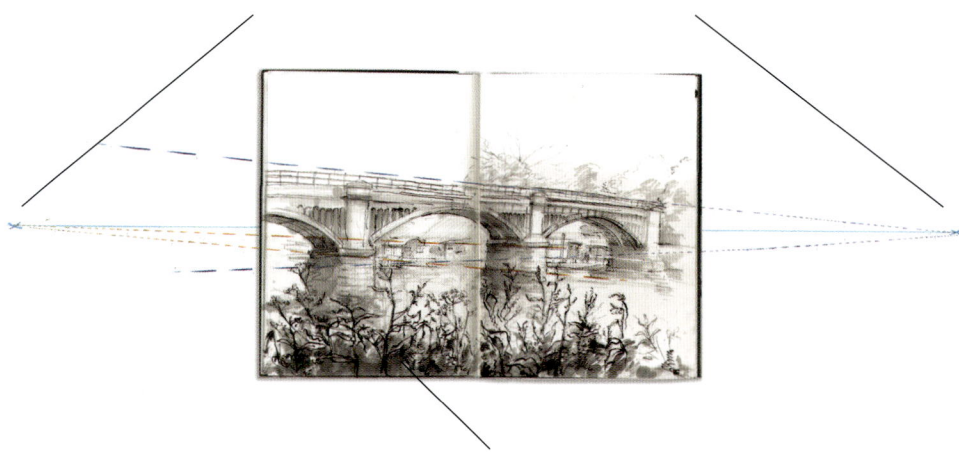

Placing the foreground in shadow can also help the illusion of depth.

Background
Here tonal values are at their lightest
and closest in contrast.

Middle ground
Atmospheric perspective makes shadows
and dark-coloured objects appear lighter
than the foreground. Apply mid-tone
values in the shadows.

Atmospheric perspective

There is a technique in photography called HDR, or High-Dynamic-Range, which takes several exposures and can put the fore-, mid- and backgrounds all in sharp focus. However, we don't see this way and objects in the distance are not as sharp to us. A loss of focus creates an atmospheric perspective. So, when you're painting, make sure that objects that are further away have less detail than objects closer to the viewer. There should be moments of rest, a relief for the eye, in any study.

Tone and depth

In the monochromatic study in Raw Umber shown on the right, notice how the modulation of tonal values (see page 21) creates the illusion of a depth of space. This is similar to a theatrical proscenium, where vertical planes of set dressing sit in front of one another.

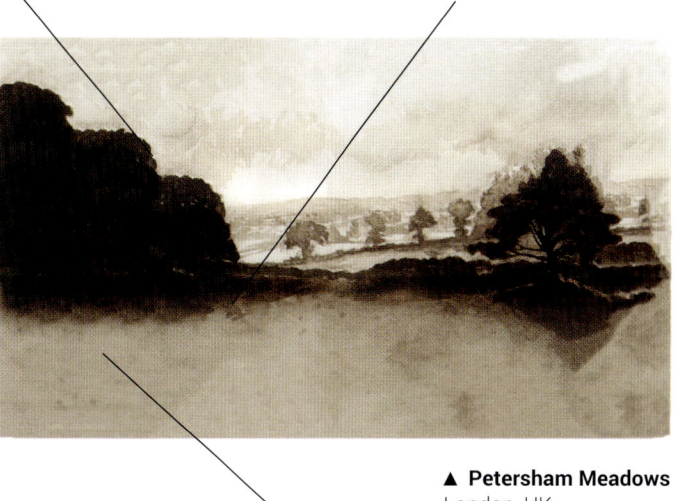

▲ **Petersham Meadows**
London, UK.

Foreground
Here colours are at their darkest, both in the shade and the local colour. Create accents with significant contrast where the darkest notes contrast against the light to pull them forward on the page. Create dark shadows, although not too dark, so that the paint loses its translucent qualities.

Foreshortening

Foreshortening is a technique used to create the illusion of an object receding sharply into the distance or background. The illusion is created by the object appearing shorter than it is, making it seem compressed. You can easily explore foreshortening by standing in front of a mirror. Simply hold up an arm straight from the shoulder to the side of your body, with fist clenched, here your arm is at its visually longest. Now rotate your arm so that your fist is facing you. As your arm rotates, it becomes shorter or more compressed but has greater depth in space. With your fist facing you, you can barely see the arm at all, only the clenched knuckles (see right).

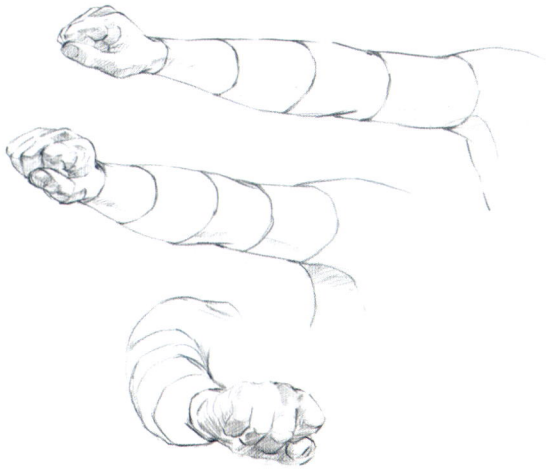

▲ **Practising foreshortening**
Explore foreshortening by moving your arm in front of a mirror.

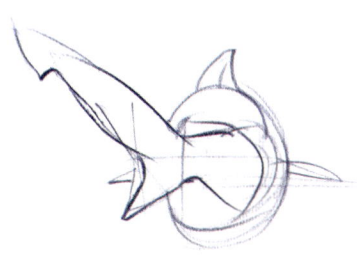

◄ **Shark foreshortened**
Here a shark swimming away from the viewer is drawn using foreshortening. Its length is greatly compressed. A shark swims with its entire body, moving in a series of sinuous waves passing from head to tail. This type of movement is called anguilliform, meaning an eel-like locomotion.

There are various techniques we can use to maximize the depth and dimension of paintings and drawings. Try to fight your unconscious preconceptions, particularly with animals – in specific foreshortened poses the length of the foot can appear longer than the length of the leg. Anything that is not exactly parallel to your eyes will have a degree of foreshortening, which is pretty much everything.

Extreme foreshortening

Forms that are closer to you can be delineated with a darker, thicker line to give them more emphasis. Overlap lines to create the impression that segments of the body are in front of other parts. Body parts in the distance can be sketched with a lighter mark. Challenge yourself with extreme foreshortening poses to create the illusion that the form is coming out of the page to the viewer, achieving a sense of perspective.

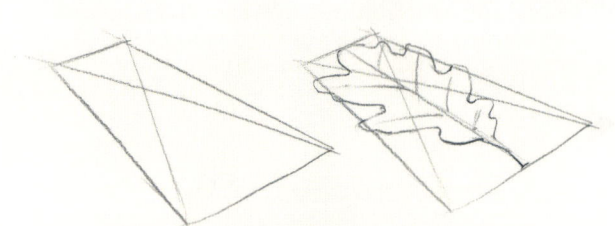

▲ Perspective frame
A perspective frame is a light sketch of a rectangle in space that can you structure and a framework for placing organic forms in space.

Foreshortening tips

- Purposefully seek out foreshortened poses to work from rather than avoiding them. Practice makes perfect!

- Create drawings that help you learn, rather than drawing subjects you are comfortable with, and persevere with the challenge.

- Draw your subject from angles that you are not used to.

- Start with light mapping or plotting lines that capture the sense of pose.

- Forms that are closer to you can be drawn with a darker, thicker line to create emphasis.

- Use lines that overlap each other to give more visual information that one form is in front of the other.

- Get away from preconceptions about the length of arms and legs. Learn to look at your subjects as an abstract set of shapes.

- Placing plants and animals in a perspective frame can help with foreshortening (see above).

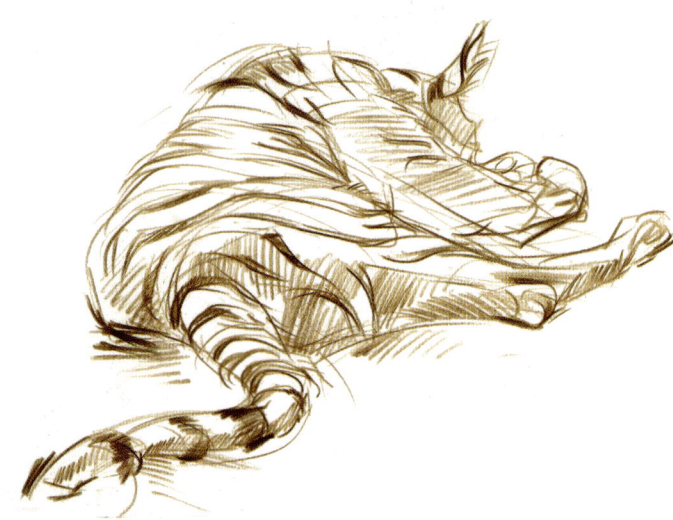

▲ Sumatran tiger sleeping
While to our eyes tigers appear to stand out thanks to their colouration, to their prey who see in black and white they appear grey because orange is one of melanin's mid-tones.

Colour and depth

Objects and landscapes that are further away are cooler/bluer in colour temperature, closer in tonality and in normal light conditions tend to be lighter. Distant colours lose some of their vibrancy due to moisture in the air and other particles.

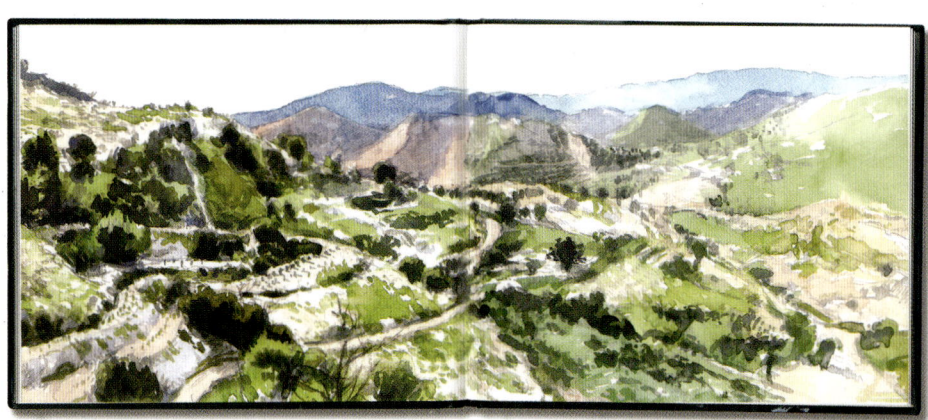

Overlapping lines

The overlapping line can create the illusion of form and depth. Press harder on the lines in the foreground to create bolder lines that push toward the eye. Experiment with this convention by creating an abstract landscape doodle.

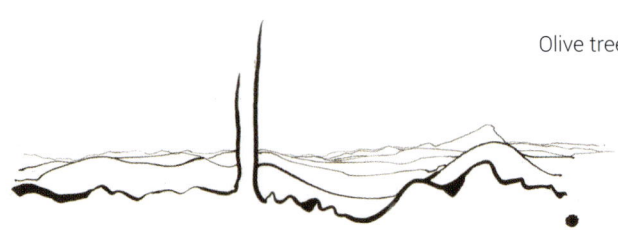

▲ Cypriot mountains
Olive trees pepper the foothills of the Troodos mountains.

◄ Overlapping lines
Imagine a landscape rolling for miles in front of you.

Tonal Value

The words 'tone' and 'value' are interchangeable and mean the same thing, which can be a little confusing at first. In painting, tone refers to the relative lightness or darkness of a colour. Watercolour is about exploring the range of tones available to you primarily through dilution (although White Gouache can also be added to lighten them). The more water you add, the lighter the tone will be; the more concentrated it is, the darker it will be.

The transparency of watercolour means you need to formulate a plan at the beginning of the painting process. What colour and tone are you going to begin with? With watercolours, once you give a form a specific value, it is difficult to lighten it. Try the following exercises to familiarize yourself with tonal variations.

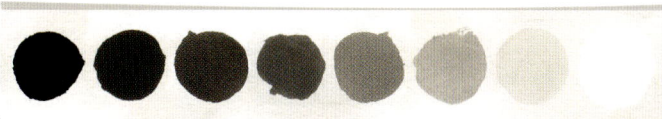

▲ Eight-step tonal value scale
This eight-step value scale is created using a black watercolour. See if you can create incremental steps from black to white by simply adding more water. The lightest value can be either the paper or white gouache. Try to see if you can keep the steps equal in their tonal value without a significant jump between a pair. Using a full range of tones such as this scale can enrich a watercolour.

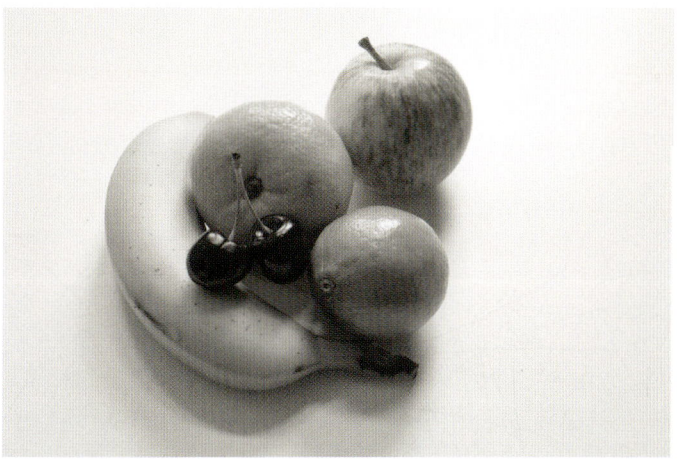

▲ Tonal economy
Look at a black-and-white photograph. Establish where the darkest notes are and then the lightest. Now look for the other gradations between. Allow yourself no more than five tones in total. Typically in a painting you would not need more than eight to nine tonal variations; with any more it can make it difficult for the eye to discern the difference.

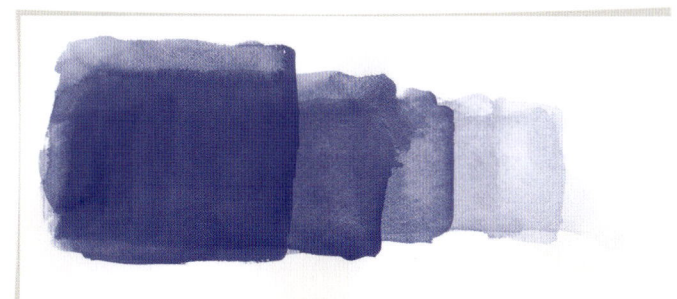

▲ Building up washes
Create a range of tonal values to any colour by building up washes on top of a dried wash beneath.

High, mid and low key

The tonal range of a scene depends on the amount of light it receives. High-key colour describes the set of colours ranging from mid-tone hues to white, while low-key colour spans the range from mid-tone to black. The high-key range is light and bright, while low-key colours provide more dramatic tones.

Chiaroscuro (see page 117) is an example of low-key painting, where edges melt into darkness and forms emerge from the gloom. A misty-morning painting may require a pale pastel palette with lots of diluted washes, while a nightscape will have more concentrated, darker colours. However, most paintings end up in the mid or intermediate key, where middle values dominate the picture with solid darks and bright highlights.

Activity
Seek out J M W Turner's paintings. Watercolour is the ideal medium to capture the illusion of light and there is no better exponent of this than J M W Turner, who created the briefest of observational watercolour sketches full of illumination. The illusion of light coming from the page is partnered with its opposite, that of shade. Learning to mix colours in the light and getting the relationship right for colours in the shade captures light on the paper.

Composition

The composition of a painting refers to its key elements and how they are arranged in relation to one another. The focus is on the main shapes, not the detail. An initial sketch will help with planning a composition. For instance, you can play with how much sky or sea you might like to include; whether you wish to place a tree centrally or off to one side; and discover if you can fit all the elements in. Artistic licence allows you to move elements in the frame of the picture to balance the composition. There is no obligation to recreate a photographic rendering of the world – you can put in, take out and move as you so desire.

Landscape or portrait?

Over the years, I have storyboarded for both films and adverts. They have always been landscape format, as they represent the television screen. However, artists have the flexibility to also work on portrait, square and even panoramic images. When storyboarding, different types of shots can help convey a range of emotions, moods and atmosphere, in just the same way that a watercolour painting can be composed. A long or wide shot can tell us about the setting and give a sense of place. A close-up can reveal more about the emotion a character is feeling. The composition can inspire awe, drama, tension and dynamic action. Whether you choose to focus on a wave crashing on a rocky cliff or include the entirety of the seascape can create what I call 'the agony of choice'. Before embarking on a large-scale composition, I recommend creating quick sketches to avoid the pitfalls that might arise at the end of a long painting.

Focal point

Many beautiful paintings have been created without the artist planning the composition and instead working intuitively. Nevertheless, it is worth mentioning focal points or an area of focus. Picture in your mind a stage of dancers all dressed in white with the lights on full. Your eye darts from one dancer to the next, not fully knowing where to focus your gaze. Now imagine the principal dancer appears in dark blue, and the lights dim to a spotlight. Of course, a painting can have more than one focal point: imagine a dancer in red now takes to the stage, and your eye is happy to view both.

Within any painting, there is usually an area of visual interest that attracts the artist, an element that is inspiring and entertaining to the eye.

How to select your focal point

Before you start to paint, ask yourself what attracted you to the scene. What is the element that drew you to capture that location or subject? It could be anything – a triangular mountain, an autumnal yellow tree, a view of olive groves in the Cypriot mountains... If there is no individual element that you can think of, then perhaps it is the whole view you like. Then it is the case that it might be worth picking something out. Off-centring this visual element can prevent the composition from becoming too static.

Scale

Visual hierarchy is when some elements tend to 'stand out', or attract attention more strongly than other elements, communicating to a viewer's eyes what to focus on and in what order. I tend to think of it as an orchestra with a lead musician and supporting players. If everything were the same size, each element would fight the eye for equal attention.

Unusual angles and cropping close

Refresh landscape compositions by exploring new angles such as high or low viewpoints by looking up at tree branches, for instance, or sitting on a stool looking into a hedgerow. One exciting way to create compelling compositions is to zoom in on a fragment. Even the most familiar view can become a dynamic composition or an intimate portrait by zooming in close. After a field sketching trip, sometimes I spread the entirety of my studies across a large table, then select one or two that have potential for a composition. Interesting areas can be isolated by using two cut pieces of mount board.

Tried-and-tested compositional guides

On the facing page are some methods for creating harmonious compositions. Take time to explore these.

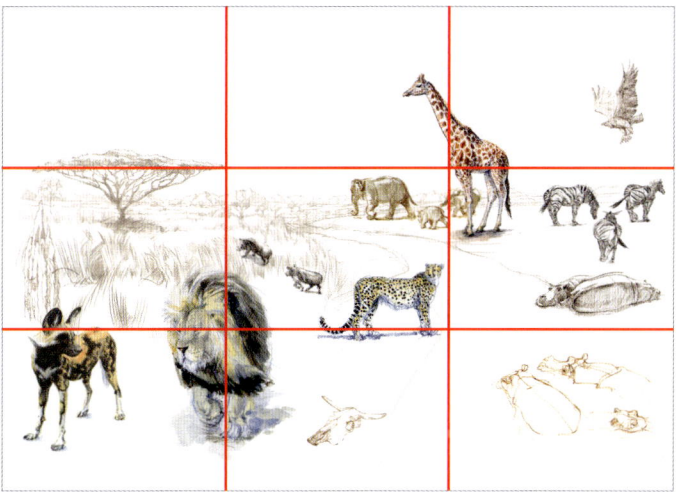

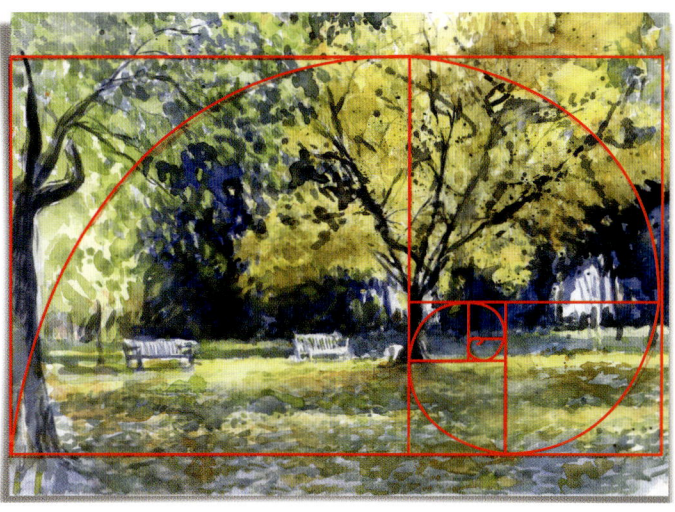

The Rule of Thirds

Break a composition into thirds – vertically and horizontally – then place the key elements of the image along these lines or at the junctions of them. The arrangement achieved will be interesting, pleasing and dynamic.

The Golden Ratio

The art world has felt the influence of the Golden Ratio for centuries – the smaller proportion has the same relationship to the larger one, as the larger one does to the next portion, approximately 1 : 1.618. There is a kind of peacefulness and beauty in these proportions that relates to nature's design and growth patterns.

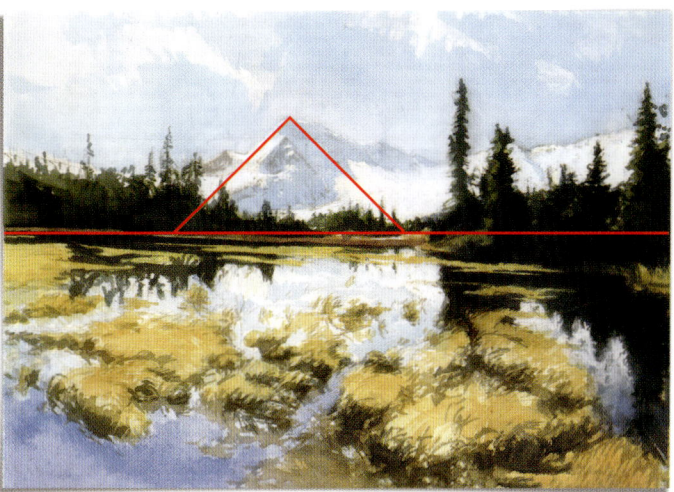

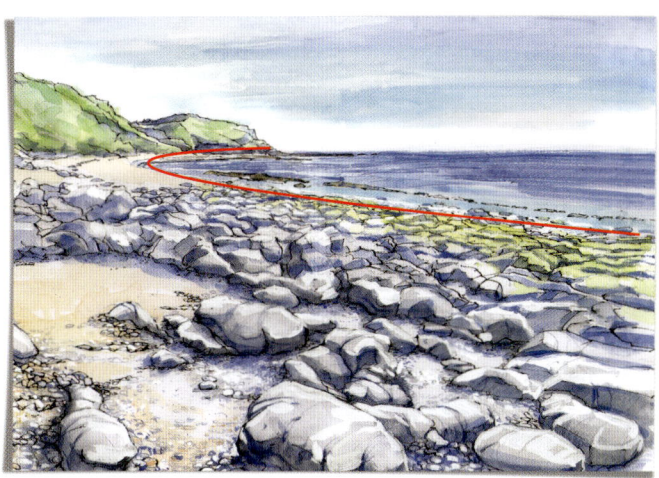

Triangular

In the classical tradition, triangular or pyramidal compositions were popular because they created balance and harmony by arranging the elements into a stable overall geometric structure. Looking at the picture above, I can still remember my excitement as we hiked out of the forest and were greeted by this fantastic scene. In painting it, I placed the mountain slightly off centre to create a sense of informality. The muskeg, which are patches of boggy grass in the foreground, help to develop an understanding of depth as they get smaller towards the horizon.

C-shaped path

A path or any delineation in the landscape can lead the eye through the painting to the intended focal point – here, that is the far headland.

S-shaped path

S-shaped rhythms lead the eye gently through the landscape. It is a very effective technique, with the artist leading the viewer on a gentle meandering journey through their painting.

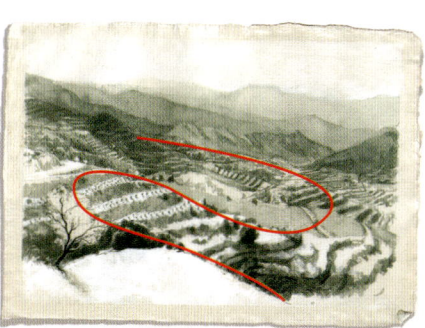

Colour Theory

At its most basic, colour can be broken down into the following categories: primary, secondary and tertiary. In theory, all the other colours could be mixed from just these. In reality, it is helpful to have a good range of around 24 colours to extend the possibilities and let you get as close as possible to nature's hues. By mixing complementary colours, the ones opposite each other on the colour wheel, you can create neutral and dark tones, which will help your paintings look more sophisticated. An artist's use of colour is often highly individual, and their choice of palette can become part of their signature style.

Primary colours

The primary colours consist of three colours: yellow, red and blue. They are called the primary colours because there are no two colours that can be mixed to create them. Red, yellow and blue are the primary hues from which all the other pigmented colours can be made.

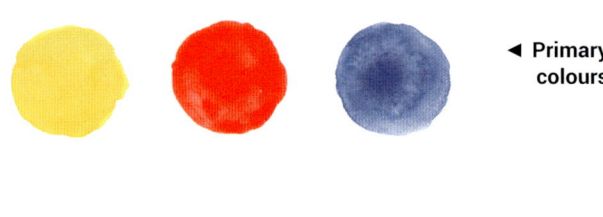

◄ Primary colours

Secondary colours

The secondary colours consist of three colours: orange, violet and green. These colours are made by mixing roughly equal amounts of two primary colours.

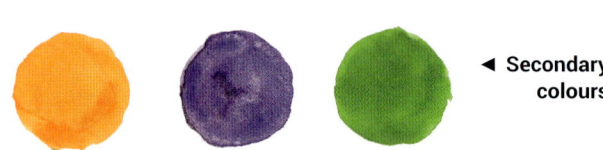

◄ Secondary colours

Tertiary colours

The tertiary colours consist of six colours: yellow-orange, yellow-green, blue-green, blue-violet, red-violet and red-orange. These colours are made by mixing a secondary colour with the closest primary colour on the colour wheel (see facing page).

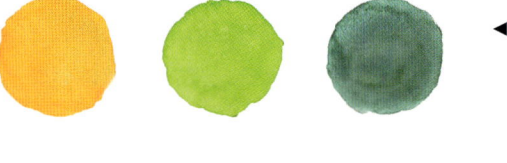

◄ Tertiary colours

Complementary colours

Just as the opposite to black is white, so do all the other colours have opposites. The complementary colour of the primary hues is the mixture of the other two. For example, the complementary of blue is orange – that is red mixed with yellow.

The complementary colours lie opposite each other on the colour wheel. For example, the complementary of red-orange is blue-green.

Complementary colours can enhance the vividness of the paint by juxtaposing them side by side and cancel each other out by mixing them to achieve neutral tones.

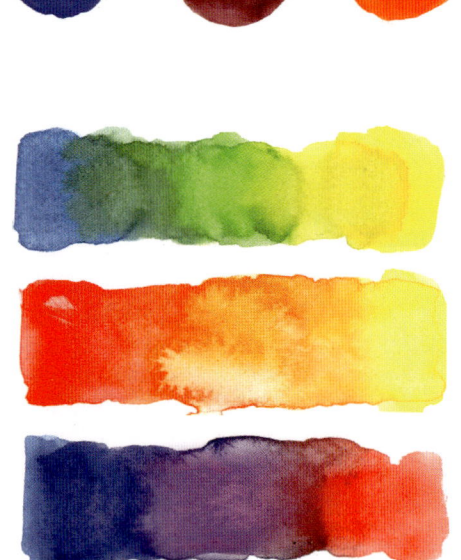

► Complementary colours

Tip
The complementary colour will gradually desaturate
the other to create smoky greys. The most neutral
shade is created by adding equal quantities of both.

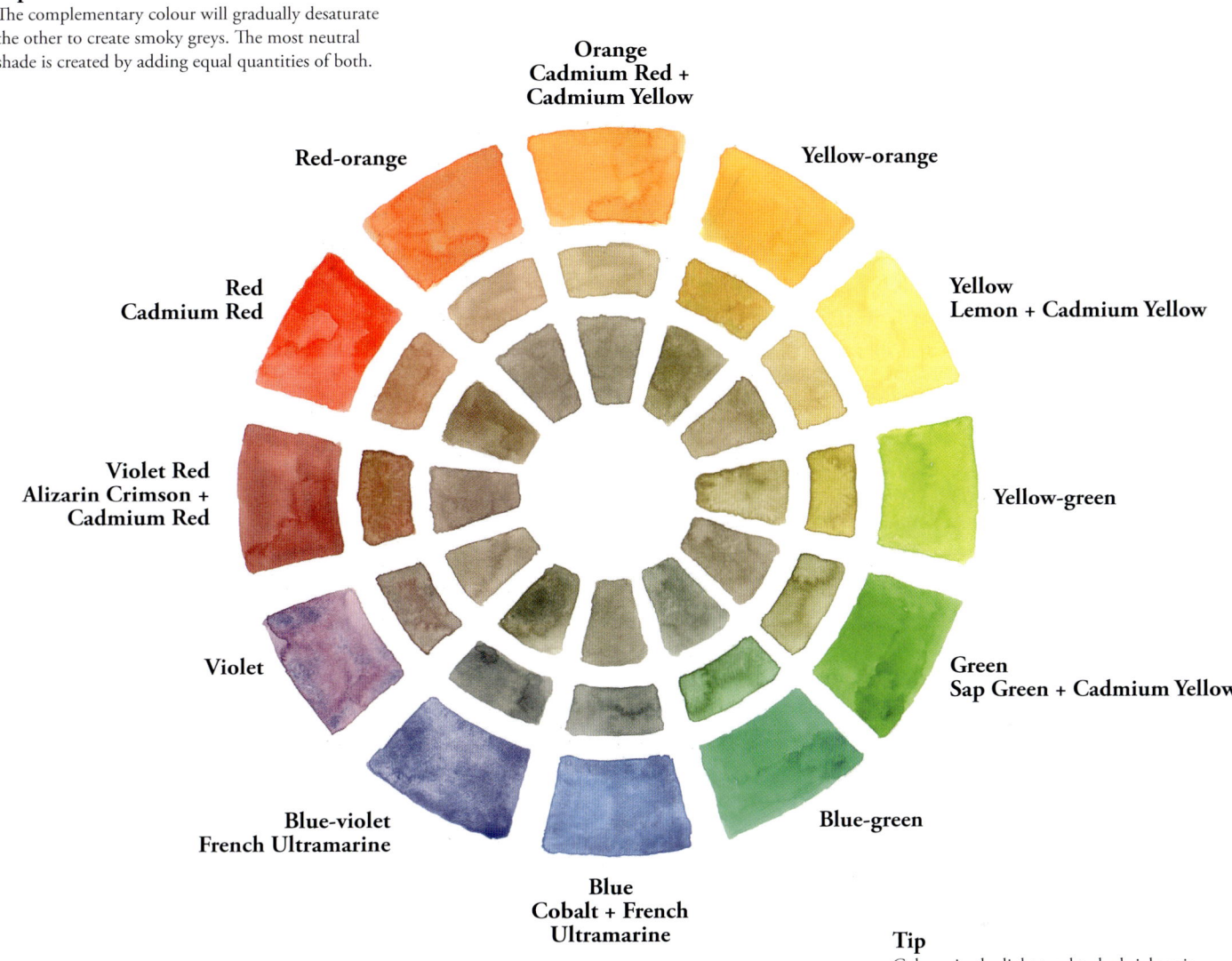

Orange
Cadmium Red +
Cadmium Yellow

Red-orange

Yellow-orange

Red
Cadmium Red

Yellow
Lemon + Cadmium Yellow

Yellow-green

Violet Red
Alizarin Crimson +
Cadmium Red

Green
Sap Green + Cadmium Yellow

Violet

Blue-green

Blue-violet
French Ultramarine

Blue
Cobalt + French
Ultramarine

Tip
Colours in the light tend to be brighter in
saturation than colours in the shade while
also being lighter in tone.

The colour wheel

The colour wheel is a circular display of 12 hues of colour,
arranged according to their relationship to one another. It
is an excellent tool for understanding how to mix paint and
make the pigment look as bright as possible; for example, a
French Ultramarine mixed with an Alizarin Crimson will give
you a much more successful violet than a Cobalt Blue with a
Cadmium Red because of their position on the colour wheel.

The colour wheel helps you to understand how to degrade your
colour by using its complementary rather than black. The more
you add of the complementary colour, the more neutralized
the initial pigment becomes. While I recommend black as a
pigment to be used in specific situations, such as creating
lovely smoky greys, this colour's overuse to degrade and
darken a tone can kill a painting.

Warm and cool colours

Hues that contain a higher quantity of blue appear cooler
from the violet to green range. Those that contain more red
or yellow, the colours of sunshine and fire, seem warmer on
the yellow-green to violet. Warm colours are the reds, oranges
and yellows and give the impression of colours coming
forward. Cool colours on other hand – greens, blues and violets
– are referred to as recessive colours because they give the
impression of dropping back and can be used to enhance the
feeling of spatial depth (see page 20) in a painting. Changes
in colour temperature and intensity can be observed in the
atmospheric effects in landscape painting (see page 19), where
the colours of distant forms become colder, greyer and bluish,
as well as lighten in contrast of tonality.

Getting Started with Watercolour

There are several traditional and experimental watercolour techniques that you can explore. This is an introduction to the techniques that I most commonly use.

Layering

Because watercolour is a transparent medium, you'll need to build up tones gradually as your image emerges, a bit like a photograph in a developing tray. Once a colour has been laid down and allowed to dry, another layer of a different colour can be laid down on top. You'll notice that where they overlap, the pigment mixes and you're left with a different shade. You might also need to compensate for your next move, depending on which colour you are laying down on top of and how mixing the two will affect the final shade. For example, if you lay an initial wash of yellow, then overlay it with a blue, the yellow will tinge the blue to create a greenish shade. A red overlain with yellow will create an orange shade, and so forth.

When laying down watercolour, work from the lightest colours to the brightest. Here I will demonstrate that principle with a painting of a rooster.

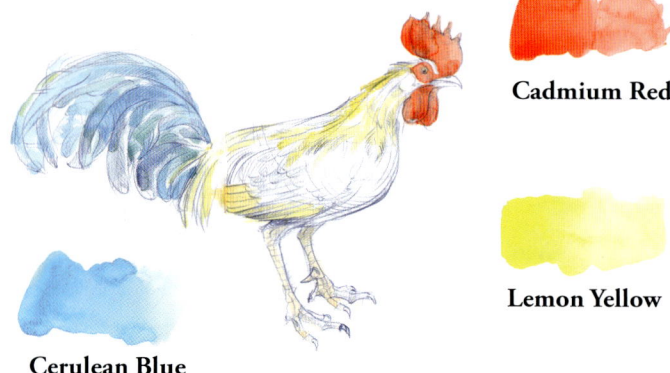

Cadmium Red

Lemon Yellow

Cerulean Blue

1   *Start by asking yourself, which are the lightest and brightest colours? Spend time carefully mixing the closest shades. Lay these colours down with plenty of clean water from a large brush such as a No. 6. Leave gaps where you require white.*

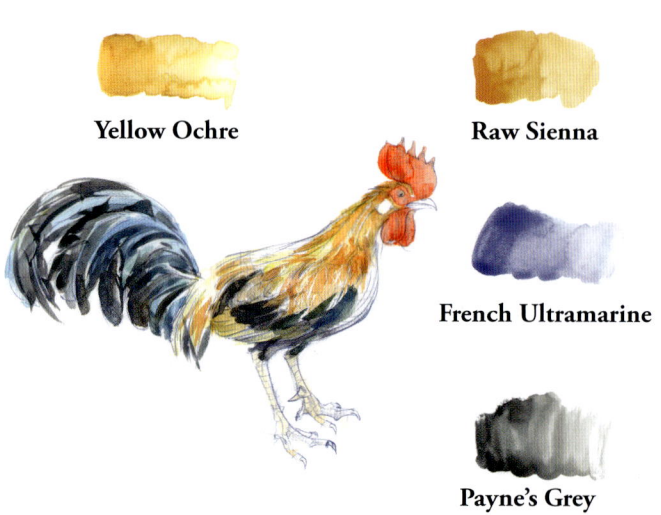

Yellow Ochre

Raw Sienna

French Ultramarine

Payne's Grey

2   *Once the first layer is dry, add mid-tone values using a medium-size brush – I tend to use between No. 4 and No. 6. Vary your brush marks in relation to the size and quality of the different feathers to add visual interest.*

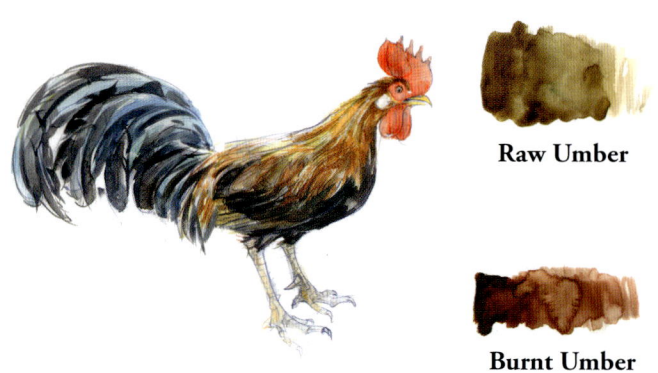

Raw Umber

Burnt Umber

3   *Apply the darkest colours at the final stage. Use smaller brushes to add detail.*

Wet into wet

To practise this technique, using pure water and a single pigment, create a broad stroke with a thick brush. While it is still wet, add colour to the tail end of the water. Watch how the colour blooms in the water, bleeding into the pure water, creating stimulating effects and a smooth, natural colour gradient. Now explore this technique with two colours at either end.

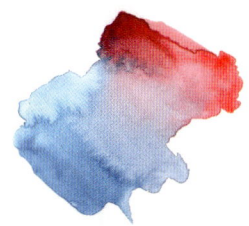

The blobbing technique

'Blobbing' means applying more saturated pigment to a wet area by simply tapping it in with the tip of the brush, pumping pigment into a wet pool of lighter colour to create a gradient.

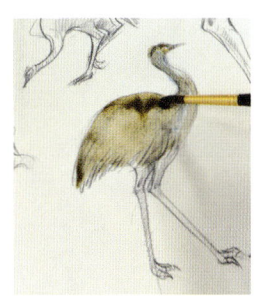

Lifting out

The term 'lifting out' means to remove or erase watercolour from the surface of a painting. Often the need arises to lift watercolour paint from the image to lighten it. I only do this when the paint is wet, although some people use an eraser to scrub off dry pigment, which can damage the surface of the paper. Primarily, I use a dry mop brush that acts like a sponge, sucking up the pigment into its bristles to create soft highlights. I do this in many situations, from forming the highlight on a cherry, as shown here, to creating clouds. Instead of a dry brush, you could also use a natural sponge or a paper towel.

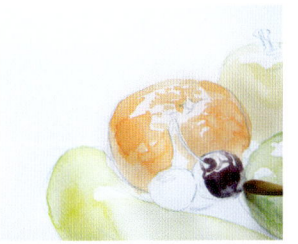
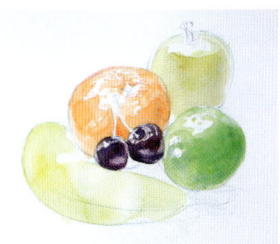

Underpainting

An underpainting is a monochrome wash that underpins a painting. It is more typically seen in oil painting. Creating an initial French Ultramarine tonal underpainting will help to unify the scene or subject.

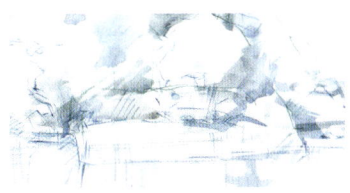

Draw with the brush

Let your brush marks show in your final work. Accept happy accidents rather than trying to control the media too much and tie it down. Life is in the brush stroke and has more personality than handwriting. The artists' objective is not to create a photographic copy of what you are looking at but an interpretation. Always remain focused on your subject and draw with the brush rather than fill in a sketched shape.

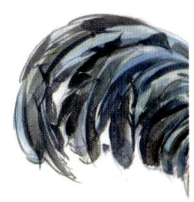

Scumble strokes

Scumbling is a technique used to create soft hues of layered pigment. Scumbling can be likened to scribbling, and artists have differing views on the scumbling process. For me, it is when I drag in a relatively haphazard way a dry amount of pigment over a dry base, allowing the speckles of the base layer to show through on the paper's tooth to create a texture effect, such as a stormy sky.

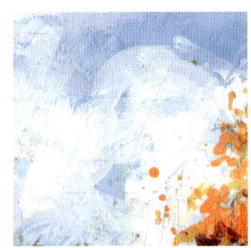

Wax resist

You can use a sharpened slither of a candle to make resist wax lines. Here, wax resist has been used to emulate texture on a pebble. Always create your underpainting first. After adding the wax resist, apply the mid-tone values and watercolour over the resist. This will create interesting textural marks as the watercolour forms bobbles on the waxy surface.

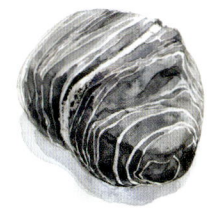

Granulation

Granulation breaks the pigmented watery solution back into its particles, which clump together adding visual texture to a painting. The older pigments generally granulate well, such as the earth colours of the ochres and umbers, cobalt, ultramarine and black. Granulation happens naturally; however, to encourage the granulation process to a dramatic effect, Winsor and Newton have developed a granulation medium. I place a drop in the palette and pump in the pigment with a brush. Bashing the solution around seems to help the creation of the flecks and specks, which can capture the texture of a dead leaf butterfly wing.

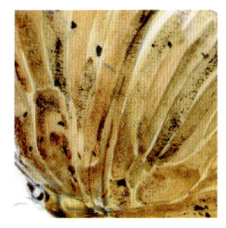

Working from a Photograph

It may not always be practical or feasible to work from life, and it is a shame to exclude all those plants and creatures we may not have an opportunity to be able to see, so it's a good idea to learn how to work from a photograph.

The use of a grid enables you to replicate an image accurately. Artists since the Renaissance have used this transfer technique to copy a preliminary drawing onto a new surface to start working it up into a finished painting, often to upscale to a much larger image. I also do something similar when I am working from a photo, where there is a lot of visual information and it is challenging to keep track of where I am. Cutting a square aperture through a piece of paper allows me to concentrate on a particular area of the painting without distracting the surrounding visual noise. To demonstrate this technique, I have chosen a photograph of daisies that is full of light.

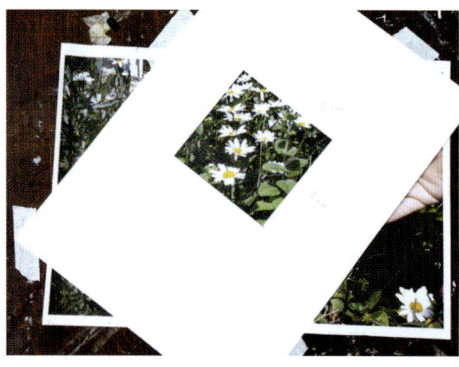

1 *Start by selecting a photograph and print it out at 8¼ x 11¾in (A4) or 11¾ x 16½in (A3). Using a set square and scalpel, cut a square aperture that is 4¾ x 4¾in (12 x 12cm) through a piece of cartridge paper to create a square frame. Move the aperture over an image until you find an arrangement that is pleasing and manageable in detail. On a separate thick piece of cartridge paper lightly draw a square box the same size.*

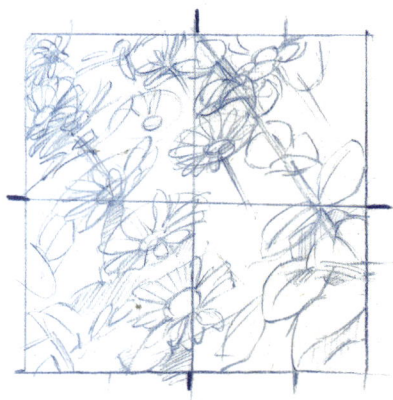

2 *Next is 'squaring up'. Squaring up, also known as 'scaling up', means using a grid so you can transfer with some accuracy to scale. Lightly draw a cross on both your paper and photograph, then copy the contents of each square of the original into the corresponding square of the reproduction.*

3 *Now make a blue-grey tonal underpainting in watercolour. In this image, it helps to unify the flowers and create a single scene. Rather than starting with the lightest colours, the underpainting technique begins with painting in the negative shapes of shadows by working up to three or four tones (see right). Think of it as a watercolour in reverse. Identify light and dark areas and sketch them in, drawing with the brush a mix of French Ultramarine and Payne's Grey. Squint at your photo to reduce the detail and identify the areas of light and dark. Create contrast – light against dark and dark silhouetted against the light.*

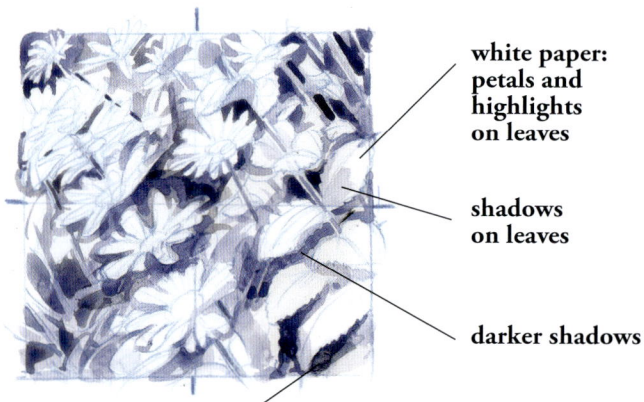

white paper: petals and highlights on leaves

shadows on leaves

darker shadows

Add in your darkest values while still drawing with the brush. Make sure that these are not too dark so that the paint retains translucent qualities, which also helps with spatial qualities.

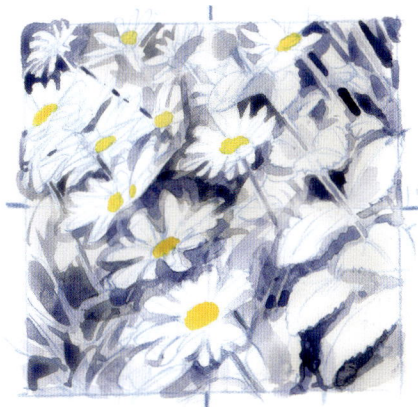

4 *Add your lightest and brightest colours. In this study I have used Cadmium Yellow Deep with Lemon Yellow to capture the disc florets. Notice that objects at the bottom of the composition tend to be closer to the viewer.*

▶ **Daisy gizmo**
The petals closest to you appear shorter because of foreshortening

ray florets

disc florets

Tip
Make sure to mix your colours accurately. I test my colour mixtures on the photo to see if they match and tend to spend longer mixing the colour than painting it on the page. It is important to remember that you are creating an interpretation of the photograph, not an exact replication, so be flexible and creative in your colour choice.

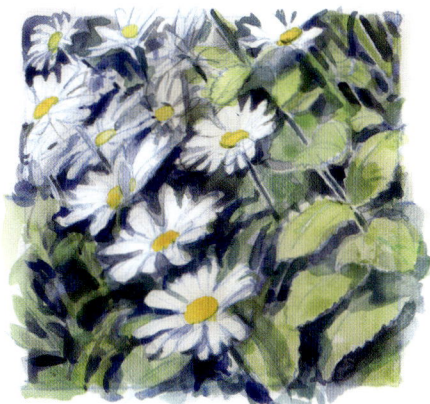

6 *When finishing off, you can push the contrast. Create accents and accentuate the lights and darks so that your image pops from the page.*

Colour in the light is lighter and tends to be more highly saturated in purer colour.

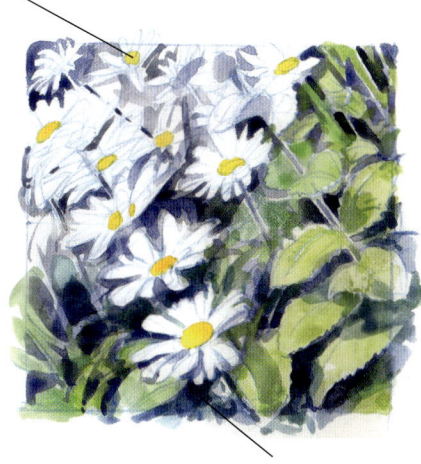

Colour in the shadow is darker and tends to be more degraded in pigmentation.

5 *Next, paint over the tonal underpainting with a light yellow-green wash for the colour of the leaves in sunlight. Achieving the impression of light coming from the page is about tonal values (see page 21) and the relationship between the colour in the shadow and the colour in the sun. Colour in the light is both lighter and tends to be more highly saturated in purer colour, except in situations such as light reflecting off water or glass. The colour of the shadow is darker in tone and tends to be more degraded in pigmentation. Use a combination of the complementary colour and French Ultramarine blue. Ultramarine was very popular among the Impressionists who used it in abundance in their shadow colours to bring a feeling of air and space to their paintings.*

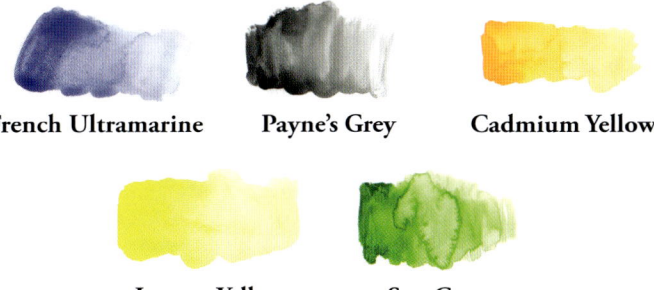

French Ultramarine   **Payne's Grey**   **Cadmium Yellow**

Lemon Yellow   **Sap Green**

Activity
Go out for a walk with a camera and take photographs of nature's details that might otherwise go unnoticed. Look for unusual compositions and angles. Try to capture details such as the light caught on a petal or the glowing sap green of a backlit leaf. Notice when looking up at a tree how the leaves overlap to create darker tones, just like in watercolour.

Working from Life

The most significant difference between working from a photograph and working from life is that when a subject is physically there, you inevitably form a relationship with it. You pick up on subtleties, such as its character, emotions and energy, and these create a range of responsive feelings that help inform the marks that go down on the page. Working from life, you get to know your subject intimately, leading to moments of humour when your subject is being playful.

Study sheets

One of the best ways to establish a relationship with your subject is to make study sheets of it. (There is also no better way to develop your observational skills and hand-to-eye coordination.) A study sheet combines quick gestural studies (see pages 32–33) and more sustained work. It can be an inquiry into anything, a rock, plant or animal, and can include whatever you want it to, from detailed studies of parts of the anatomy to written notes or daubs of colour.

Study sheets help us discover; they are not about creating a polished result. So, don't be worried about the appearance of the page (although your drawings will improve as you become more acquainted with your subject). What is important is that your hand has been activated with your eye giving instruction. Try to feel like you are almost touching the plant or animal and ensure your focus is fully engaged.

Tip
For study sheets, I tend to use a large piece of paper, usually 16½ x 23⅜in (A2 size), bulldog-clipped to a lightweight drawing board, or the open double-page of a 11¾ x 16½in (A3 size) sketchbook. I find anything smaller doesn't give me enough room to fit everything I want in (and it is annoying when there isn't space for a foot or a tail).

Study sheets of animals

When working from an animal enclosure I try to keep drawing without stopping. I move rapidly from one sketch to another. Every time the animal moves I start again, and then go back to a sketch as the animal returns to a similar position. I end up leaving lots of unfinished studies scattered on the page.

Animals that aren't sleeping tend to be in continual motion, and quick sketches have a lively, attractive quality that will bring a drawing to life. Wild animals certainly aren't going to sit for a portrait. Rear views, hanging-upside-down views and stretching-out-in-the-sun views are all part of the action.

Every subject has a unique character that you get a sense of when working from life, which cannot be gained from sketching from a photograph.

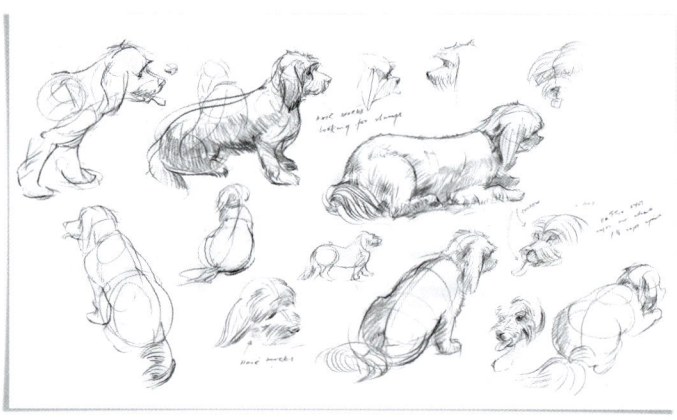

▲ **Early studies**
Pets are an accessible way to begin learning to create study sheets.

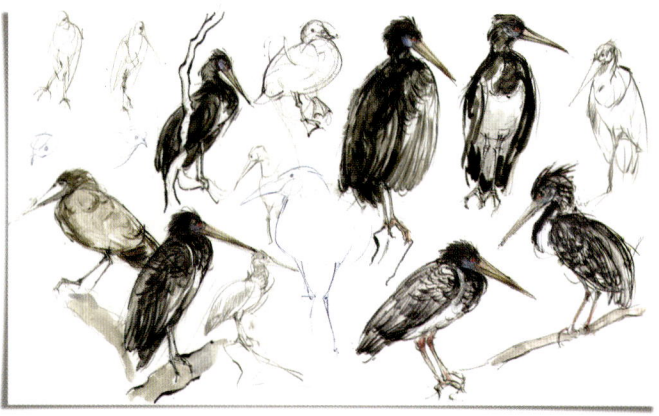

▲ **Close-up studies**
Experience sketching inside an aviary where you can get close to your subject without the frustrations of mesh or glass.

Tip
Don't just use your eyesight to inform you, use your sense of smell and sound to capture the character of your subject.

When the subject of your artwork is an animal, it is vital to approach it with a calm and quiet mindset so as not to cause it stress. Take a deep breath and for a few more, simply observe the animal and contemplate what you are about to do.

An observational drawing appears convincing when it's most truthful, when the artist is trying their very best to record what they see. A single line can capture every nuance of the animal's shape and can convey a remarkable amount of information. Create continuous flowing lines that capture the physical boundary of the animal and inner contours resembling what you witness.

Carefully observe, don't make assumptions. Look at the animal more than the page. If you can, start with a side pose to familiarize yourself with the body parts from nose to tail. Then become more ambitious, capturing more unusual postures,

even if the animal has its back facing you. As frustrating as it is, your model could constantly be moving, but this will give your drawing energy. Work quickly. Even though your animal might be standing still, he/she will soon move! Fast, vigorous lines imply power and make your animals come alive on the paper. Create lines that capture the character of form and bite into the edge of the form. Each time your subject moves, start a new drawing on the same page. Return to the unfinished sketch when your subject returns to a similar pose. Be prepared to work on more than one drawing at once. Be surprised by what you see! Don't dictate. You are combining a series of abstract shapes together as something that can be read as an animal.

Tip
Early on, check the proportions of the size of the head in relation to the body, as there is a tendency to sketch the head too big.

Example study sheet: Penguins

The first question is, where to begin? Each pose might suggest a new starting point. In poses where the head is visible, I often begin my sketch by starting with a mark for the eye. I try to sketch an abstract shape that is characteristic of the eye shape. Look hard before striking the mark. Once the shape is secured,

I shade it with vigorous sideways marks. Starting with the eye helps me get the head and body in proportion to it by working beak to tail, shape to shape, building out from the proportions of the head. Other times I begin by just throwing out a line, the curve of the back, for example, or a series of light loops.

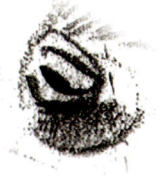 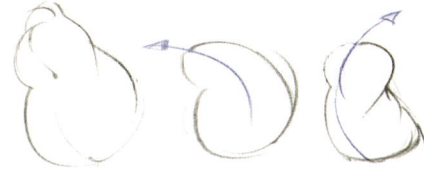 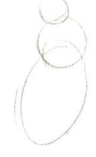 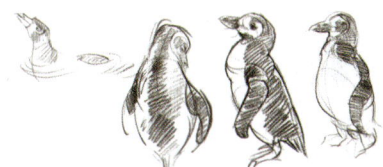

▲ **Eyes**
Try not to have a preconceived idea of what eyes look like; represent them with an abstract mark corresponding to the shape you are genuinely observing.

▲ **Dynamism and tension**
Imagine the body as a dynamic stress ball or a rubber egg. Experiment with creating dynamism and tension with this blob form, just like a stuffed pillow bent into different positions. The line of symmetry creates the line of action of the body.

▲ **Beak**
In repose, the beak of the penguin is often angled pointing up.

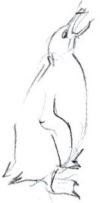 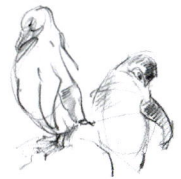 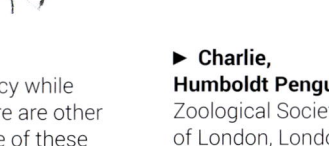

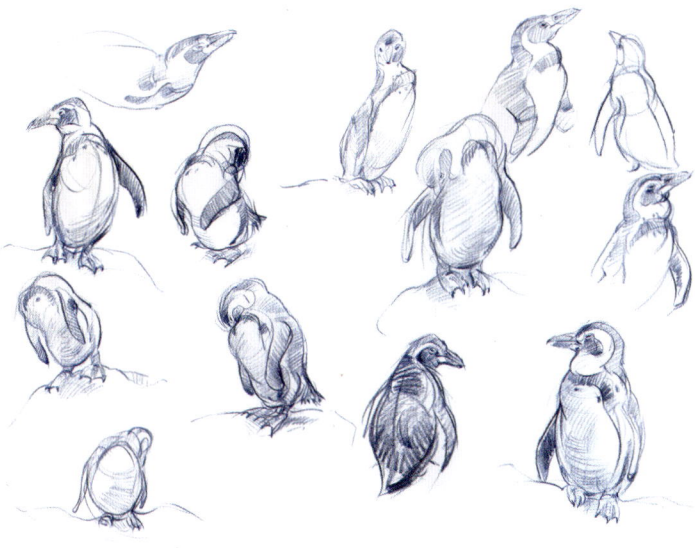

▲ **Capturing behaviour**
Besides the struggles of accuracy while sketching animals from life, there are other equally important elements. One of these is capturing characteristic behaviour, from vocalizations to preening.

▶ **Charlie, Humboldt Penguin**
Zoological Society of London, London Zoo, UK.

Gesture Drawings

To portray the characterful poses and unique movements of an animal, you can create what are known as gesture drawings. Gesture drawing is about capturing what your subject is doing rather than its appearance. A good place to practise this is at a farm or a zoo.

Choose a subject and try to capture the main thrust of its movement, as if you are experiencing the same action with your own body. Work rapidly and with determination. At first it might feel like you are scribbling, but this is part of the process. You are not looking to create a precise edge but the main 'oomph' of the pose. Don't worry about being messy; energetic mark-making will bring your subject to life.

Marks are created quickly and with vigour to capture the energy and character of the subject.

Tip

I suggest working with a soft pencil. I prefer a waxy colouring pencil over graphite, such as Faber Castell Polychromos. The pencil is a direct and uncomplicated medium that can quickly block in and force you to work boldly. You need to be able to capture the essence of the pose in a few fleeting marks.

A good understanding of the construction or anatomy of your subject supports any action analysis. Understanding the basic anatomy can aid in understanding an animal in motion and draw a convincing pose. Familiarize yourself with the pivot points of the skeleton and clearly understand where the elbow, wrist, knee and ankle are. Remember, though, you are not a camera, and gesture drawing can be interpretative – it's mainly about getting to the heart of the pose.

Freeze moments in time by capturing the gait of animals running, leaping and bounding.

Tip

The time it takes to capture the pose will take longer than the animal maintains the posture. With practice, try to develop a visual memory. Think of limbs as simple articulated tubes and the body as a flexible trunk with a bilateral line of symmetry.

Activity
Discover the drawings of Daumier. He brings a sense of drama and dynamism to his courtroom drawings. His characters are brought to life by picking out particular moments of heightened emotional tension – seizing the split second.

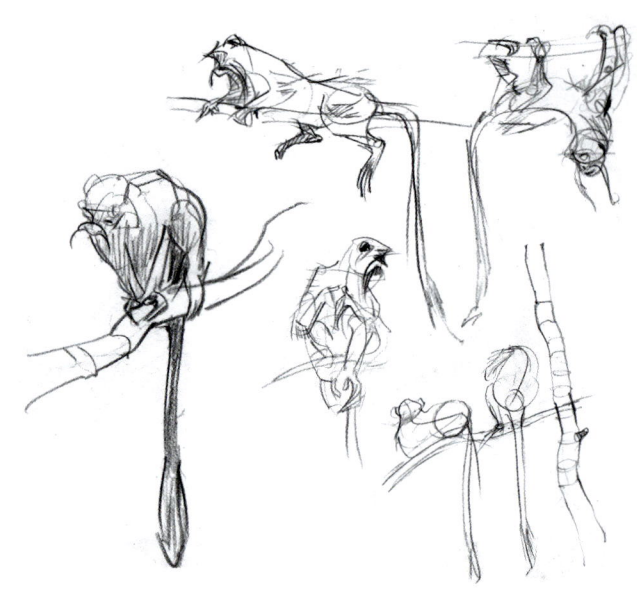

▲ **Emperor tamarin**
Zoological Society of London, London Zoo, UK.

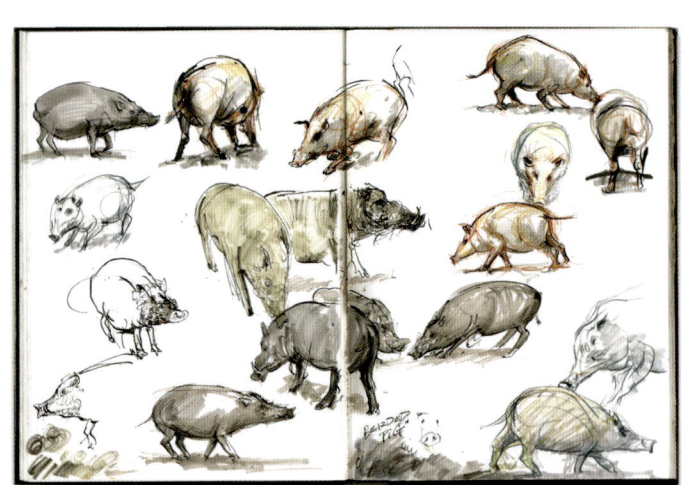

▶ **Pig study sheet**
The bearded pigs are snuffling and grunting, rooting around with their long snouts and propensity to get a bit muddy!

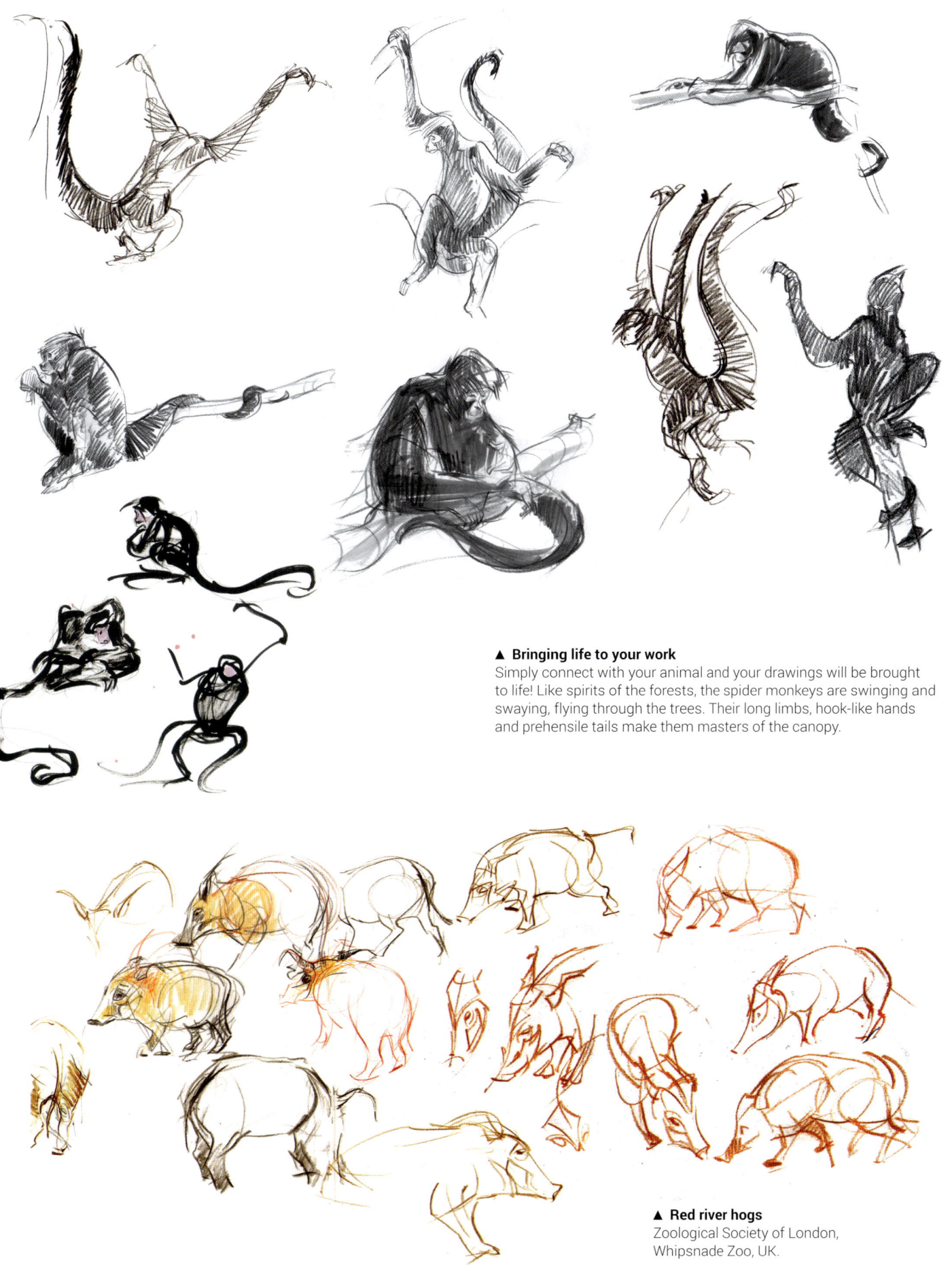

▲ Bringing life to your work
Simply connect with your animal and your drawings will be brought to life! Like spirits of the forests, the spider monkeys are swinging and swaying, flying through the trees. Their long limbs, hook-like hands and prehensile tails make them masters of the canopy.

▲ Red river hogs
Zoological Society of London, Whipsnade Zoo, UK.

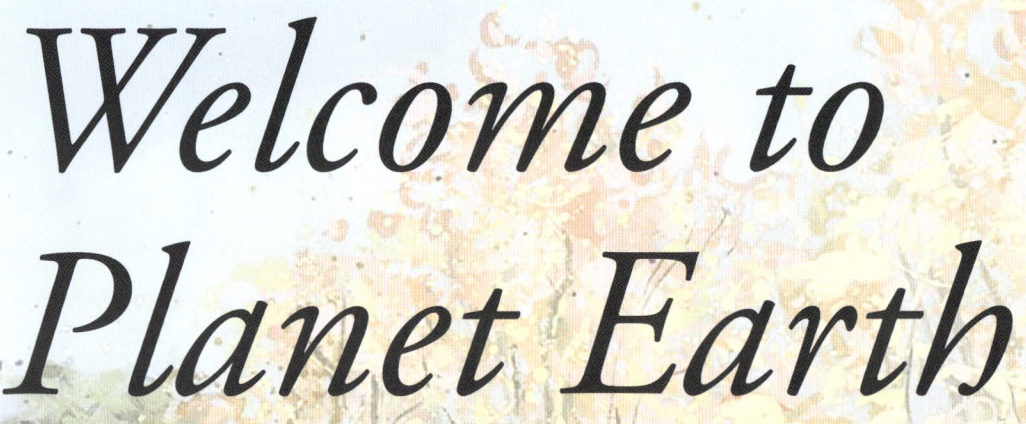

Welcome to Planet Earth

The Earth is the only planet in the Universe known to support life. Animals and other living organisms exist in a rare, oxygenated air and water zone, from the largely unexplored floors of the oceans to the sky. The deepest known point is the Mariana Trench, located in the western Pacific Ocean; measurements place the deepest portion at 36,200ft (11,034m). The highest-flying bird is the Rüppell's vulture, reaching equally staggering heights of some 37,000ft (11,300m) above sea level – higher than the death zone, where there are insufficient oxygen levels to sustain human life, which is considered to begin at 26,247ft (8,000m).

There are currently an estimated 8.7 million species of plants and animals in existence. Modern genetics shows that all this abundant life is related to each other. The story began some 3,000 million years ago, with mysterious yet humble beginnings, when molecules began to clump together to form cells. These were the seeds from which the tree of life has grown until we reach the present day, and what life we find is quite extraordinary!

From the humid, warm climes of the tropics that harbour an abundance of species, to the sun-baked deserts and the frozen poles, where the conditions for life to survive are at their harshest. Here, animals have evolved specialist adaptations to pioneer a place to live.

The Earth has a vast diversity of habitats, from rolling rivers and open seas to grassy plains, mountains and forests. In all these places, plants and animals have forged their way and over time adapted to them, not only to survive but to thrive.

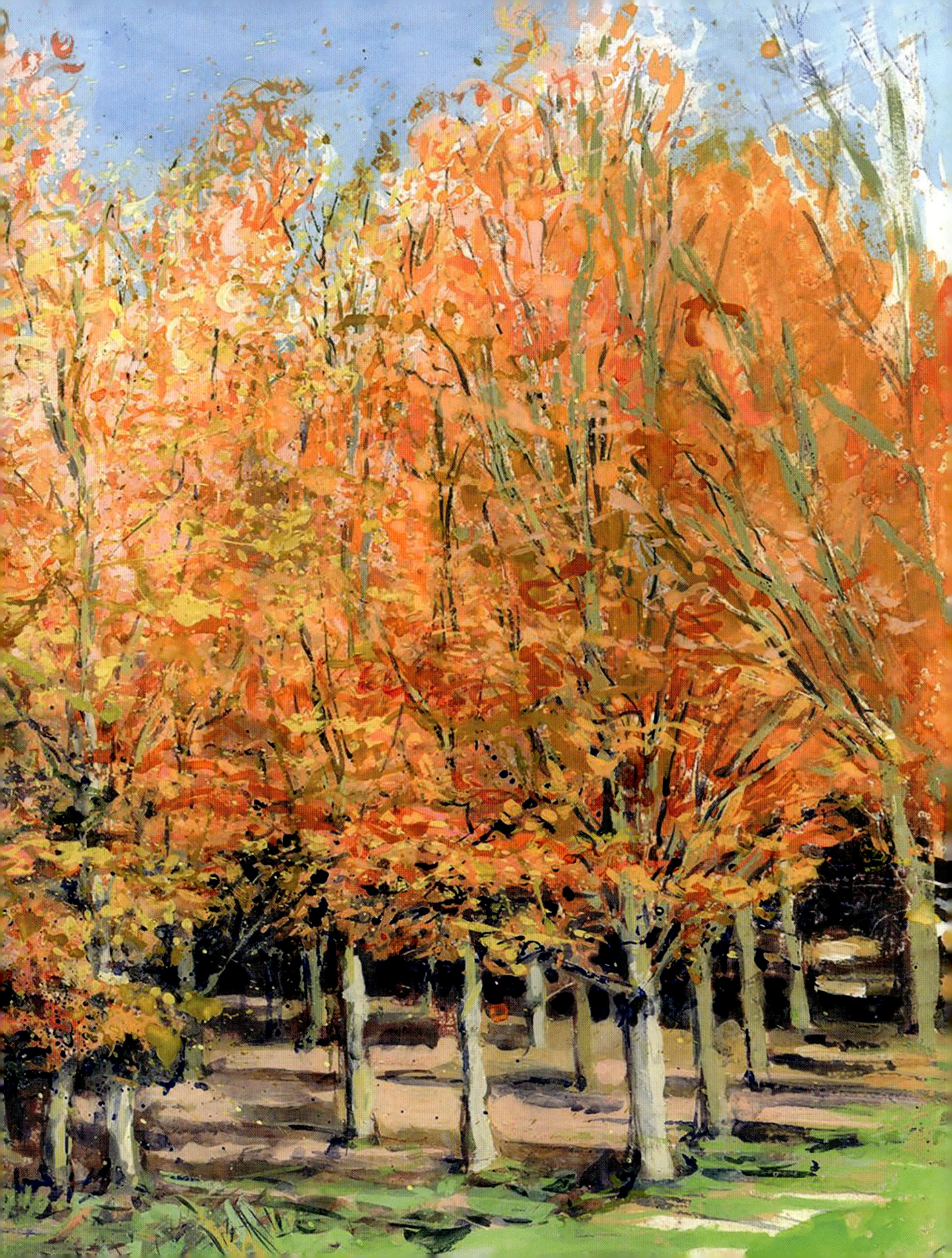

Animals and Plants: The Pioneers of Places

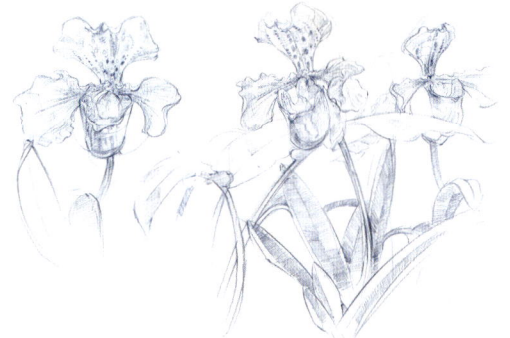

The foundations of the ecosystems of planet Earth were laid some 500 million years ago with the evolution of land plants and animals. Some 200 million years before that, life had begun in the sea, where more stable conditions existed. For many millennia, Earth was a barren and hostile place, with fierce winds, a baking sun and freezing nights, which were inhospitable for life to take root. When the land became green with the evolution of land plants, animals could abandon their previous home of the sea. From the ocean, which is the source of life, animals were able to clamber up and take advantage of land plants instead of those in the sea.

Ancestors such as millipedes were one of the earliest to venture onto land, with their segmented and armoured bodies. The hard carapace of their shell, an exoskeleton, now did an excellent job of keeping them moist out of the water. Their legs that worked in the sea adapted to the land. The shrimp is an ancestor of the garden woodlouse. All these animals that left the sea adapted to life on land and turned to breathe air rather than extract oxygen from water in sometimes unique ways. Insects, for instance, draw in oxygen through holes in their bodies known as spiracles, and the Bornean flat-headed frog has no lungs, getting its oxygen through its skin instead.

There is a fantastic array of different habitats on planet Earth, which have set forth a myriad of marvellous adaptations, enabling both animals and plants to take advantage of their environment. A spiky cactus, for instance, is adapted for sandy soil, dry climates and bright sunlight, and grows well in arid desert areas. It would not do well in hot, damp, fertile jungle habitat where, like overwatering a cactus at home, it would simply rot. An African elephant has enormous ears that they flap to keep cool in their tropical habitat. Animals such as a polar bear have thick white fur to stay warm in cold habitats and blend in with snow so they can hunt their prey more successfully. There are also nature's curiosities, such as the giant spring-like legs of the red kangaroo, enabling them to bound across the vast distances of the Australian outback.

Both animals and plants have adapted to survive the worst that the habitat may throw at them, from tropical storms and baking deserts to freezing polar nights.

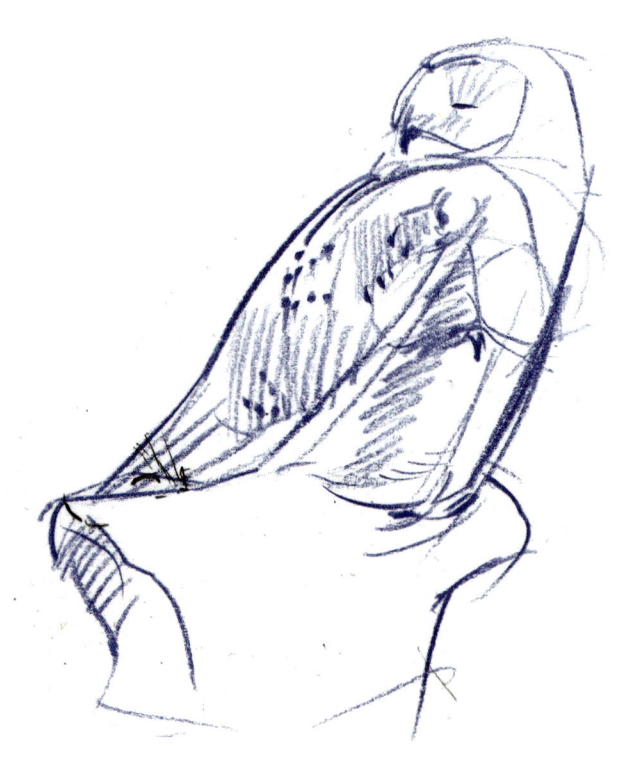

▶ Snowy owl
Some animals have made their way to the coldest places of them all, the northern mountains. Species have to be highly adapted to be able to survive here. The ghostlike snowy owl has brilliant white plumage that echoes its Arctic backdrop and acts as camouflage. They also have feathers on their feet to keep them warm.

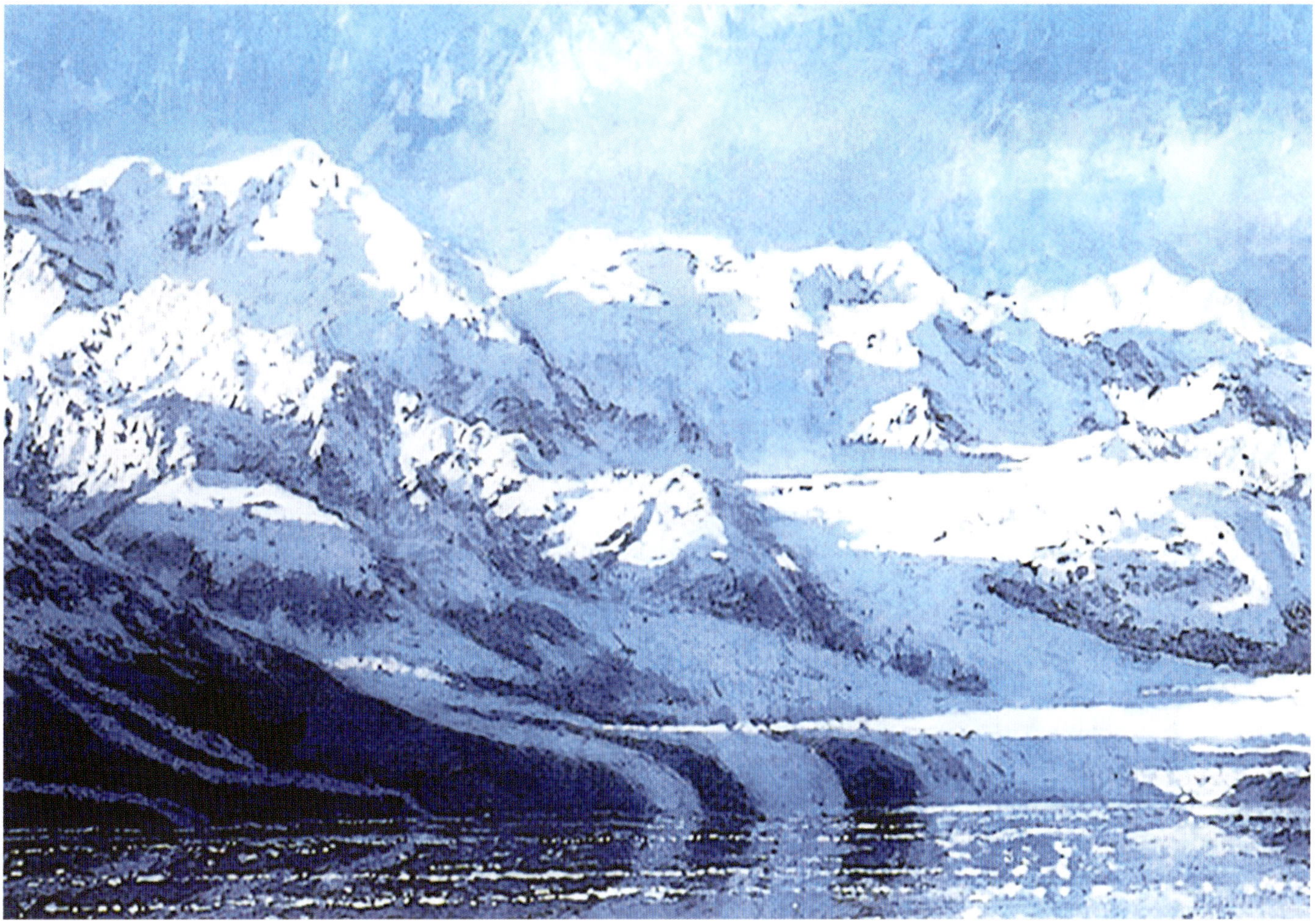

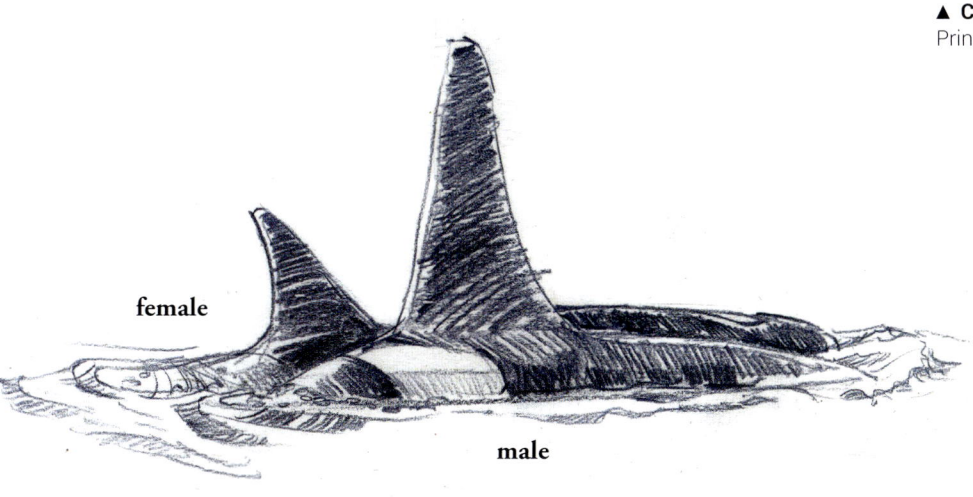

▲ Chugach Mountain Range
Prince William Sound, Alaska, USA.

▲ Orcas

Killer whales, also known as orcas, flourish in the pristine clear waters of Prince William Sound in Alaska, USA. Orcas are members of the dolphin family and are not whales, as their name implies. They are the largest, fastest and most powerful dolphin family members and live in groups called pods. Breathing air, orcas are sea mammals and have evolved from land animals that went back into the sea about 60 million years ago.

Orcas in the food chain

In the sea, at the base of the food chain are plants called phytoplankton, which provide food for the smallest animals, zooplankton. Zooplankton are in turn eaten by small fish, which are then prey for predatory fish and mammals. At the top are the apex predators, including orcas, who consume seals, fish, squid and sea birds. This is beneficial to the ecosystem as orcas keep seal numbers in check and stop them from overeating the fish.

What Are Habitats?

A habitat is a place where an organism, plant or animal makes its home. Differences in habitats are created by many factors, including the distance from the equator, height above sea level, weather patterns and topography. Some habitats, such as coral reefs are inhabited by a cornucopia of life with abundant biodiversity; others, such as the ice poles, have more challenging conditions, but they still support a uniquely varied life.

The earliest and most unexplored habitat is the marine environment. Marine habitats include smaller, more specialized habitats, including the open ocean and the ocean bed, coral reefs and rock pools, pure freshwater – ponds, rivers, lakes and even temporary freshwater puddles where life still finds a way – and brackish water (partly salty, partly freshwater) such as estuaries and mangrove swamps where different sources meet.

Terrestrial habitats range from the inhospitable polar caps to hot, humid rainforests, and from precipitous mountain ranges to flat, sunburnt deserts.

Plants vary the world over and have adapted to all the continents on earth. Their habitat needs to provide them with the right combination of light, air, water and soil.

For animals, their habitat has to provide everything that they need to find and gather food, select a mate and successfully reproduce. For residential animals, their habitat might be a single location; while for migratory species and those with a vast range or territory, their lifestyle depends on various habitats. Animals that live a double life and metamorphose, such as a dragonfly, breed and pupate in the water, an aquatic habitat, then graduate to lead their adult life in the air. For some animals, their habitat could be as temporary as an Indian muddy puddle created by a seasonal rainstorm, where a frog relies on incubating its eggs.

Habitats are occupied by more than one species. Over millennia animals and plants have evolved alongside each other, giving rise to symbiotic relationships. An example of this is the miraculous co-evolution of plants and their pollinators, from insects to hummingbird birds. Some hummingbirds'

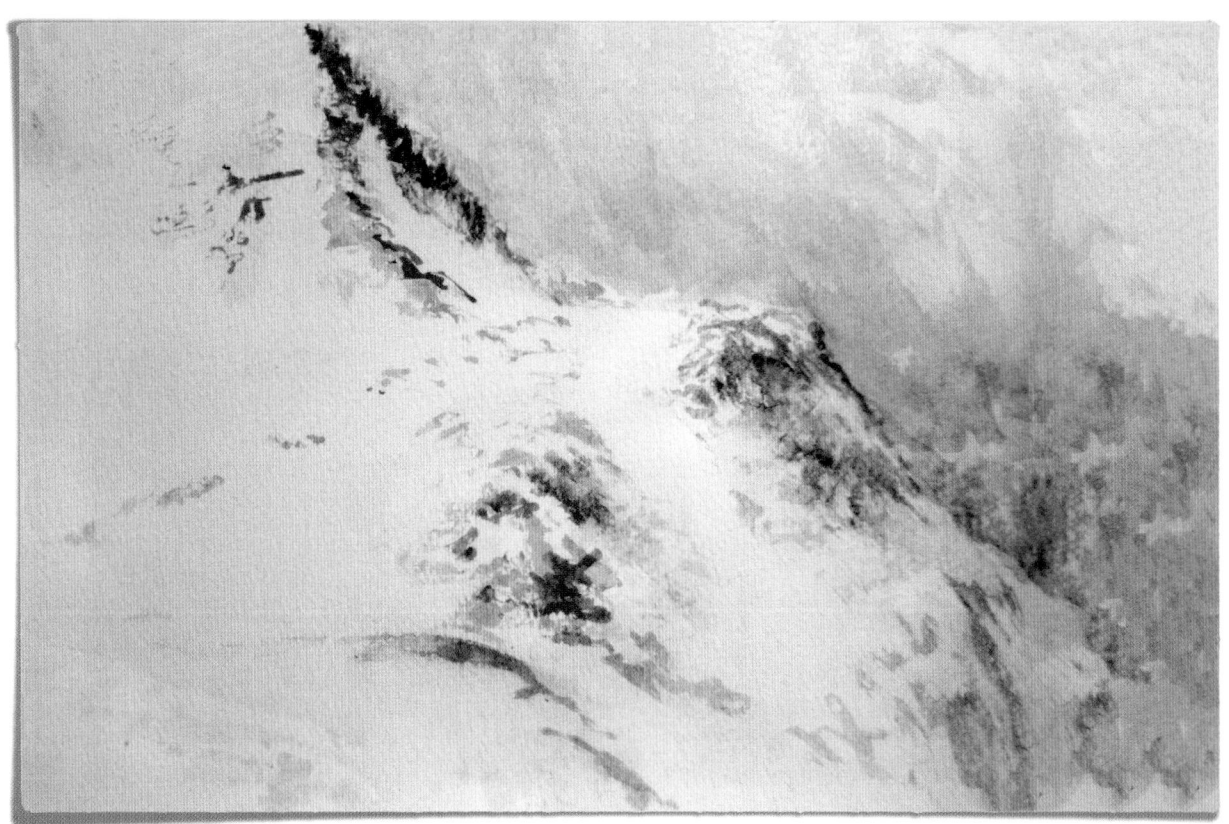

▲ **Whiteout clearing over Raven Glacier**
Chugach Mountain Range, Alaska, USA.

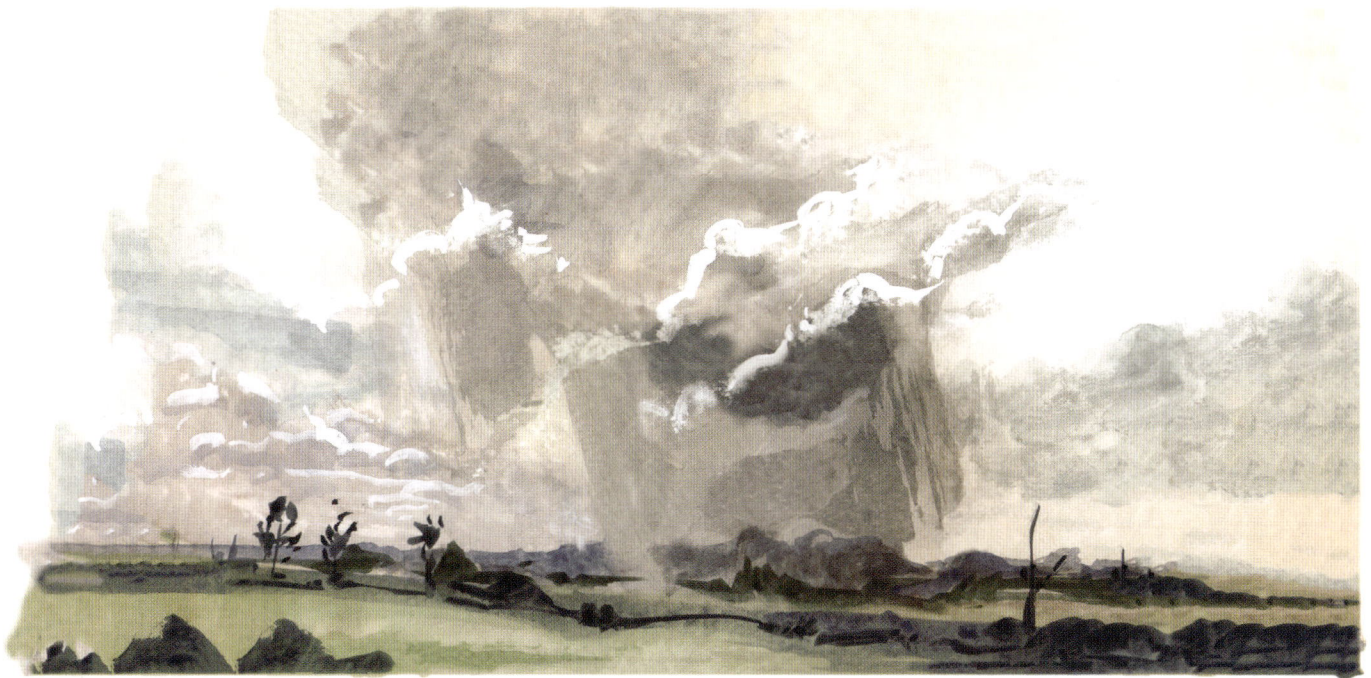

▲ Fields
Bury St Edmunds, Suffolk, UK.

beaks are so specific as to feed on only one type of flower, resulting from the flower and bird having evolved together.

Home

A home is a place within a habitat, where a particular animal species can protect itself and its young from the weather and predators. There are many different types of animal homes. Some examples include birds' and ants' nests, a beaver's dam, and a mole's burrow. For many spider species, home is a silk-woven web that catches its food. Bees and wasps create wax inside their bodies that is the building material for hives. Bats make a home from caves, as do conger eels in the sea, staying safe during the daylight hours and coming out to feed at night.

Microhabitats

An oak tree is a home to countless species and could be considered a myriad of microhabitats. Bugs make a home within the multitude of nooks and crannies of the bark. Naturally formed hollows create cavities for nesting owls; a large trunk and branches with ridged bark are ideal for a treecreeper to grip and climb and build a nest behind a flap of loose bark. Squirrels typically build their homes, called dreys, in the forks of tree branches out of twigs, dry leaves and grass. A wren shelters from the rain beneath the leaves. It is cool and damp at the oak roots, creating just the right conditions for fungi to grow. Around the roots scavenging insects such as beetles feed on dead animals and fallen leaf material, thereby recycling nutrients back into the soil and aerating it. As decomposers, insects help create topsoil, the nutrient-rich layer of soil that allows the oak and other plants to grow.

What is the difference between a biome and an ecosystem?

A biome is a community of plants and animals with common characteristics for the environment they exist in. These are shaped by various factors, such as temperature, altitude and rainfall. These areas that share common features can be found worldwide, over a range of continents, and include examples such as the polar deserts, tundra, grassy savannah and sandy desert.

An ecosystem is a term used to describe how all the living plants and animals and the non-living, the temperature, rocks and humidity, interact to form a circle of life. Each organism has a role to play within the ecosystem.

A biome can be made up of many different ecosystems. For example, an ocean biome can contain coral reefs, kelp forests and hydrothermal vents.

Seasons of the Year

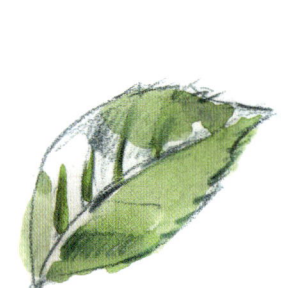

The powerhouse behind all life on Earth is the Sun. The Sun, just another star, sits at the centre of our solar system. Spinning around it are the spherical planets with their moons, in an accidental arrangement, rotating like clockwork. Without this radiating warm light, there would be no life. And we are just the right distance away in what is known as the Goldilocks Zone.

Leaves lie at the base of the food chain; they create the foundations of life and have evolved to convert the energy of the light of the Sun into oxygen through photosynthesis. Harnessing the power of the Sun, these leaves are beautiful life-creating machines. Photosynthesis is the process by which green plants use the energy of the sun to convert carbon dioxide and water into sugars that are the plant's food. A by-product of this process is the creation of oxygen, which is released into the air and enables the rest of all life to survive.

Oxygen, Earth's life-support system, is created as a by-product of a plant's feeding mechanism.

The Moon

4.5 billion years ago, the Earth was struck by a Mars-sized body called Theia. This massive object hit the Earth at an oblique angle knocking the Earth out of kilter and sending a vast amount of rubble into orbit. Following the scientific laws of the potato formula that states objects in space above a certain mass will coalesce to become spheres, it happened that rubble combined into one to become the Moon. This collision also pushed the Earth off its balance by 23 degrees, which means in August, the Northern Hemisphere is tilted towards the Sun and has warmer summer weather.

The Moon creates distinct habitats, such as rock pools, with the ebb and flow of the tides, and it also affects the mechanisms of life on the planet. Once a year, entire colonies of coral reefs simultaneously release plumes of tiny eggs for a universal synchronistic breeding event triggered by the light of the Moon.

Seasonal impact on behaviour

The seasons affect the behaviour of animals – some hibernate or migrate – and plants can become dormant. One of the most spectacular natural phenomena is the annual migration of the monarch butterflies across North America. The migration starts in September in southern Canada and takes the butterflies several months to arrive in central Mexico around November. No individual completes the entire trip, but rather the butterflies reproduce along the way. It takes at least four

generations to enable the butterflies to complete this incredible journey. It is interesting to think that the sole reason for this migration was the collision with Theia.

The two polar seasons

Because of their geographical position at the poles, both the Arctic and the Antarctic receive less energy from the Sun and have only two seasons, as the Earth's tilt pivots them towards and away from the Sun. In the height of summer, the Sun does not set, and in winter, the Sun does not rise, creating conditions of 24-hour light or dark.

Located in both the extreme northern and southern hemispheres, temperatures can both drop to below -40°F (-40°C) in their winters, making it hard for both plant and animal life to survive. Both locations are vulnerable ecosystems to climate change – as the Earth warms, more dramatic effects can be witnessed here than anywhere else on Earth.

The Arctic summer lasts from June through September, being in the Northern Hemisphere, while Antarctica's summer is from October to February, being in the Southern Hemisphere. Here the hostile freezing conditions create a challenging environment for life; however, beneath the dark water, life is abundant with a rich diversity of sea anemones, starfish and jellyfish creating a vibrant and colourful display on the seabed. However, life becomes a matter of grim survival between predator and prey in these relatively plantless places on land.

The four temperate seasons

Every year, four spectacular seasons transform the landscape in the temperate zone. They each bring with them opportunities and enormous challenges for both the animals and plants. Between May and August, the Northern Hemisphere is exposed to more direct sunlight because the hemisphere faces the Sun. The same is true of the Southern Hemisphere between November and January. This creates the four seasons governed by changes in the intensity of sunlight that reaches the Earth's surface. These changes in temperature cause plants to become dormant in winter and animals to undergo hibernation or migrate.

Each of the four seasons inspires different feelings. The ancient cycle of spring buds giving way to flower-filled meadows, the blazing riot of autumn's decay to the drifting of blue-white snow has inspired countless artists over the generations. There is no better way to experience the effects these seasonal changes have than to get out into nature, where you will notice these changes with greater intensity.

The one or two tropical seasons

The tropics lie on the Earth's equator, like a belt around the middle of the planet. These regions are closest to the Sun and receive the strongest rays of sunlight all year round. This tropical region is least affected by the Earth's tilt being at its middle, the result being that it has one or two seasons. Each day is pretty much like any other in some areas, with one hot season all year round. In other regions, there are two seasons, a dry and rainy one. It is often recommended not to visit these areas in the rainy season, where hefty rainfall can last between one to three months.

▼ Migration formations
Some migratory birds fly in a V formation for efficiency. Flying just behind and to the side of the bird in front, timing their wing beats to catch the uplifting eddies. The birds in this painting are pink-footed geese, which breed in eastern Greenland, Iceland and Svalbard. Every year flocks migrate to spend the hostile winter season in northwest Europe.

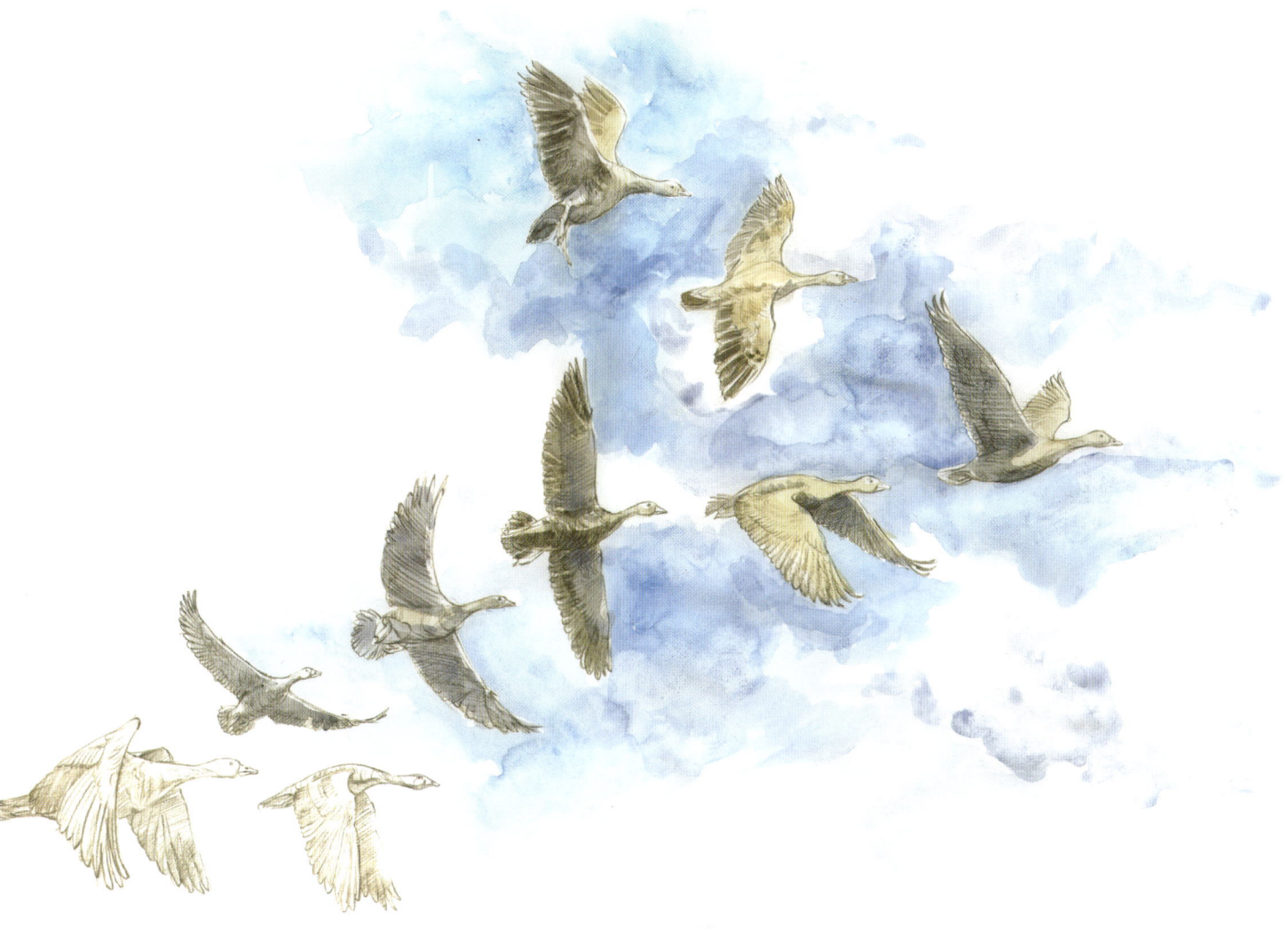

Weather Patterns

Across the Earth, the different climates create distinct weather patterns. As the sky often provides the backdrop and sets the atmosphere for a painting of the natural world, I think about what I want to capture from it before I focus on anything else.

Watercolour has to be one of the best mediums for painting skies. You can explore wet into wet (see page 27), letting one colour bloom into another; you can experiment with lifting out (see below); and you can enjoy painting the smoky blue-grey shadow of cloud forms and their cast shadows.

Clouds

Clouds don't have a specific colour because they are water vapour evaporated from our seas, freshwater lakes and rivers, which float through the air. As light falls on the water vapour it is reflected, giving the clouds their form.

The typical snow-white depiction of clouds can be created by leaving gaps on the paper, lifting out, adding White Gouache, or a combination of these techniques. You can even be more experimental and use a wax resist (see page 27).

Lifting out

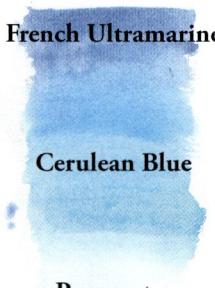

French Ultramarine

Cerulean Blue

Pure water

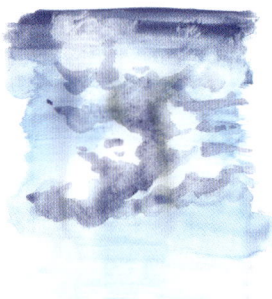

1 The sky is lighter at the horizon as we look through more of the atmosphere. On a clear day, this creates a smooth gradient. Apply a line of very watery French Ultramarine at the top with a thick, soft brush and work your way down the paper in long horizontal strokes. Start to dilute the wash with Cerulean Blue, working in more dilute washes as you progress until you end at the bottom of the gradient with pure water.

2 When the paint is still wet, lift out pigment with a sponge, cotton wool or a wipe. This is also a good technique for cirrus clouds characterized by thin, wispy strands, taking its name from the Latin word cirrus, meaning a curling lock of hair.

3 Add in the bottom of the clouds to create a generic cloud. As clouds are formed of water, use plenty of French Ultramarine and paint with feathery brush strokes.

Positive and negative shapes

The shapes formed by changes in space are referred to as positive and negative shapes. Negative shapes represent the space between objects, while positive shapes represent the space where they exist.

1 Create the negative shape of a cloud by leaving a gap as you draw with the brush.

2 Create a shadow colour mix by carefully observing the colour of the base of the cloud. Clouds are like sponges to reflected light, particularly at sunset.

Blue skies

Light travels in a straight line unless it knocks into something. Sunlight is scattered in all directions by the tiny molecules of air in Earth's atmosphere. As blue is the shortest wavelength, it scatters more and creates a blue sky. Although there are many moods of blue sky, no two days are the same and there are many ways the colours can be interpreted so that the land and the sky work in harmony, setting the scene, the time of day and weather conditions.

Light levels and direction

The intensity of light and the direction of the sun defines the level of contrast in the lit elements of the landscape. Direct sunlight creates a strong contrast, and the range of tonality is wide, while overcast days soften the distinct tonal contrast and create a more subtle range.

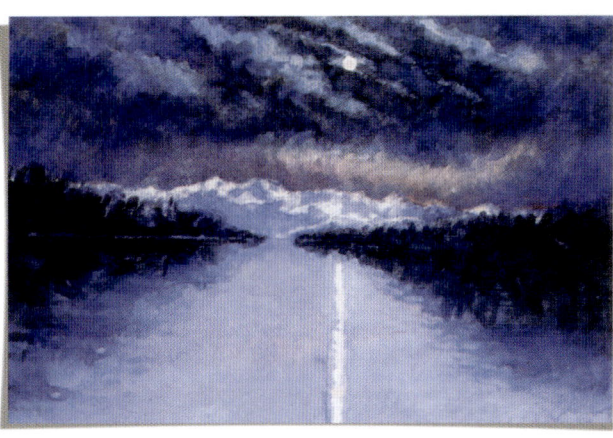

▲ **Back light**
Known as 'contre jour', against the light throws the clouds into silhouette against the moon beams.

▲ **Top light**
This stratus cloud study was painted at midday when the light is directly overhead and at its brightest. I used the negative shapes technique (see opposite), which is the technique I predominantly use.

▲ **Evening light**
I used wet into wet gradients (see page 27) to capture the changing colours on the horizon after sunset.

Moody skies

I believe we see with both the eye and heart; stormy weather conditions can lead to some really lively brushwork and subtle tonal variations and a hot summer's evening can result in a lot of warm colours on the horizon.

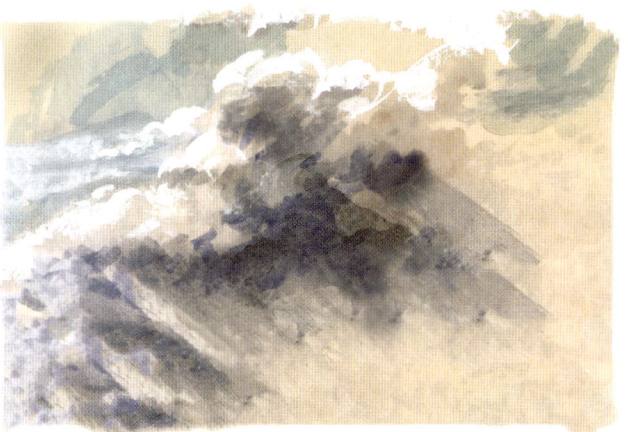

▲ **Showers on a summer's day**
To capture sheets of rain as they descended from storm clouds, I applied an overall wash of Yellow Ochre mixed with Alizarin Crimson, then dragged my brush at an angle to show the wind direction. I used a combination of Payne's Grey, French Ultramarine and Ivory Black for the bottom of the clouds and left areas of white to capture where the sunlight hits the top of the fluffy mounds.

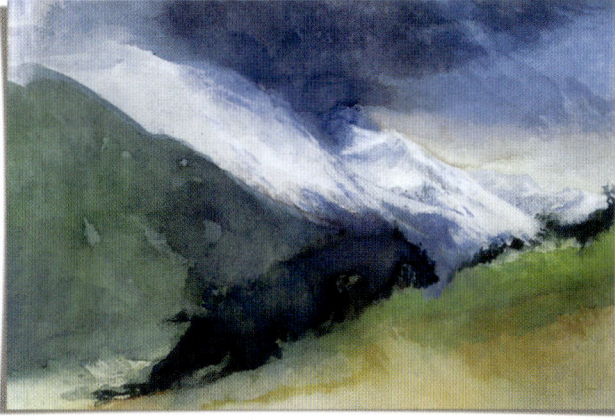

▲ **Storm clouds**
Encroaching storm clouds above Eagle River, Chugach Mountain Range, Alaska, USA, create a sense of foreboding and heightened drama.

Mountainous Regions

Mountains are a challenging habitat with high altitudes and rugged slopes. They can be found in all polar, temperate, tropical and sub-tropical climates. Here the air is thin, and food can be scarce, as vegetation decreases the higher up the mountain you go. There is more space with fewer animals and predators adapted to this rugged and treacherous zone than the lowlands.

In Alaska's Arctic, animals have adapted to walk through the deep snow found on the lower slopes of its mountainous landscape. Both predator and prey have evolved adaptations in their feet and legs. The ptarmigan, for example, has feathery feet that serve as snowshoes, enabling them to move more easily across the snow. Other Arctic wildlife, like the snowshoe hare and caribou, have enlarged feet that stop them from sinking into the snow. The lynx, which relies heavily on the snowshoe hare as a prey species, also has highly adapted large paws. Moose, on the other hand, have long, thin legs that help them walk through the snow when it is at depth.

In the temperate zone, the Alpine ibex can climb a near-vertical rock face. These animals have adapted to life in rocky mountainous regions of the European Alps. Their split hooves and rubber-like soles create an excellent climbing shoe, and they can traverse the steepest cliff faces.

In the tropics, the warm climate means that vegetation tends to extend higher up the mountainside. As their name implies, mountain gorillas live in forests high in the mountains, at elevations of 8,000–13,000 ft (2,400–4,000m). The mountain gorilla has thicker fur, and more of it, than the lowland species. The hair helps them to survive in a habitat where temperatures often drop below freezing at night.

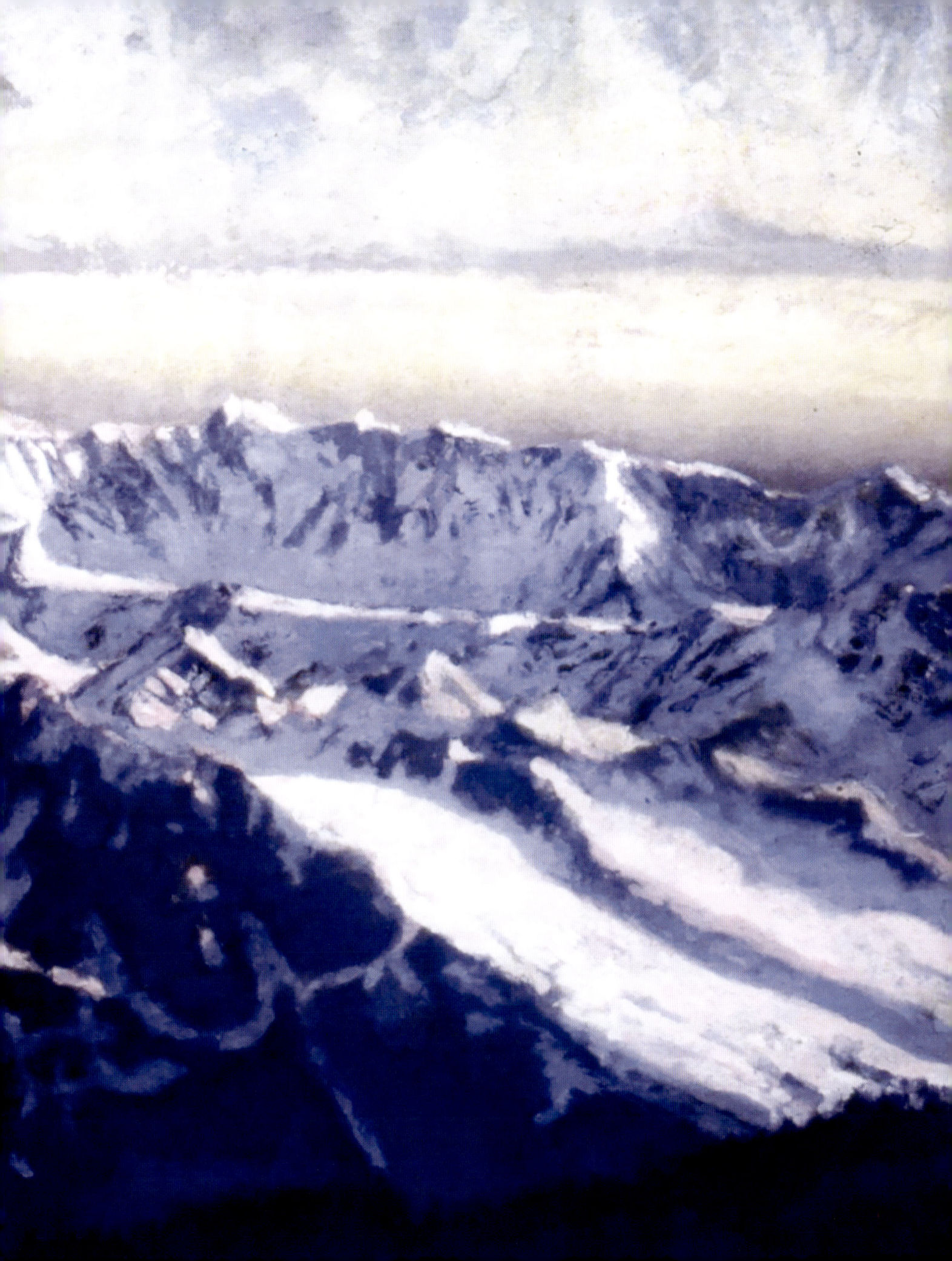

Mountain Ranges

Mountains make great subjects for practising atmospheric perspective (see page 19); from a low viewpoint, they spire into the sky with majestic splendour and a jagged silhouette. From a high viewpoint, mountain ranges can be seen as a series of flat, sharp-edged, proscenium-like layers that become lighter in the distance.

I painted this series of mountainscapes en plein air (in other words, outdoors, from life). There is no underdrawing, and they were created by placing a patchwork of colours together on a French Ultramarine underpainting. The mountain contour was created by painting the negative shape (see page 42) of the sky with a Cerulean Blue. After this, I added the vegetation with a light wash of green in varying shades.

I selected the mountain's peak to be the focal point, and this is where I started. You can visualize the top of the mountain as a triangle, where one side is generally in blue shade, as the sun hits the form from one side. I think of the abstract shapes of white space and blue shadows as snow shadow patches.

The negative shape of the Cerulean Blue sky creates the skyline. Carefully I paint towards the mountain contour, trying to capture the character of the form. I try to shape the mountain as I feel its grandeur.

I begin these outdoor sketches with no underlying drawing but by creating abstract snow shadow patches of French Ultramarine.

Lower down where the mountain vegetation was sprouting, like creating a jigsaw puzzle, I juxtaposed a piece of green, the lightest shade, and in the same shape I saw.

I break the rock outcrops down into two shades and paint the lightest shade first.

Finally, the darker notes of the rocks and plants are added.

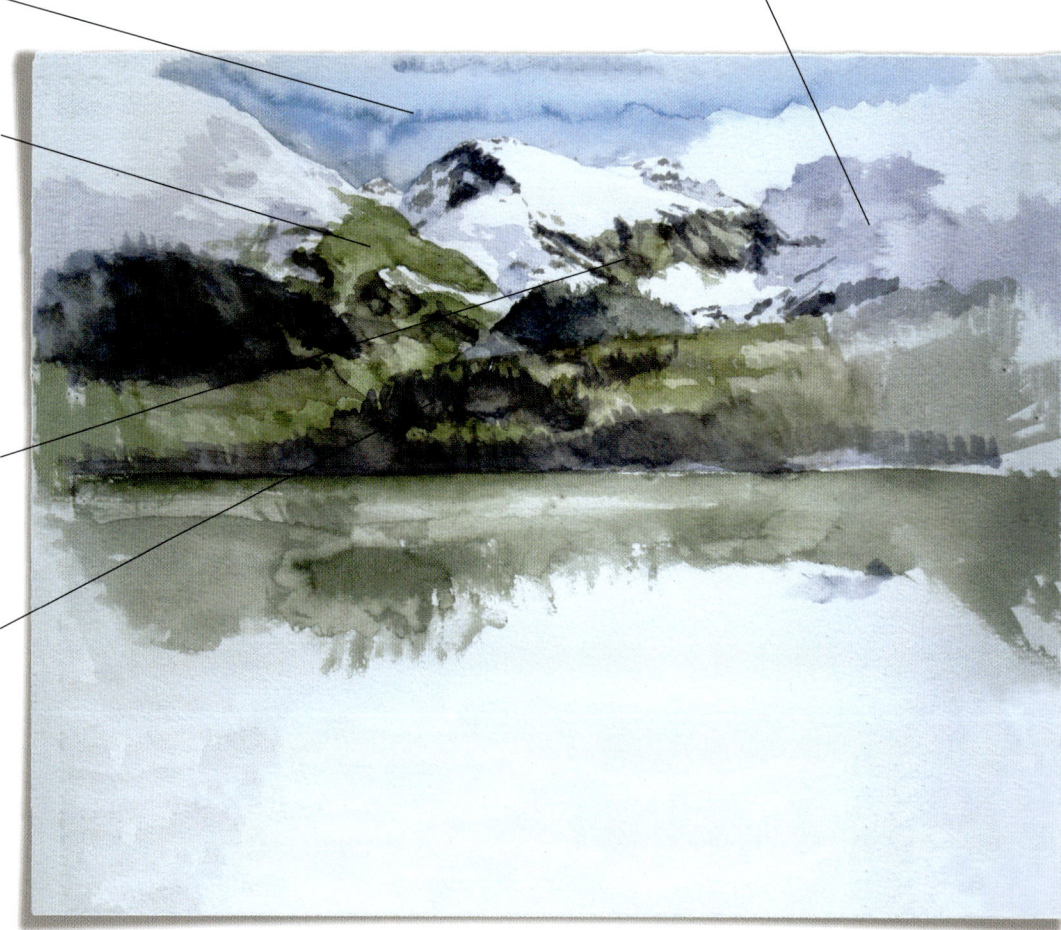

Tutorial: *Distant Mountains*

In this simple tutorial, the aim is to simplify what we see and to view the landscape almost as a stage set or proscenium, where vertical planes of stage furniture overlap to create depth.

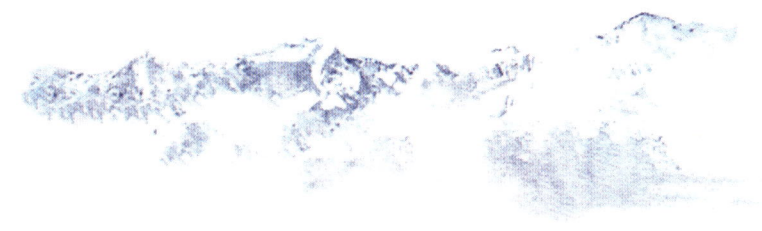

1 *Using French Ultramarine, a thin No. 1 rigger brush and other small watercolour brushes, first create bright blue shadows. Simplify and mass together the ridges and gullies to create an impression of the mountains in the distance.*

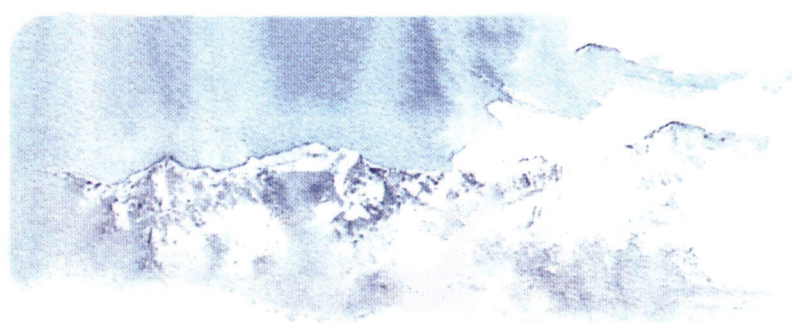

2 *Now with a medium-sized brush, wash in the sky with Cerulean Blue, leaving a small white lip on the peaks of the mountains.*

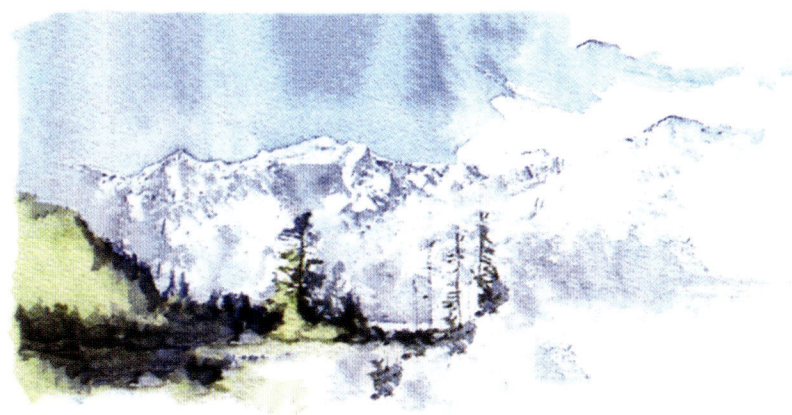

3 *Next, wash in a light Sap Green for vegetation in the light. Once dry, you can bring in the darker shadows with a mixture of Viridian Green and French Ultramarine.*

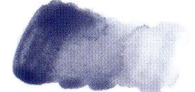

French Ultramarine

Cerulean Blue

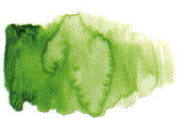

Sap Green

Viridian Green

Tip
Using clear water and a clean brush is key to capturing the snow's vividness and the clear blue sky.

Tutorial: *Craggy Rocks*

Spectacular rock formations on mountainsides are created by the weathering howling winds. They are excellent subjects for practising perspective and capturing shadows. In this study, by gradually layering the shadow of form and cast shadow the rock formations appear to be bathed in light.

I created the composition by taking elements I liked from a couple of photographs. You could do the same or use my picture as a reference.

Playing with perspective

The primary rule of two-point perspective (see page 18) is that any object with parallel sides, such as a box, will recede to a vanishing point on the eyeline. Cuboid shapes at different angles to the viewer will therefore recede to a variety of vanishing points along the eyeline.

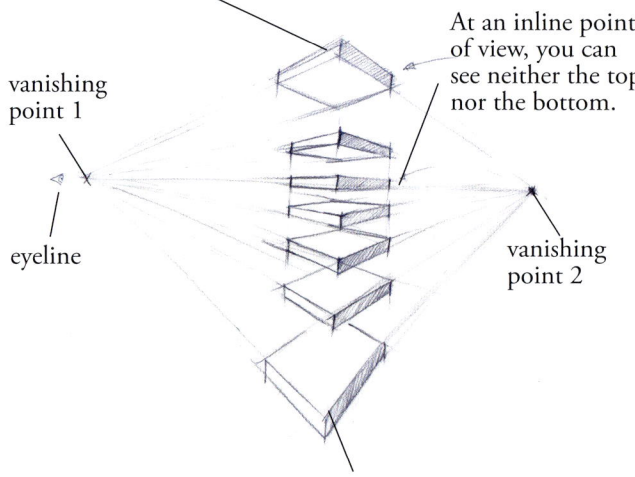

The higher above the eyeline, the more you can see of the base.

At an inline point of view, you can see neither the top nor the bottom.

vanishing point 1

eyeline

vanishing point 2

The further below the eyeline, the more you can see of the top.

▶ **Widget**
Shadow of form is a uniform shade over the plane in shadow.

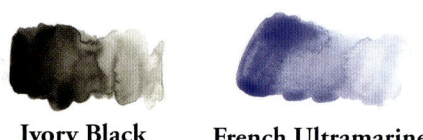

Ivory Black   **French Ultramarine**

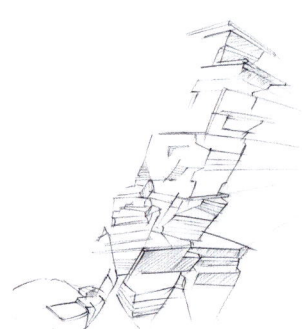

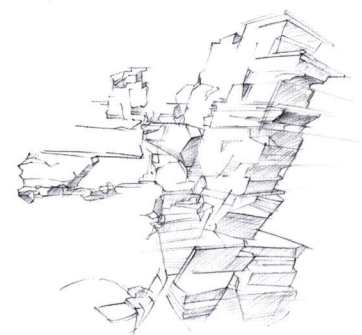

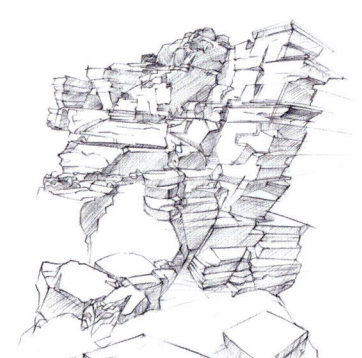

1 *First pick an area to start blocking in the basic shapes. I used a dark blue Polychromos pencil for this. Be aware of the parallel lines receding to a vanishing point on the left and right. Remember that these vanishing points will move along the eyeline depending on the angle of the cuboid shape.*

2 *Now add shading to clarify the boundaries between light and shade and emphasize changes in the planes with the direction of your mark-making.*

3 *Move from shape to shape, using the cracks as landmarks as your pencil traverses the craggy stack.*

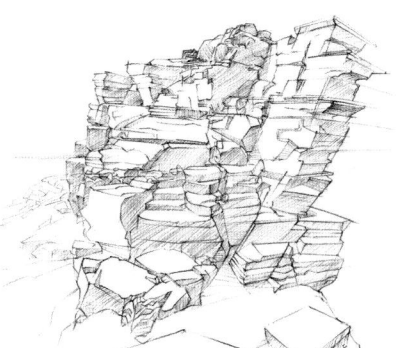

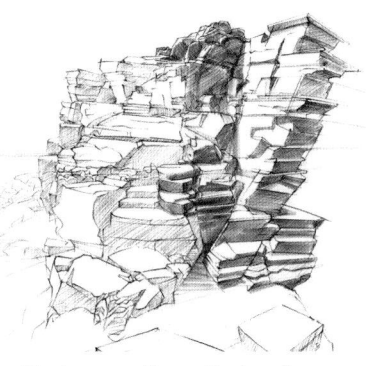

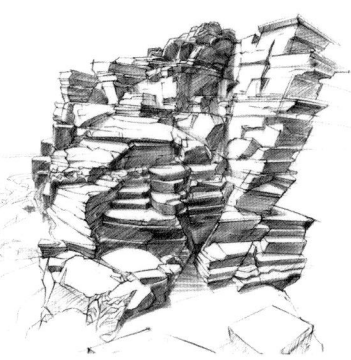

4 *Gradually allow your drawing to grow.*

5 *Next, cover the entirety of your drawing with a light wash of Ivory Black and French Ultramarine. If you wish, you can add a touch of granulation medium (see page 27) into the mix to create a speckled texture.*

6 *Squinting at the image reduces detail, allowing you to focus on the main areas of light and shade. Using a more concentrated mix of colour, paint the shadows with a No. 6 medium-sized brush.*

7 *Emphasize the cracks and use them to help model the form by wrapping them around the boulders – a rigger brush is a good tool for this. Try to capture the interplay between light and shade of abstract shapes that combine to create the illusion of a rock stack.*

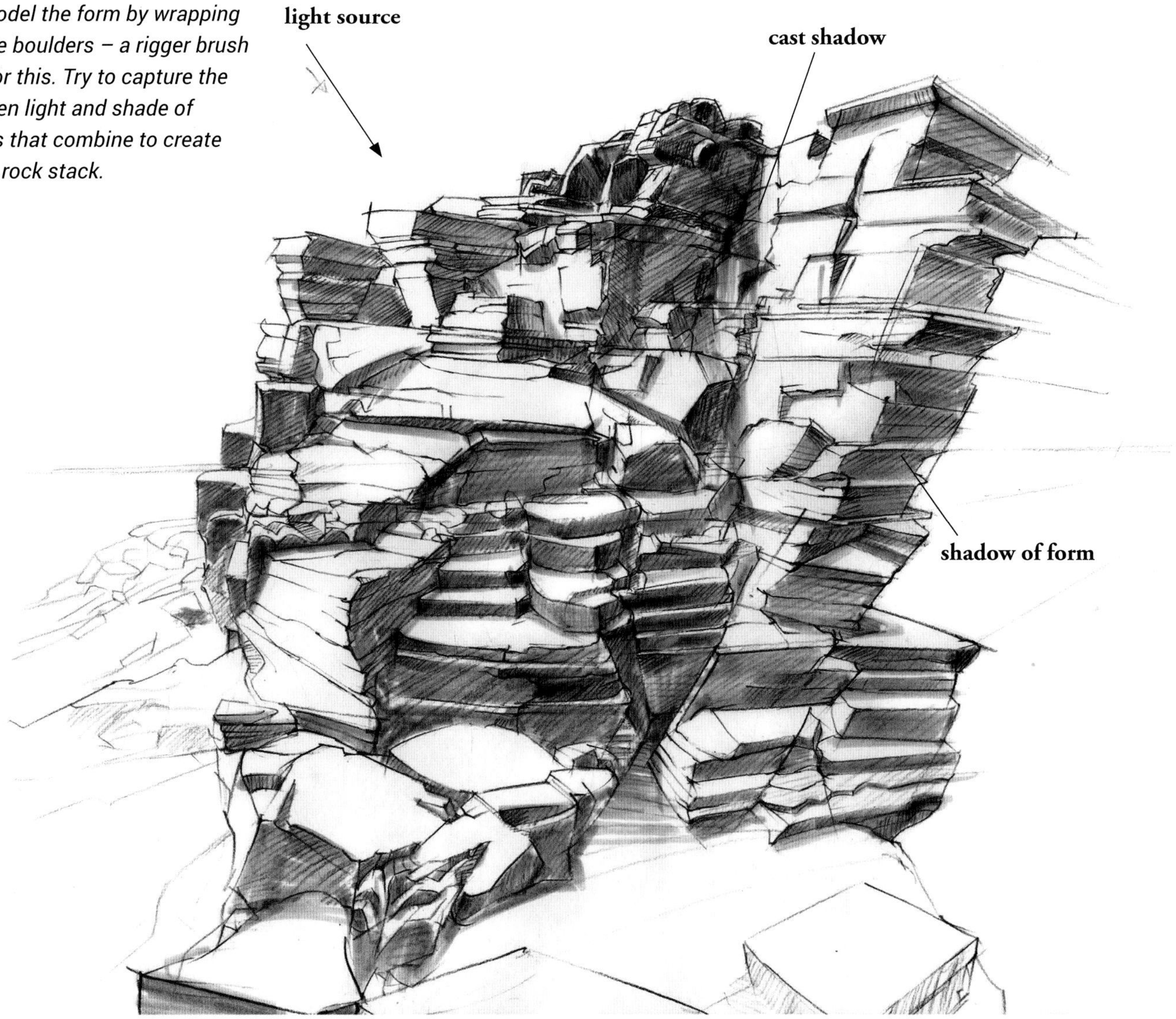

light source

cast shadow

shadow of form

Study Sheet: *Lynx*

Cats are a supple and elastic subject to sketch, combining incredible speed, agility and coordination into a single bound, and none more so than the powerful lynx.

There are four species of lynx (Canadian, Iberian, Eurasian and bobcat) that enjoy the cool conditions of North America and Eurasia. It is one of the most adaptable of all the wild cats and has a vast territory, from rocky mountain slopes to woodlands.

All lynx are noted for their characteristic pointy ears and a moustache-shaped sweep of fur on their cheeks. They have a lithe, muscular body with powerful hindquarters. An acute sense of sound and binocular vision combined with lightning reflexes makes them a very successful predator. Their principal prey is deer, goats and any hoofed mammal up to four times their size and even smaller animals such as hares, which is a speciality of the Canadian lynx.

The Eurasian lynx inhabits both mountainous and woodland regions from Northern Europe to East Asia. They have a white underbelly, as do all lynx, and a rusty ochre back. To help break up the body's shape, the cat's coat is peppered with spot and stripe markings.

As climates get colder and more northerly, different species of lynx gain progressively thicker and lighter coloured fur and their paws become larger and more padded so that they can walk on the cold, soft snow.

Anatomy
Knowing a little about the anatomy can help you understand what you are looking at and inform your painting.

Ears
The ears are large and funnel-like, which can point in different directions to draw in information about the prey's whereabouts.

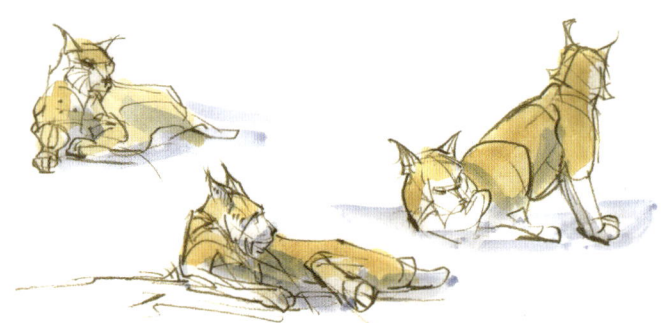

▲ **A relaxed family group of Eurasian lynx**
Zoological Society of London, Whipsnade Zoo, UK.

Muscles
This Canadian lynx muscle anatomy illustration applies to all species of lynx and all cats in general.

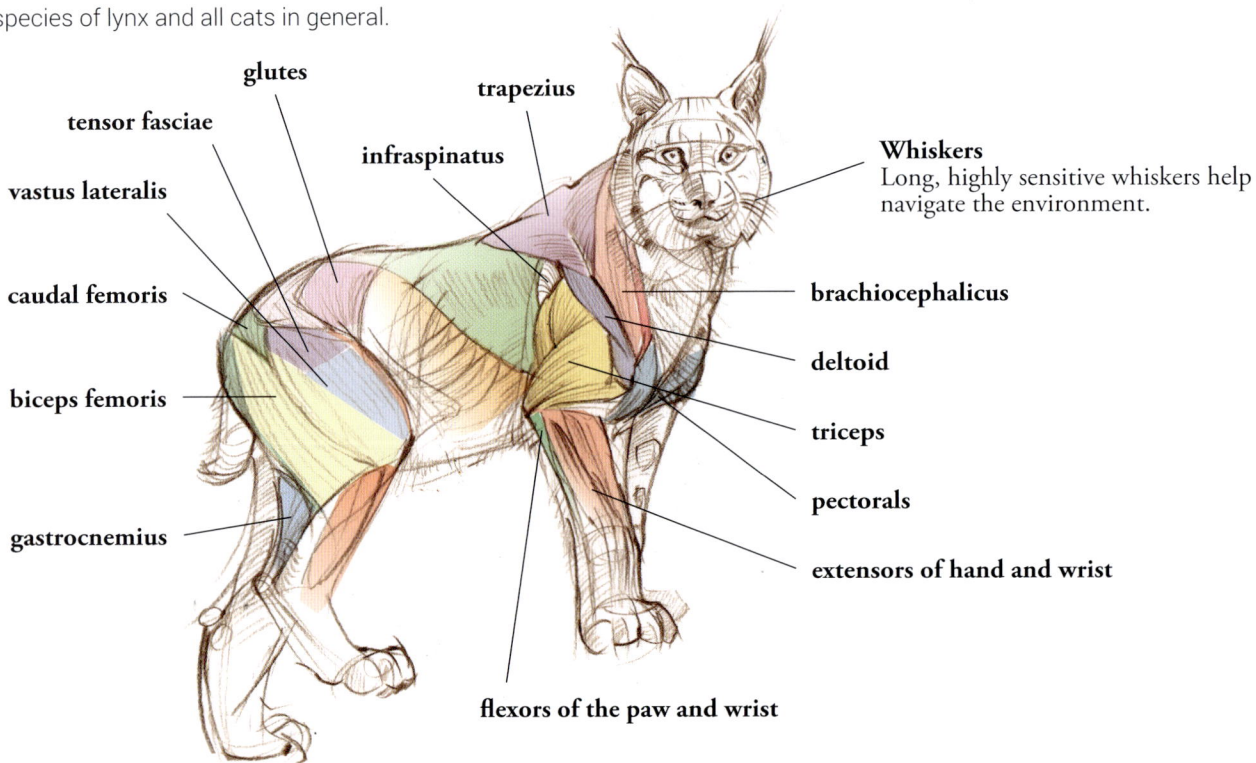

glutes

tensor fasciae

trapezius

infraspinatus

vastus lateralis

caudal femoris

biceps femoris

gastrocnemius

Whiskers
Long, highly sensitive whiskers help navigate the environment.

brachiocephalicus

deltoid

triceps

pectorals

extensors of hand and wrist

flexors of the paw and wrist

Predator stance

The foot stance of all cats is digitigrade (walking on toes). There are five digits on the front foot and four on the back. Each digit has a curved retractable claw that sits above the pad on the bottom of the foot. These pads are surrounded by fur, which assists in silent hunting and insulation.

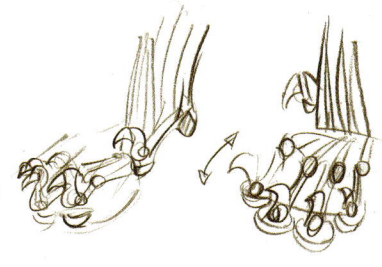

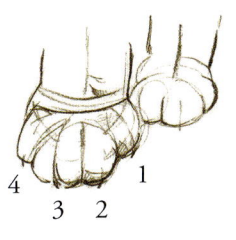 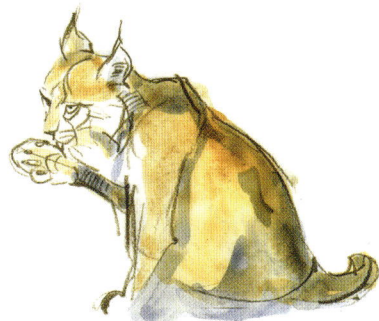

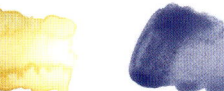 

▲ **Hind paw**
four claws

▲ **Front paw**
five claws

Stereoscopic vision

Forward-facing eyes that can contract to a slit to create the classic cat-eye shape and dilate to a large pupil disc are excellent for night hunting.

Snowshoe paws

The Canadian lynx has really big paws that look disproportionate to the size of its body. These are an adaptation to help them walk in deep snowy conditions without sinking.

Movement and action

Watercolour is ideal for capturing the movement of animals because of the liveliness and immediacy of this watery medium. Particles of pigments floating around in the water are in themselves a kinetic medium full of spontaneity and happy accidents. In this study, loose brushwork helps capture the lynx as it leaps and preens. Lively brush marks capture the pelt of the animal as it wavers in the wind. Form and detail can simply be suggested without getting tied into intense detail and destroying the feeling of the animal being alive on the page.

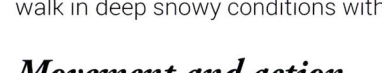

Yellow Ochre   **French Ultramarine**   **Raw Umber**

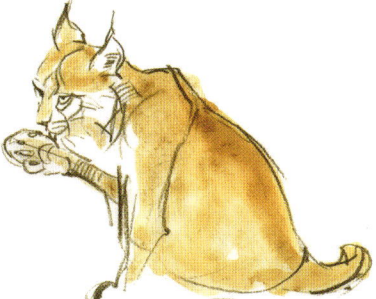 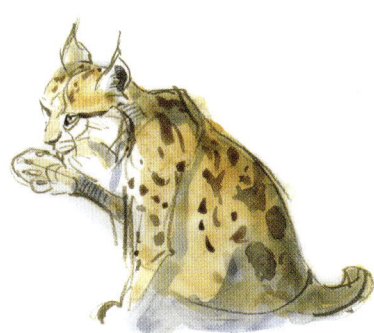

1 *Apply Yellow Ochre with a granulation medium (see page 27). The coat is darker on the top and lighter on the stomach. Apply more water to create the gradation.*

2 *A light wash of French Ultramarine helps to solidify the form and capture the light and shade.*

3 *Finish by adding the spots in a Raw Umber.*

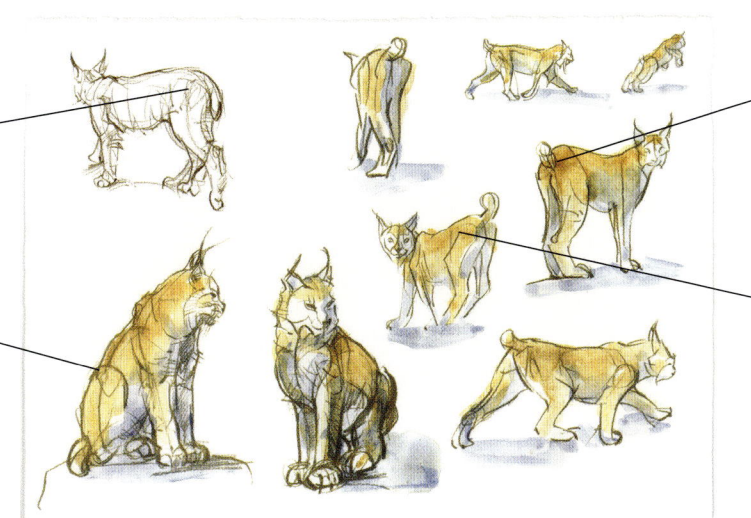

Look out for grooming behaviour and use short flick marks to suggest hair.

Capture the character of the sweeping shape of the moustache-like cheek.

Lynx have a short tail.

Notice how the powerful rump can appear higher than the shoulders.

Frozen Habitats

Frozen habitats are one of the most extreme and inhospitable environments on Earth, yet some pioneering plants and animals have turned these hostile places into their home.

The Arctic and Antarctic frozen regions are dominated by large amounts of snow and ice and contain vast polar deserts that receive little annual rainfall. With average winter temperatures dropping below -22°F (-30°C) in the Arctic and -58°F (-50°C) in the Antarctic, these are no places for animals that can't cope with the cold and long periods without food. Altitude creates freezing conditions too. Almost nothing grows above the snow line, and only the hardiest animals can eke out an existence. The thin air, freezing temperatures and strong winds become harsher the higher one goes, and there is progressively less food for an animal to live on.

In the Arctic, a polar bear has thick white fur, which helps to insulate and camouflage; when the sun's rays hit the polar bear's pelt, some light energy travels into the hair and gets trapped. This energy bounces around inside the hollow part of the hair, creating a reaction called luminescence. Whales, seals and penguins use their blubber for insulation; it can also be used as a food reserve in times of hardship. Male emperor penguins huddle together for warmth during Antarctica's brutal winter while they incubate their eggs.

Plants must also be highly adapted to survive these sub-zero freezing conditions and make the most of a short growing season. In the Arctic, plants grow in the seasonally thawed soil above the permafrost and tolerate frozen earth in winter. This thin layer of soil is called the active layer; it only makes room for shallow root systems and prevents larger plants from growing.

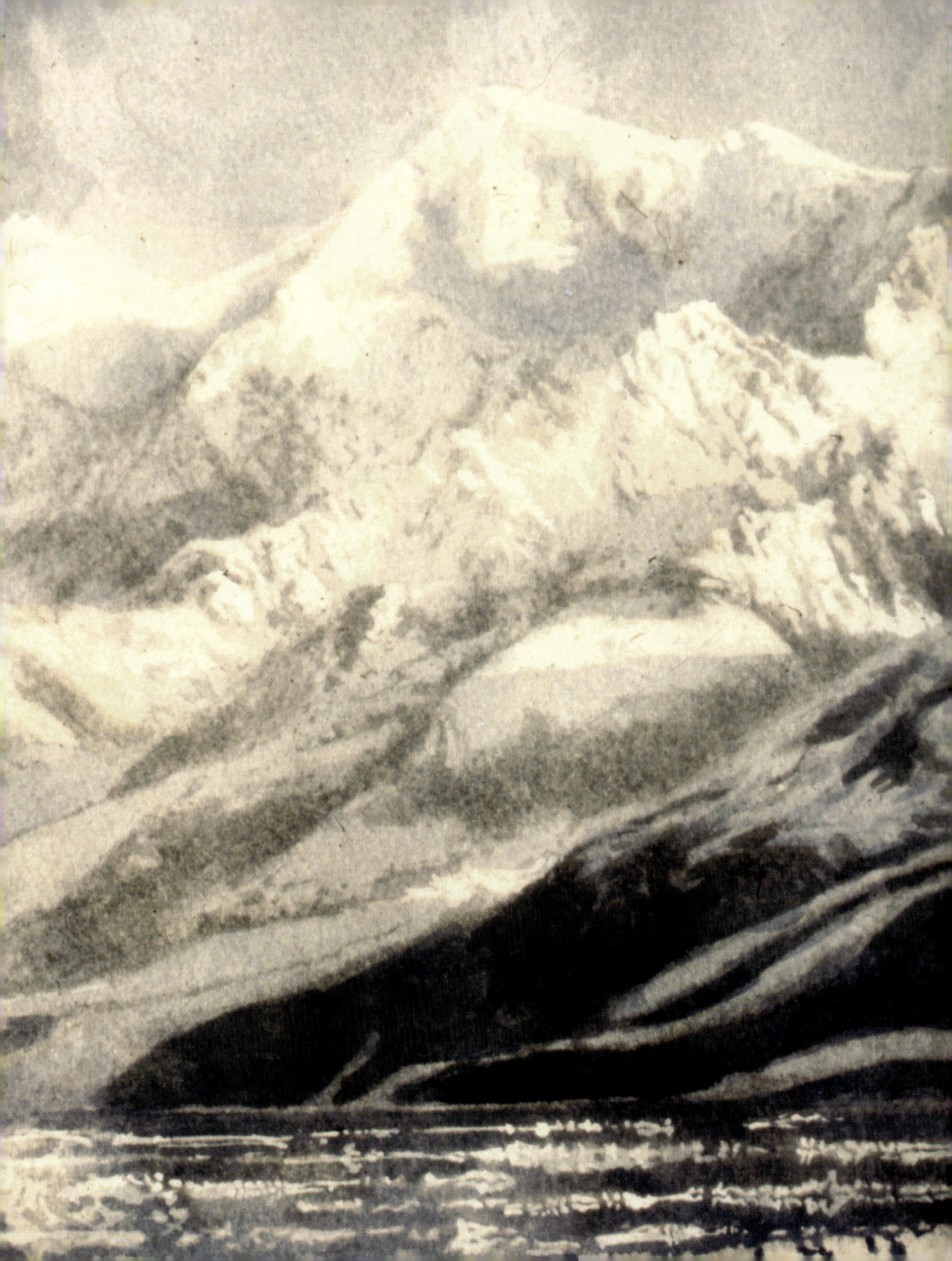

Snowscapes

Snow transforms the landscape creating many inspirational subjects, from snow-laden trees and frozen streams to icicles and wintry skies. It acts like a giant photographer's reflective light screen, bouncing dazzling light around the landscape.

I always use a bright white watercolour paper for a daytime snowscape, when the white snow is blinding with intense blue shadows. I love the challenge of leaving the paper unpainted to represent sunlit snow. In a way, I don't paint the snow at all, just the blue shadows.

For a nightscape, a mid-tone paper can be an advantage at getting the composition down quickly. Watercolour can still be laid down translucently for the darker values, and White Gouache can be added to create the ice-cream colours of the lighter shades.

A snowscape is very much about tonality and a limited palette.

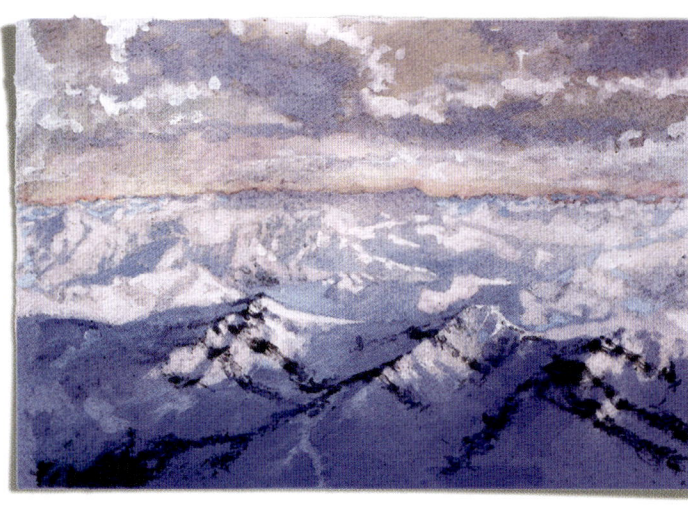

▲ Morning light
Snow often reflects the colours in the sky. To capture the pink morning light falling on these peaks, I used White Gouache mixed with an Alizarin Crimson. The blues are darker and warmer in the foreground, graduating to a cool blue on the horizon. I created buttery cloud marks to create the impression of clouds in the light with an Alizarin Crimson and French Ultramarine underbelly.

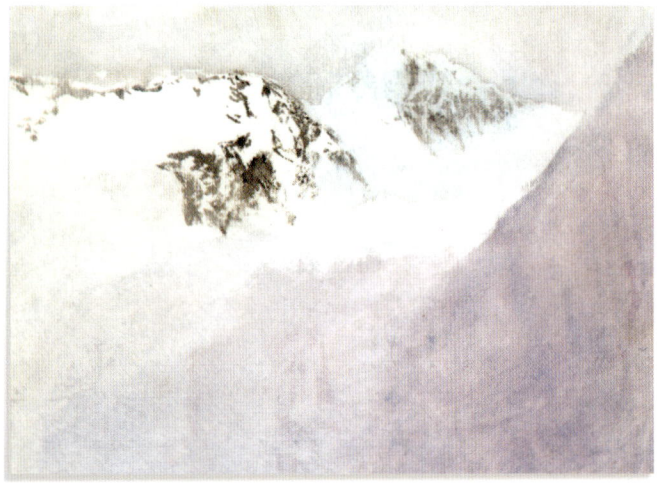

▲ A whiteout descends
Before I paint a snowscape, I always plan where to save the white of the paper for my brightest values. In a whiteout on a glacier, there are many whites, from pure white to silvery greys. When I lay down my first washes, they are very light – water with just a touch of pigment to knock it down a fraction. In this painting, after I built up an atmospheric base, I sketched in the rocky outcrops with a feathery mark. A note on the back of this painting reads, 'It was a "whiteout" when we arrived, and the freezing temperatures drove us quickly to the warmth of our tents. When the whiteout cleared, I made this quick sketch looking up Raven Glacier.'

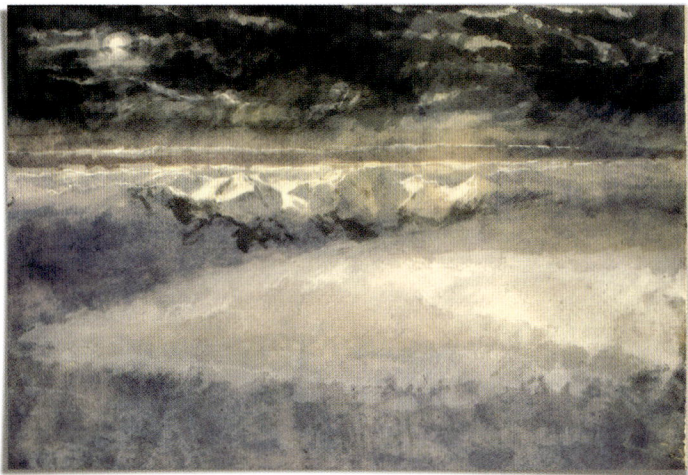

▲ Night snowscape
The memory of waking up in the middle of the night and being greeted by this scene after unzipping the tent door was breathtaking. Thousands of nameless mountains receding in the distance with the lip of the peaks caught in the moonlight. While I sketched this nightscape from a photograph, the image was infused with the magical moment that caught my attention. Behind the Payne's Grey clouds is a Cerulean Blue silvery sky, and the horizon glows with a tinge of Alizarin Crimson. Using White Gouache and a thin brush, I picked out the ridges of light at the end.

Tutorial: *Glacier*

Pictured here is Eagle Valley River, in the Chugach Mountains, Alaska. Flowing down the gulley between the slope of snow in the foreground and the mountain is Raven Glacier. Glaciers can be a challenge for the artist. They are heavily crevassed and composed of the most compact molecules of ice. These molecules absorb all the colours of the spectrum except blue, which is reflected in a dazzling bright blue. In this tutorial, however, you will see how with just a few sweeps of your brush you can capture a glacier.

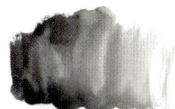

Payne's Grey

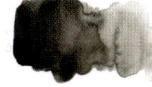

Ivory Black

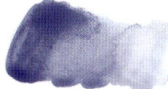

French Ultramarine

Cerulean Blue

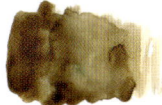

Raw Umber

White Gouache

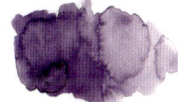

Cobalt Violet

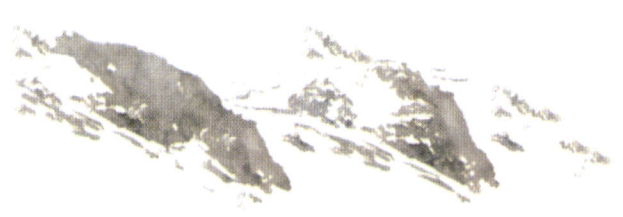

1 *With a mixture of Payne's Grey and Ivory Black, start by painting in the black rock outcrops that contrast vividly with the pure white of the snow. Squint at the picture to reduce the visual complexity. Look at both the positive and negative shapes and allow your painting to grow.*

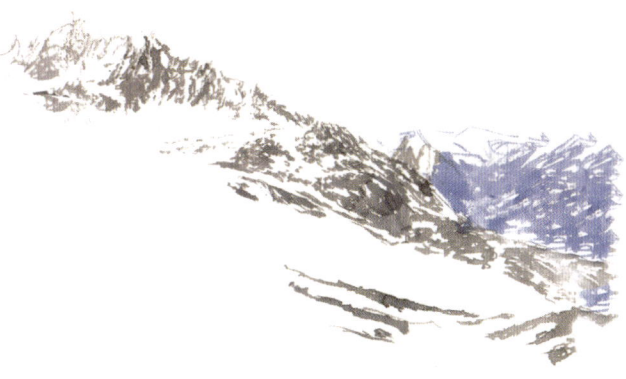

2 *Make the areas in the distance softer, with less tonal contrast. For the areas where the light hits, you can make them more distinct, using French Ultramarine to increase the feeling of depth.*

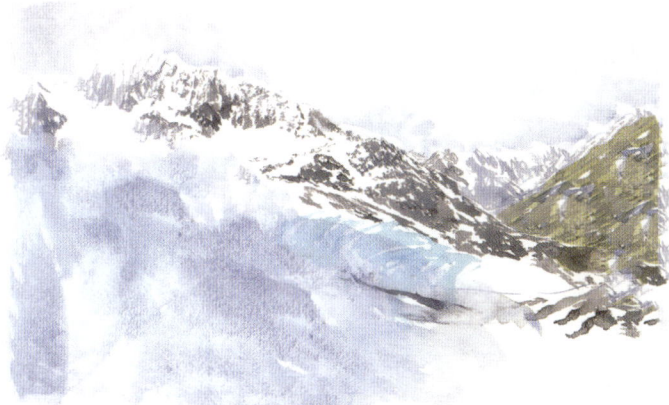

3 *With a few sweeps of your brush, indicate the glacier with a Cerulean Blue. Next, softly blush in the foreground. A slope of snow in shadow can be loosely captured with a wash of French Ultramarine. The bare rocks have a rusty colour that can be depicted with Raw Umber.*

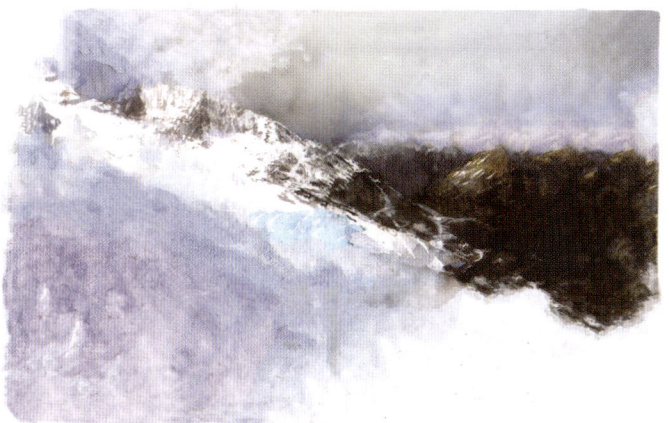

4 *As your painting develops, try to respond to it intuitively, enhancing the odd tone here and there or crisping up contrasts where you feel you need them. Use plenty of sooty Ivory Black, graduating from smoky greys to coal black and White Gouache to pick out flecks of snow. The purplish tints of the snow in the foreground is created by a light wash of Cobalt Violet.*

Study Sheet: *Reindeer*

Reindeer, called caribou in North America, are a species of deer found in the Arctic. There are two varieties: tundra reindeer and forest reindeer. Tundra reindeer migrate between tundra and forest in vast herds of up to half a million in an annual cycle covering 3,000 miles (5,000km). Forest reindeer are far less numerous.

I was thrilled to discover that a farm local to me had a herd of 19 male reindeer, so I headed off with my telescopic easel to join them in the paddock. I sketched them on a polar blue Mei-Tientes paper in the field and took lots of photographs so I could work from them later in the comfort of the studio.

Both male and female reindeer grow antlers, which makes them unique in the deer world. The female reindeer use their smaller antlers to defend food in small patches of cleared snow. Unlike horns, antlers are shed each year, and in males, this happens in late autumn after the rut. Females retain their antlers until spring because access to food is critical during their winter pregnancy.

I drew these reindeer as the season was turning to autumn when their antlers were covered in fur. The pelt, composed of hollow air-filled hairs for insulation, is brown and thin in the summer but was starting to turn thick and greyish-white for the winter.

Anatomy

Knowing a little about the anatomy can help you understand what you are looking at and inform your painting.

Feet

Four splayed toes on each foot act as snowshoes, floating on the snow in the harsh Arctic environment; they also make reindeer strong swimmers. The sharp toes can break through snow to uncover nutritious grass beneath.

Dew claws

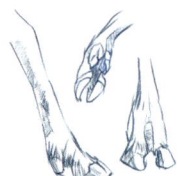

Dew claws commonly grow higher on the leg than the rest of the foot. They only make contact with the ground when the animal is running, and they provide extra traction on slippery surfaces.

Clicking ankles

While I was sketching the reindeer, I heard a continual clicking sound coming from the herd. This was created by tendons that snap over sesamoid bones in their feet. A sesamoid bone is a small round bone embedded within a tendon whose purpose is to reinforce and decrease stress. Think of a patella, for example. Experts believe the clicking helps the herd members stay in contact, especially in snowstorms or a whiteout when they could easily get lost.

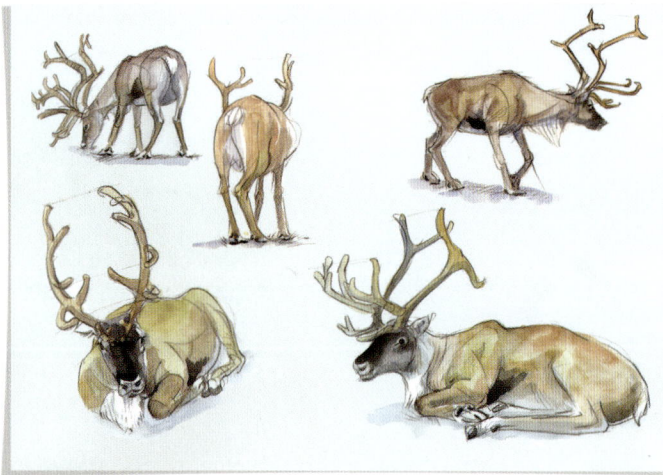

▲ Sitting pretty
Initially, I filled my paper with lots of sketches of different positions. After a while, the reindeer settled into seated positions, which allowed for more sustained studies.

Bones

Knowing the bones can give your drawing structure and the feeling that the legs are supporting weight.

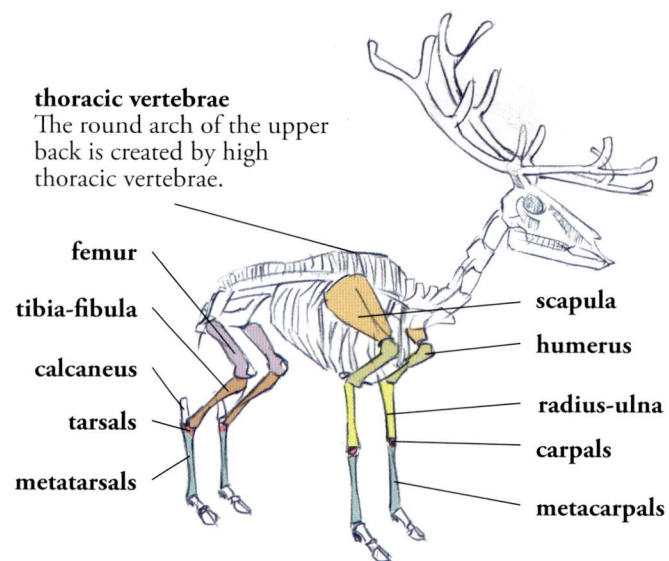

thoracic vertebrae
The round arch of the upper back is created by high thoracic vertebrae.

femur

tibia-fibula

calcaneus

tarsals

metatarsals

scapula

humerus

radius-ulna

carpals

metacarpals

Muscles

Recognizing a few key muscles can help model the form and make sense of the lumps and bumps.

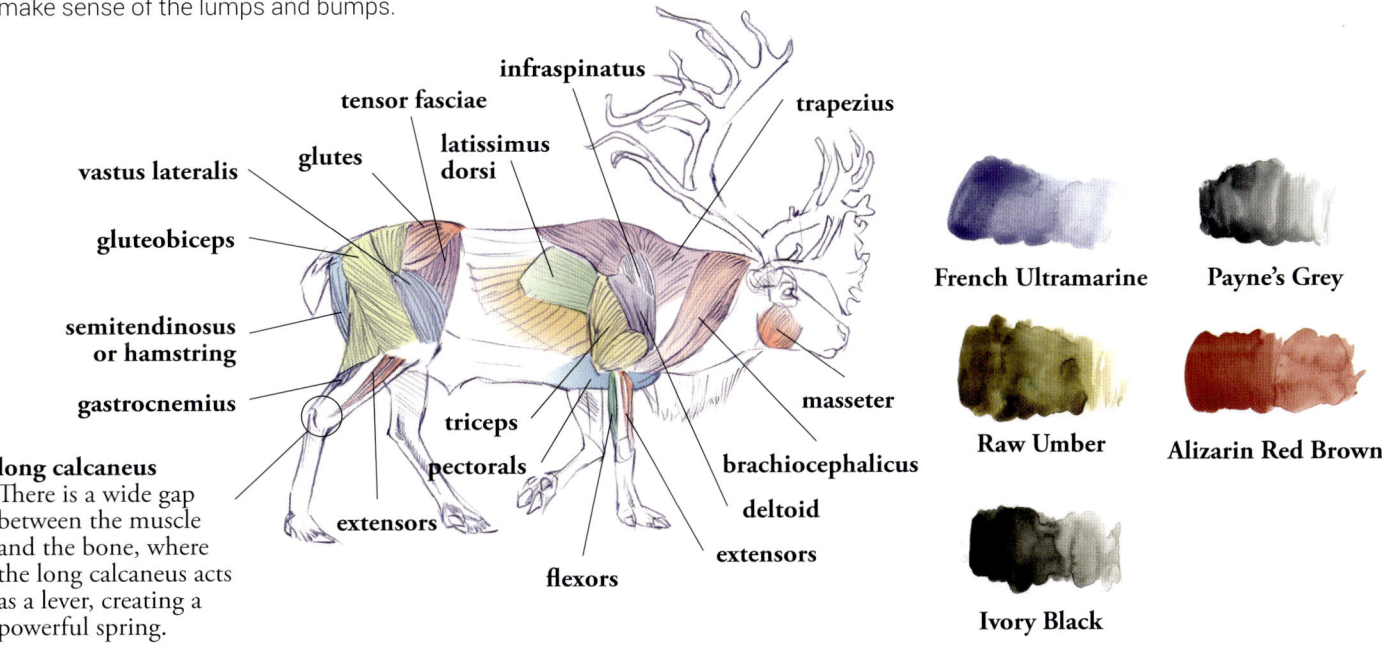

Labels: infraspinatus, tensor fasciae, trapezius, latissimus dorsi, glutes, vastus lateralis, gluteobiceps, semitendinosus or hamstring, gastrocnemius, masseter, triceps, pectorals, brachiocephalicus, deltoid, extensors, flexors, extensors

long calcaneus
There is a wide gap between the muscle and the bone, where the long calcaneus acts as a lever, creating a powerful spring.

French Ultramarine   Payne's Grey

Raw Umber   Alizarin Red Brown

Ivory Black

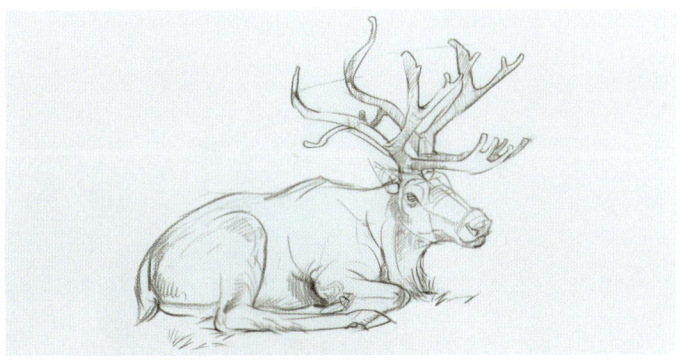

1 Begin with a loose sketch. I used a Raw Umber Polychromos pencil that's similar to the colour of the pelt. Start with the head when it is visible and fit the body to the head's scale, as there is a tendency to draw the head too big.

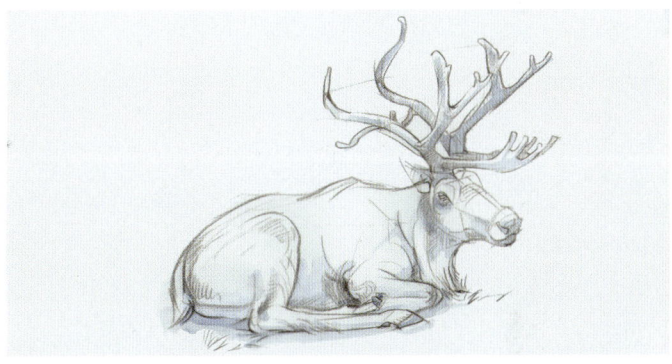

2 At this stage I went back to my studio to finish the painting. Create a tonal underpainting with a French Ultramarine and Payne's Grey mix.

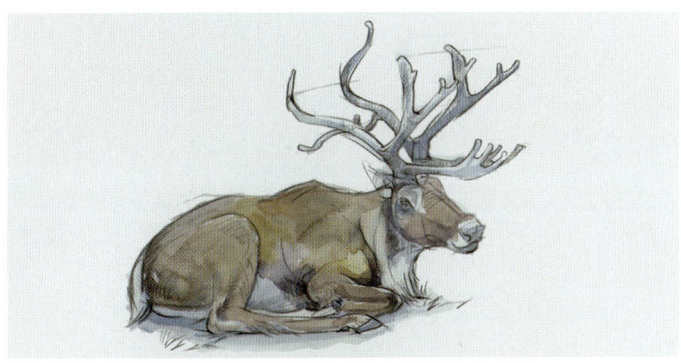

3 Put in the base colour of the pelt, varying the browns between Raw Umber and Alizarin Red Brown. I drew with the brush and followed the form.

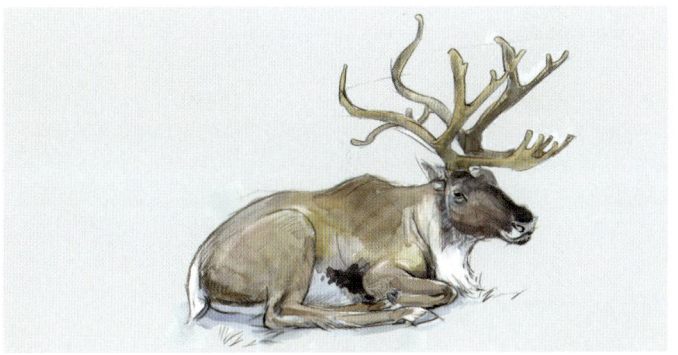

4 Finally, increase the dark notes, using Ivory Black for the bridge of the nose and watercolour pencils to create hair-flick marks.

Study Sheet: *Penguin*

Penguins are the flightless birds of the Southern Hemisphere, with only one species, the Galápagos penguin, found north of the equator enjoying a tropical climate. It is a commonly misheld belief that penguins only live in cold temperatures. Penguins have been successful in colonizing every continent of the Southern Hemisphere, including Africa.

There are around 16 to 19 recognized species of penguin. They are distributed in coastal regions and tend to get larger the further south they live. It is advantageous to be bigger in the freezing Antarctic weather with a lesser surface area to volume ratio.

Penguins are highly distinctive with their tuxedo-like appearance. Having a white belly and black back is called countershading and is a highly successful form of camouflage – seen from below, their white belly blends with the light catching on the ocean's surface; from above, their dark back disappears into the colours of the ocean's depths. Penguins are born camouflaged to their land environment and develop this adult sea camouflage as they mature. Telling male and female penguins apart is challenging and can only really be done by DNA testing.

Anatomy

Knowing a little about the anatomy can help you understand what you are looking at and inform your painting.

Fishing beak

Penguins are carnivores. Fish and krill make up the bulk of an emperor penguin's diet, along with squid and crustaceans.

An unusual tongue

Backward-pointing barbs on the tongue stop slippery prey from escaping.

Feathers

A penguin's body is covered with 70 percent more feathers than a typical flying bird. It is helpful to keep this in mind when considering the texture that you are trying to depict in your painting.

Down feathers

Down feathers are not waterproof, and chicks must remain out of the water until they acquire their juvenile plumage.

Oily secretion

Penguins continually waggle their beak on their tail, preening

Bones

Knowing the bones can give your drawing structure and the feeling that the legs are supporting weight.

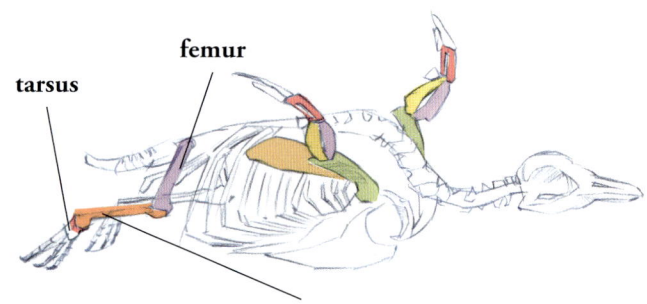

femur
tarsus
tibiotarsus – fused lower leg

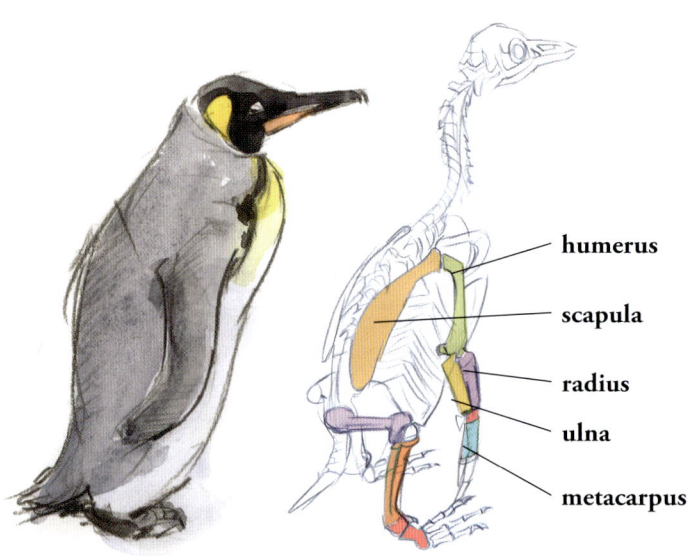

humerus
scapula
radius
ulna
metacarpus

Note that the leg goes up inside the body.

an oily secretion into their feathers to waterproof them for fishing trips.

Balancing tail

A short, stiff tail helps keep their balance on land.

Webbed feet

A penguin's feet are at the bottom of the body, giving them greater speed in the water. Think of a speed boat's outboard motor compared to a paddle steamer, like that of a duck. These feet have powerful claws on feet to help grip ice or rock when emerging from the sea. The feet are also helpful when tobogganing or sliding on their bellies to conserve energy.

Toes

Penguins have a small hallux, or first toe, which is hard to see when sketching in the field. It is a little reminiscent of a thumb.

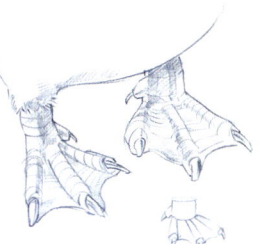

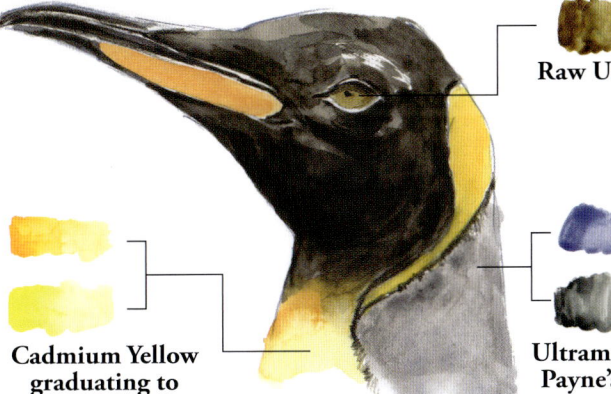

Raw Umber

Cadmium Yellow graduating to Lemon Yellow

Ultramarine + Payne's Grey

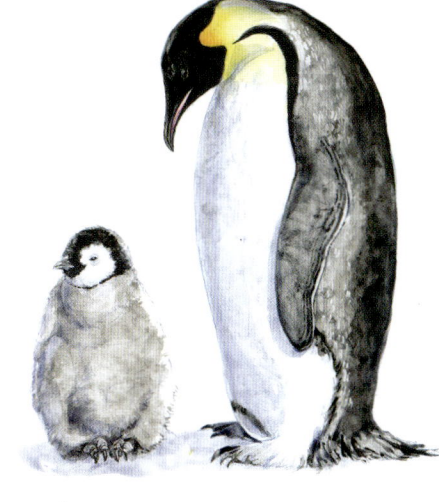

▲ Emperor penguins

The emperor penguin is bigger than the king penguin but not as brightly coloured. It can hold its breath for 20 minutes and dive to a staggering depth of 1,500ft (450m) to catch fish. Although a little ungainly on land, once in the water, the penguin is a dynamic torpedo, essentially flying through the water at incredible speeds.

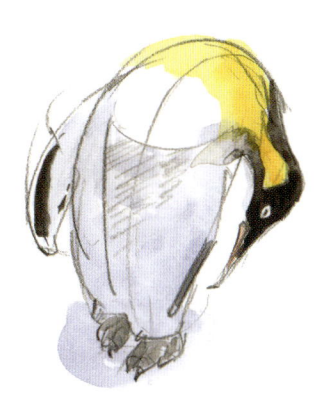

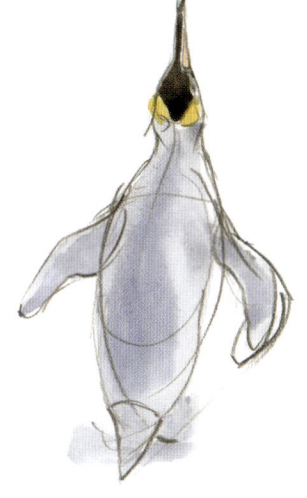

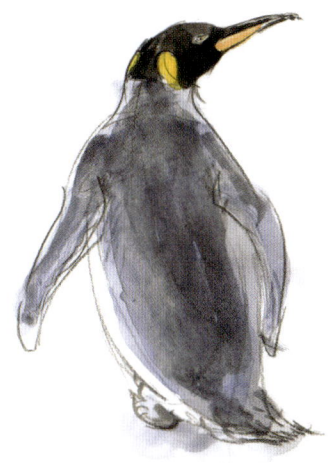

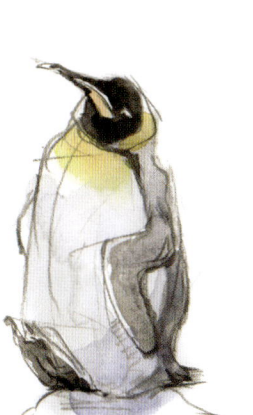

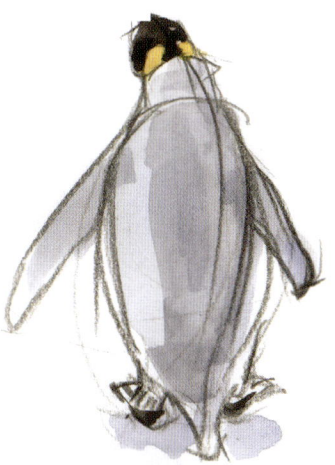

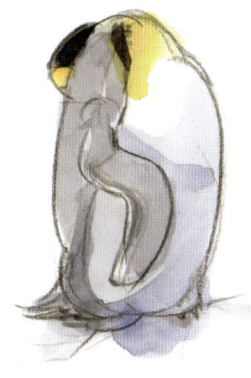

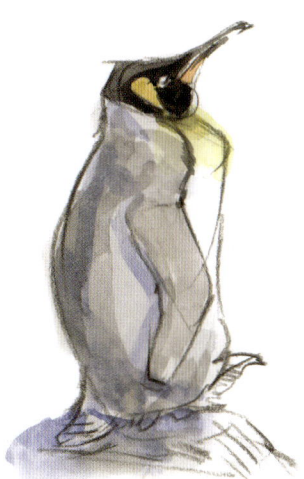

▲ King penguin study sheet

King penguins are the second-largest penguin and are found from Antarctica to the Falkland Islands.

Temperate Regions

Temperate climate refers to the zones of the Earth's surface lying between the tropic of Cancer and the Arctic Circle in the Northern Hemisphere and between the tropic of Capricorn and the Antarctic Circle in the south. These mild climate zones do not have the temperature extremes of the poles or tropical regions, but they do have a greater variety of temperatures.

They are home to a wide variety of terrestrial and aquatic plants and animals. Temperate forests include both coniferous and deciduous trees, and both create a habitat for nocturnal animals such as owls, badgers, bats and raccoons. During the day, woodlands around the world are filled with the sound of the drumming of woodpeckers, while lower down, herbivores such as deer and moose graze on the undergrowth. In the warm earth, subterranean carnivorous moles burrow for worms.

Some of the areas in this zone are closer to the sea or ocean, so they have a maritime temperate climate. Because the sea is nearby, rain may fall at any time of the year, but temperatures do not vary as widely because winds coming off the sea regulate land temperatures.

The Mediterranean climate gets its name from the environment found around the Mediterranean Sea, which is close to the equator and hence warmer. Several other places worldwide, such as California, central coastal Chile and southern Australia, also experience this climate. It is characterized by dry summers and mild, wet winters. The grass is not as lush, and scrublands are typical, created by small shrubs, grasses and herbs. Cork, conifers and cacti are well adapted for the dry summers. Prey animals without fussy diets, such as rugged goats, sheep and rabbits, thrive and are always on the lookout for their predators of jackals and lynx. Insects, the food for many lizard species, also enjoy the dry conditions.

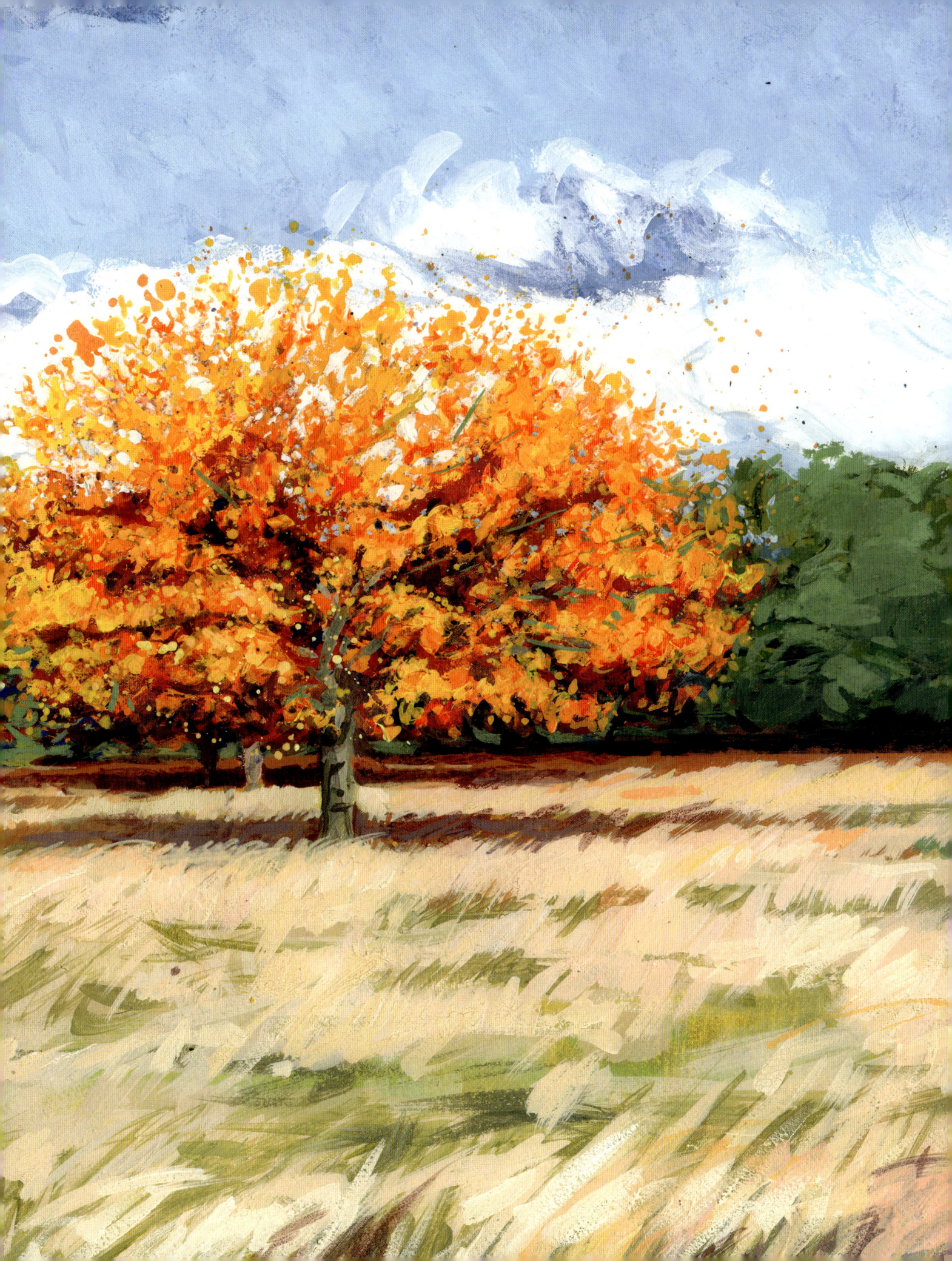

Spring

As winter draws to an end, the Earth tilts towards the Sun and the warmer air and more extended periods of sunshine trigger new beginnings for life on the planet.

At the beginning of the day, the dawn air is full of the sound of birds singing a chorus, as if celebrating the start of a new, milder, less inhospitable season after the long hard winter in which many may have died of starvation or the cold. They are calling out for a mate, the first signs of the beginnings of the next generation. Seeds that have lain dormant start to sprout roots as this seasonal rebirth begins, and buds soon start to grow from beneath the leaf litter, providing nutritious food for herbivorous animals in the seasons.

In the southern regions of Alaska, the snow begins to melt, avalanches come tumbling down the side of mountains, fresh green and yellow shoots push their way through the top thawing soil. A little below is the permafrost, where the ground never defrosts. Yet on the surface, small flowers start to bloom. On the other side of the world, spring is one of the most favourite and notable seasons to the people of Japan. Cherry trees burst into blossom, creating a spectacle that attracts visitors from all over the world, drawn to the tranquil, enchanting atmosphere that these flowers create.

▼ A dead tree by Isabella Plantation
I created this portrait of a dead tree by Isabella Plantation, Richmond Park, London, surrounded by the fresh sap green of new growth. I also perched a black crow on top as a symbol of mortality and death so that the tree becomes a sort of memento mori. I enjoyed painting the gnarled, twisting branches grasping outwards. Although dead, the tree now takes on a new life, that of a bug hotel.

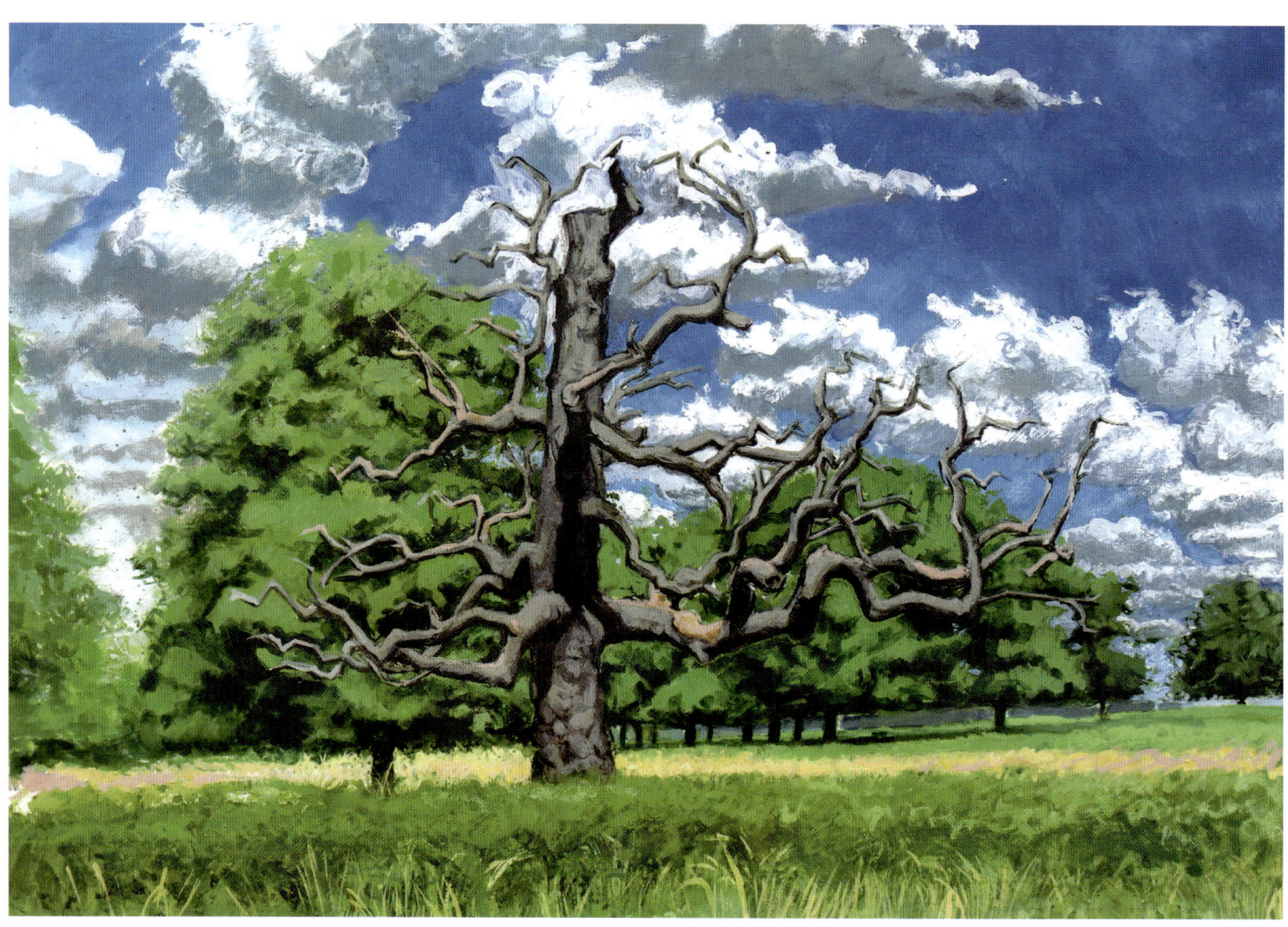

What to look for in the spring landscape

Spring is the season when animals such as hedgehogs, dormice and bumblebees awake from hibernation. Other animals begin pairing for reproduction. Mallard drakes chase female ducks. Willow and hazels sprout catkins, and the first buds of new life emerge all around. From beneath the rotting dead leaves that fell last autumn and provided essential nutrients for the soil, fresh shoots of violets and snowdrops push their expanding flower buds through the leaf litter.

Songbirds seek out twigs to build nests. Large-winged birds such as geese and swans arrive at estuaries in squadrons flying in V formation. In ponds, frog spawn gathers in its gelatinous clumps. Each black spot is an embryo surrounded by a coat of jelly ready to develop into tadpoles. In rivers, brown trout jump out of the water to catch mayflies dancing their short mating dance on the surface. After their mating flight, mayflies are usually dead by the end of the day. There's only one thing they really care about on that one eventful day, and it's not eating; they don't even have a mouth. In fact, most of the life of a mayfly is spent beneath the water in a larval stage.

French Ultramarine   **Cerulean Blue**

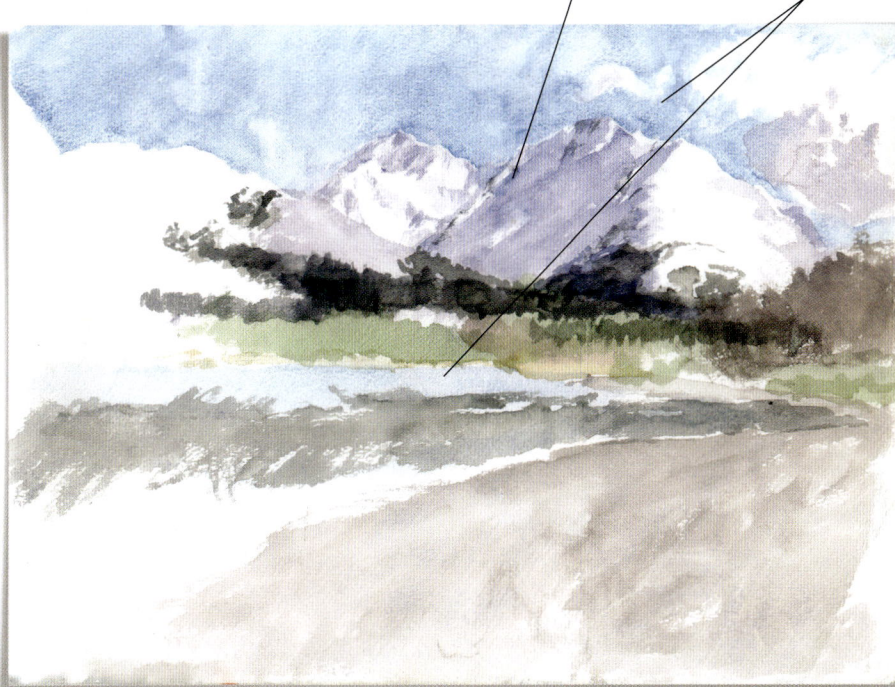

▲ **Moose Pass, early spring, Chugach National Forest, Alaska, USA**
Spring in Alaska and the snow begins to retreat up the mountainsides. In this sketch there is no underdrawing. It is created by drawing with a thin brush, starting the shadows in the snow with a pure French Ultramarine and then moving shape to shape, attempting to place the correct hue in the right place. A block of dark conifers below the snow line, a lighter shade of green vegetation beneath, a yellow line of shingle creates the shore, and the Cerulean Blue of the sky is reflected in the ice of the lake that is just beginning to thaw.

Spring, for both the animals and the plants, is a race to grow.

The spring palette

There are many colours you will see throughout the seasons. Some of these are more accentuated in spring. Fresh acidic greens and the lemon yellow of the growth of new shoots. The egg-yolk yellow of daffodils and the cerulean blue for bright, chilly, clear mornings that have made a welcome return. The light pink of the Japanese cherry blossoms creates feelings of sensitivity, femininity and romance; it is a soft colour that puts people into a state of calm. Bright pinks glimmer in sprouting crocuses too. The emergence of snowdrops is a sure sign that warmer weather is on the way; their petals are pure white droplets. White is a colour without a hue called achromatic. Throughout much of history, white has been used as a symbol of goodness and purity.

Activity
Parks are a valuable refuge for plants and animals in urban areas that can become concrete deserts for wildlife. Take a sketchbook out with you to your local park and try to capture the explosion of blossom.

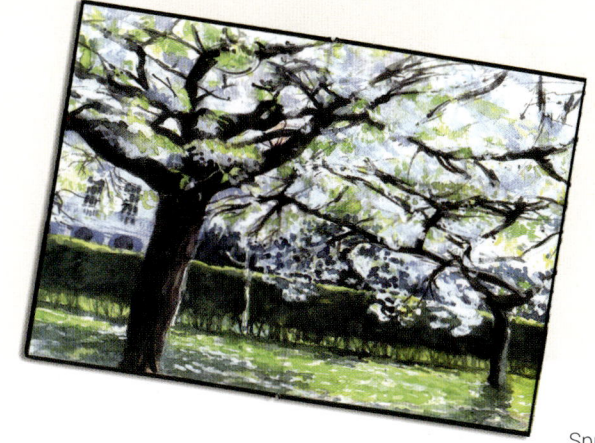

Summer

This is the season of plenty when the days are at their longest. It invokes memories of childhood, the bright blue sea, the sound of seagulls and laughter. Golden rays of sunlight caress the landscape from the breaking of dawn until sunset brings forth a vivid palette of vibrant warm hues as the sun, like the deep, orange yolk of an egg, slowly slips below the horizon.

All the landscapes in the temperate zone experience this summer light, whether coniferous or deciduous forests, mountains, coastal cliff faces or estuaries. Sketching outdoors, you get a greater sense of the atmosphere and can fully immerse yourself in the light and warm air of the day when everything seems so alive and the hedgerows buzz with life.

What to look out for in the summer landscape

The summer sun ripens fruit in orchards around the world in the temperate zone; it lights up fields of long, wavering grass and rolling meadows peppered with wildflowers and the shrill call of skylarks trebling upwards. These rays of light penetrate through the canopy of forests to create dappled light on the green grass floor. Sunlight sparkles on the backs of silverfish darting in crystal streams and shimmers on the liquid surface.

Flowers provide a host of vibrant subjects for the artist. Besides marvelling at their beauty, summer is also a time for us to marvel at one of the most remarkable examples of symbiotic co-evolution on Earth between plants and pollinators. While most pollinators are insects, there are other pollinators, such as hummingbirds, mammal pollinators, such as bats and lemurs, and reptiles like the gecko lizard.

Most flowers use colour to attract insects, sometimes helped by ultraviolet-coloured guiding marks on the petals that are invisible to the human eye. The flowers are often shaped to provide a landing platform for insects or force them to brush against their anthers and stigmas. Colours can't be seen in the dark, so scent is essential for flowers pollinated by night-flying insects such as moths.

The more the sun warms the flowers, the more nectar they produce, which is a valuable source of nutrition for the honeybee. The summer is a busy time for honeybees, for they are already starting to harvest the nectar to create honey to keep them going over the following winter. All worker honeybees are female; to produce 1lb (454g) of honey, two million flowers must be visited. A female honeybee visits 50 to 100 flowers during a collection trip. A single bee will produce only around

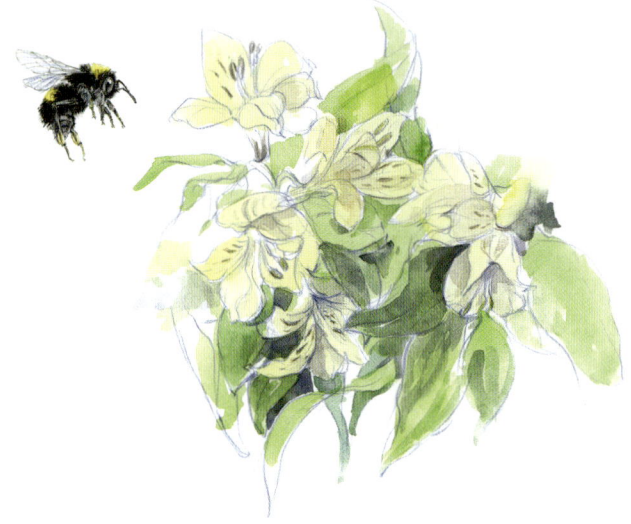

▲ **Full bloom**
Summer is a glorious time of abundance.

a twelfth of a teaspoon of honey in their lifetime despite their earnest industry, so it helps to be part of a cooperative colony. The distinctive sound of the buzzing of honeybees, which we associate with summer, is created by their wings beating 11,400 times per minute.

In North America, brown and black bears will, in turn, raid beehives. Bears are not fussy eaters and will eat the lot – grubs, honeycomb, even the bees themselves – putting up with the occasional sting to fatten themselves up for their winter's hibernation. Honey itself can be a vital source of nutrition over the summer period; a bear can double its weight.

Staying cool

These seemingly carefree days can also bring sweltering temperatures and carry their own challenges; it is a time when animals need to keep cool. Some animals such as dogs and birds pant to lose heat. Birds, such as owls, open and drop their wings to do the same, while others fluff out their feathers or take a birdbath to cool down, much like us diving into the sea.

Finding shade

Many animals use the shade beneath trees to keep cool. Fallow deer blend almost seamlessly into the darkness with their spotted backs in the dappled light. Freshwater fish seek cooler, deeper waters of rivers, lakes and ponds during the summer heat. In ponds, insect life shades beneath rotting leaves. Reptiles such as lizards and snakes, being cold-blooded and especially susceptible to heat, take shelter under rocks and in burrows.

The summer palette

The summer palette is filled with bright and vivid colours that dominate the landscapes. The dark blue and jade green of the summer sea, washing up on a yellow sandy beach, vivid oranges, poppy reds.

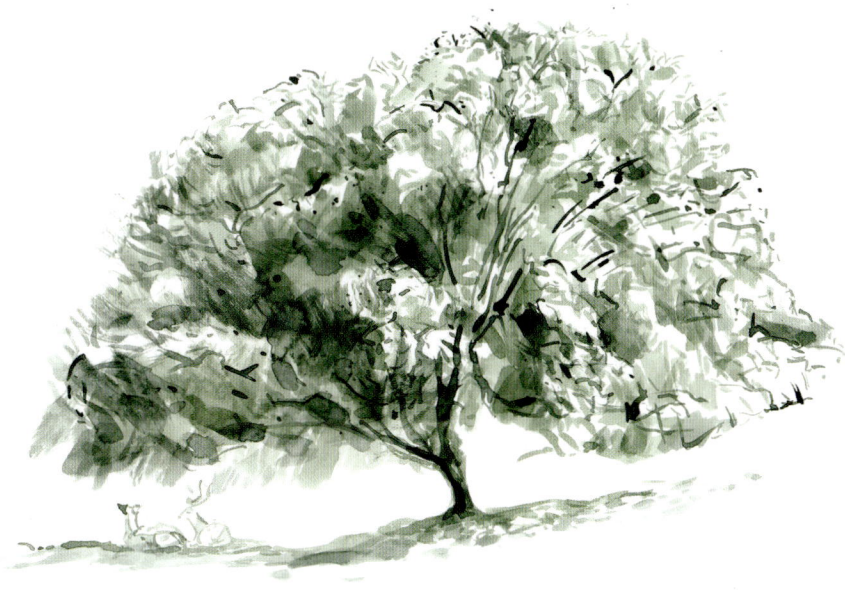

Activity
Have a go at mixing five colours that remind you of summer, and experiment with pastel ice-cream shades too. White Gouache can be added to achieve a chalky opaque finish.

▶ **Fallow deer shade beneath a beech**
Richmond Park, London, UK.

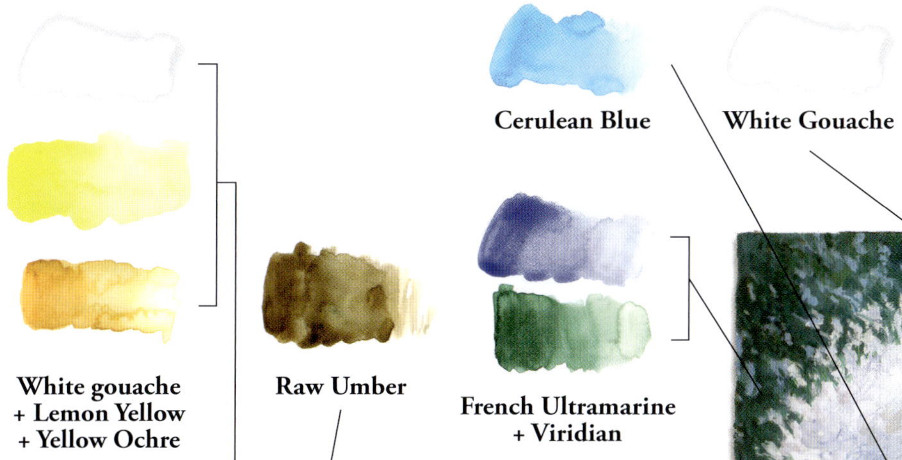

Cerulean Blue

White Gouache

▼ **Extended highlights**
Experiment with using White Gouache opaquely in the highlights contrasting with translucent darker colours.

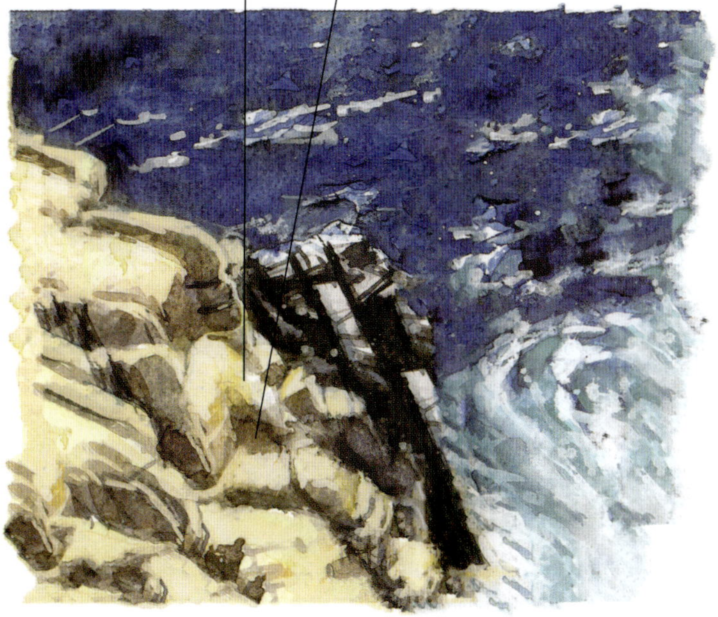

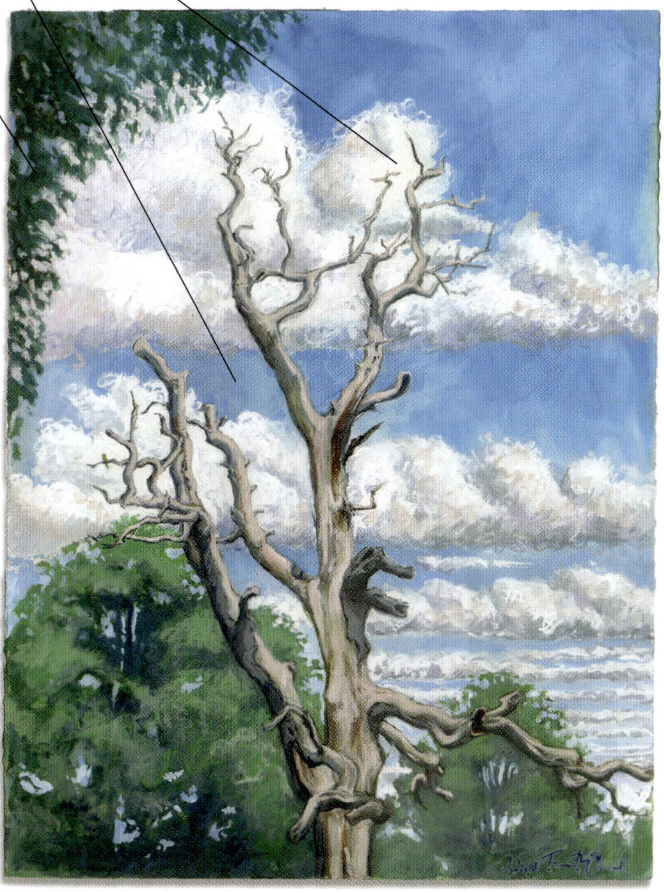

White gouache + Lemon Yellow + Yellow Ochre

Raw Umber

French Ultramarine + Viridian

Autumn

Autumn across the temperate world is one of the most spectacular seasons of them all. It is an inspirational time of year to go out into the field and sketch in watercolour. The English poet John Keats described it as the 'season of mists and mellow fruitfulness'.

The nights lengthen and the days become shorter. Vibrant colours are short-lived as winter hastens. Landscapes take on their annual display of seasonal decay, with misty mornings, frosted lawns and frozen stems of grass. At the heart of this seasonal change is the changing colour of the leaves, which creates one of the greatest shows on Earth in the temperate zone. Trees draw down all their resources from their leaves to their roots, and the colours of the leaves transition from sap green to lemon yellows, rich golds to deep Alizarin reds.

Autumn is a season of change and vivid contrast. It forces you to work quickly – the appearance of a tree can change in a matter of days as the Earth tilts away from the Sun and the Sun's rays grow shallower. Golden and russet leaves get blown in the autumn breeze – soon the branches become bare, and we will be able to trudge through the rustling leaves underfoot.

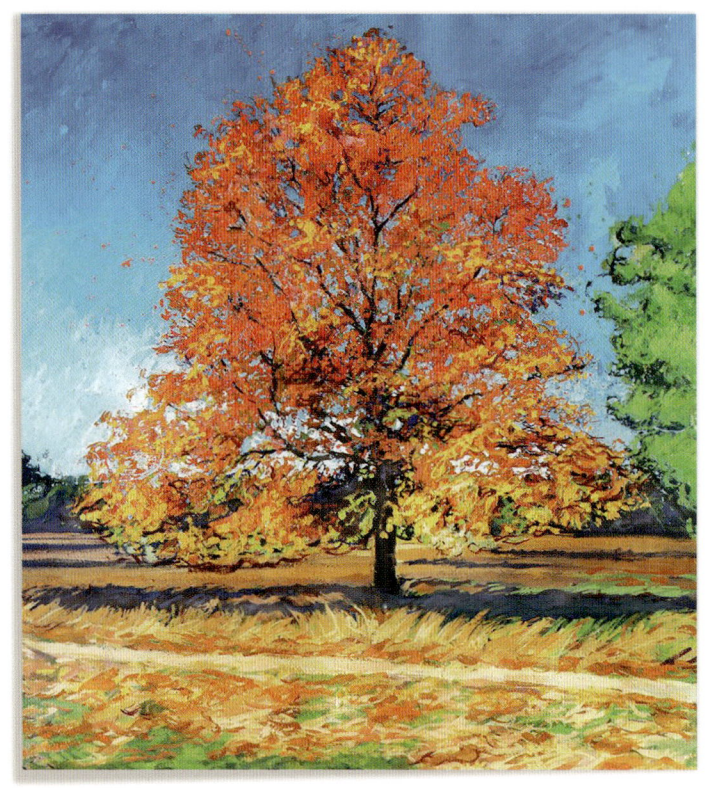

▲ **Autumnal contrasts**
Cerulean Blue is a vital pigment to capture the clear blue skies that can contrast with the lemon yellow of early autumn leaves.

Activity
Carry a small sketchbook around with you so that you can easily take it out to create a quick study.

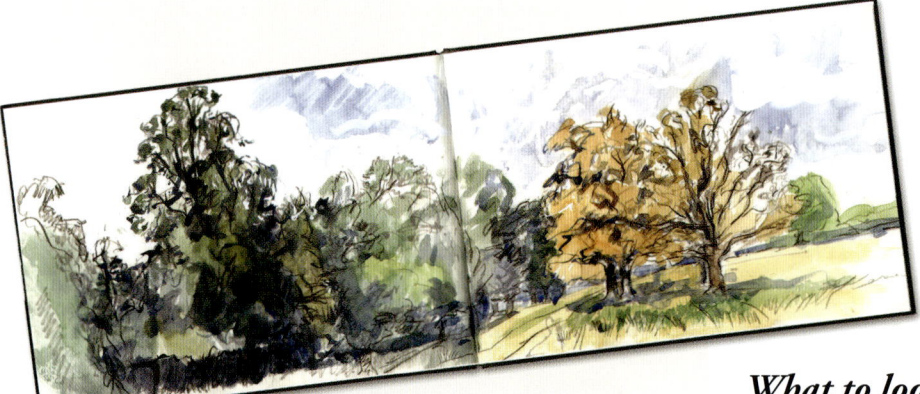

As the leaves turn brown, many animals are already preparing for more challenging times to come.

What to look for in autumn

While we can enjoy the colourful beauty of this season, animals experience an intense time of harvesting. For them, there is no time to waste; winter is on the horizon, which can bring a thick blanket of snow to hide their food, so autumn is a time of vital preparation. Autumn's harvest supper of fruit and vegetables is a critical supply of food to build up their bodies for the tough times ahead, so all animals tuck in when they can to increase their body fat or fill their larders. In North America, a beaver will stock up on plants and leaves to sustain the dam through winter. In Alaska, grizzly bears wait by the side of overflowing rivers for the arrival of Pacific salmon, as they start their ascent to their breeding grounds from which the males won't return. In the sky, annual migration begins; wildfowl take to the air in V formations in search of richer, warmer pastures.

Nuts are the ideal packed lunch to help animals get through bleak winter months when food is scarce. They are packaged in a self-preserving husk and are highly nutritious. Woodland rodents in the form of red and grey squirrels forage and stash their nut larder in secret spots marked by recognizable markers such as an oak tree. They scrape a small hole in soft earth and bury their prize, patting the soil down on top to hide it from birds. Later they will return to their secret spot with a mental map of their location. Squirrels can even sniff out stored nuts under a thick layer of snow. Smaller members of the squirrel family, the Siberian chipmunk, cram as many nuts into their expandable cheeks and store as much as 9–11lb (4–5kg) of nuts in their underground burrows. Before hibernating, they layer the burrow with a warm bedding of dried leaves and grasses and wake every few days to dine from their en-suite larder.

Why do leaves turn brown?

Because the days are shorter and the Sun is further away, trees can no longer sustain their leaves. Leaves are full of a chemical called chlorophyll that is bright green and has a unique function that can capture the energy in sunlight and convert it into sugars that the trees then use as energy. There are, however, other pigments in leaves – yellow, orange and red – that we can't see because there is just so much chlorophyll in them that it masks the other colours in spring and summer. As the trees start to produce less chlorophyll, we begin to see the other pigments. The leaves eventually die and fall from the trees. When they litter the ground at the base of the trees, they act as a natural fertilizer, and the trees survive the winter from the energy they have stored up.

The autumn palette

Autumn is a time of outstanding beauty when we are treated to a final burst of colour before the onset of winter. Autumn's sketchbook is full of russets, ochres, Burnt and Raw Umber, Raw Sienna and the all-natural, earthy browns that dominate the late autumn landscape. Earlier, the leaves varied greatly in colour from fiery lemon yellows, bright oranges to crimson. Autumn's harvest brings dark greens and warm colours, a visual feast of seasonal fruit and vegetables.

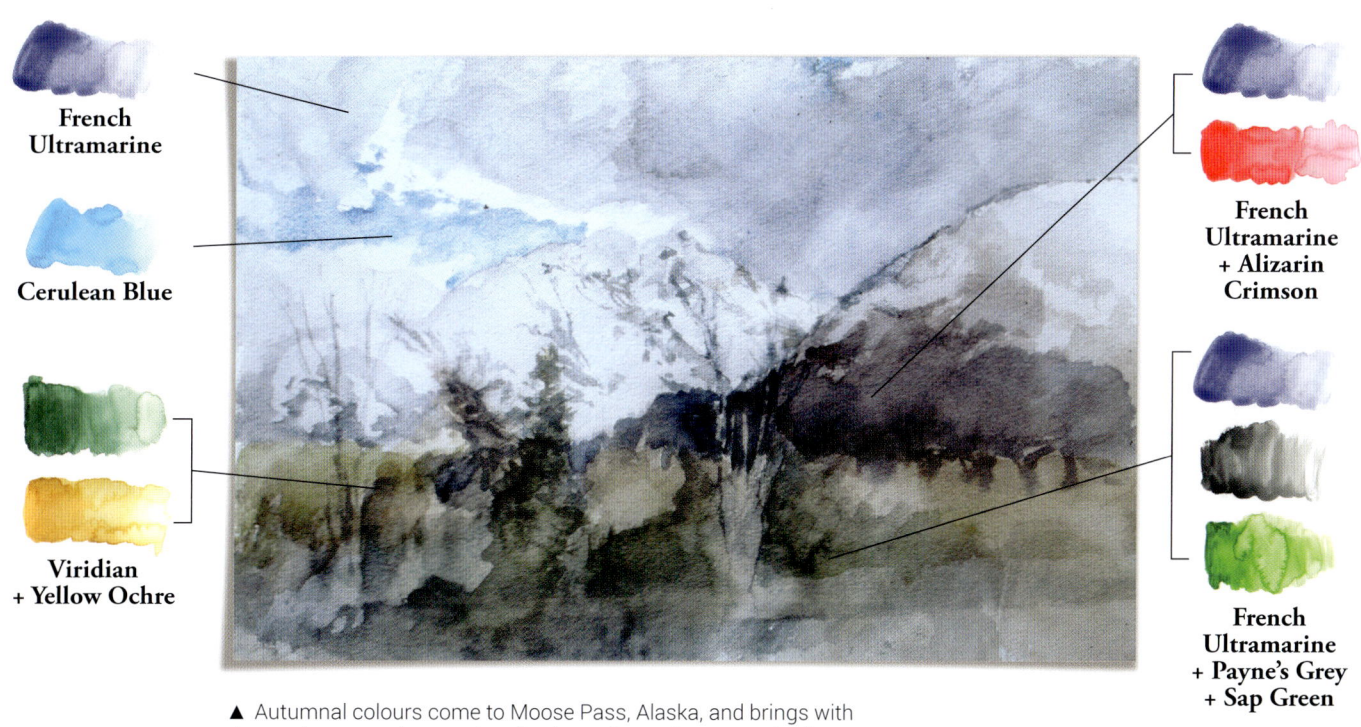

French Ultramarine

Cerulean Blue

Viridian + Yellow Ochre

French Ultramarine + Alizarin Crimson

French Ultramarine + Payne's Grey + Sap Green

▲ Autumnal colours come to Moose Pass, Alaska, and brings with them rainstorms that can last for days of an uninterrupted deluge.

Tip
Use plenty of French Ultramarine in the shadows to create the impression of shade and airy space.

Winter

As the Earth turns on its axis, the power of the Sun's rays weakens and the days shorten. Winter is a time when temperatures drop and life can go into a period of suspended animation. Snow and frost can create spectacular landscapes of a winter wonderland that are inspiring to paint and sketch.

But this time of the year is particularly challenging for animals, and only the toughest and most ingenious will survive. Dazzling displays of snowy fields, icicles and frozen waterfalls belies the struggles that animals face in staying alive and finding food. As temperatures plummet, one of the first challenges that winter brings is staying warm.

Plants can't migrate; they are rooted to see the winter through. For them, one of the most difficult aspects of winter is that water can be frozen and cannot be taken up through their roots. Deciduous trees shed their leaves to stop them from evaporating precious water into the air. Coniferous trees retain their leaves and needles, which have a thick, waxy coating to reduce water loss. This period of dormancy, where plants are ticking over but not growing, comes with the annual seasonal chill. Seeds and bulbs lay dormant, waiting for the warmth of spring to spark them into life. Plants not adapted for the cold must be brought indoors to prevent frost damage. These, too, need less watering.

What to look for in winter

In the Highlands of Scotland, temperatures can drop to as low as -22°F (-30°C). To cope with these temperatures, ptarmigan, a small grouse, grows more feathers to keep the heat in. It even has feathers on its feet, nostrils and eyelids. By covering as much of its body as possible with these insulating feathers that trap warm air, it can survive the bitter cold. Seasonal adjustments in the appearance of the animal also keep the ptarmigan out of harm's way. The ptarmigan's feathers turn entirely white in winter to blend in and become almost invisible in the snow, hiding it from predators, except for its tail and eye patch that remain black.

Snow itself is frozen cold, although it is also 95 percent air, so it can act a bit like an ice duvet. Some animals around the globe have taken advantage of this. Polar bears hibernate in dens made of snow, and until recently were thought to be the only mammals to do so. That is until a discovery in Japan where scientists witnessed the Ussurian tube-nosed bats leave their tree roosts to drop onto snow accumulating on the ground. Once there, they created an impression of their body and became covered by more snow as it fell. The bat's shuffling wing movements and body heat create a small cavity like an

igloo, in which they curl up and wait for spring. This snow hollow is warmer than the tree cavities they usually roost in, which in winter are blasted by icy winds.

Snow is also excellent for soundproofing, as it soaks up sound waves. In Alaska, the winter is called the great white silence. The aptly named snowshoe hare, found in North America, has big furry feet adapted to hopping on the surface of the snow to allow it to run quietly without breaking through. Like the ptarmigan, the snowshoe hare also adjusts its coat to match the habitat. It follows the same seasonal colour variation with the mammal's excellent insulator, fur. Fur and skin are coloured with a pigment called melanin. It is the seasonal absence of this pigment that turns the pelt to a pure wintery white. The word melanin comes from Greek and means 'dark black'. Melanin can produce a range of colours that we see in mammals' skin, hair and eyes, from pale yellow, tawny, buff and ginger to red-brown, brown and black. The light-absorbing properties of melanin act as a barrier against the damaging effects of the ultraviolet rays of sunlight. You will notice gradual tanning of your own skin after being in the sun for an extended period.

If animals can't escape the freezing conditions, they need to be well insulated. The Arctic fox grows one of the thickest white winter coats in the animal kingdom and even has warm, furry pads on the soles of its feet. Their tiny ears help to reduce heat loss. Small appendages close to the body stay warm and resist frostbite. An extreme example of this is the Chinese snow or snub-nosed monkey, endemic to the Yunnan Province of China, which has no nose to prevent it from suffering frostbite. Apart from us, this monkey is the only other primate to live at high altitudes where the land is frozen and covered in snow for most of the year.

Hibernation

Many animals hibernate, from bumblebees to bears. Chipmunks dig a burrow as far as 3ft (0.9m) under the ground and fill their larder with a store of nut snacks to see them through the dark months. Bears living in warm climates can find food all year long, so don't need to hibernate, whereas those residing in colder areas retreat to their dens. A den can be anything from a hollow tree, under the root system of trees, a cave or even a nest of leaves, ferns, moss and lichen. Over the summer, grizzly bears in Alaska have built up fat reserves to give them enough food stored on their body to enable them to make it through the tough winter months. Bears can gorge on 20,000 calories a day and really pile on the pounds.

Migration

Another strategy for surviving the winter is not to remain in the cold conditions. Some species of birds are renowned for their epic migrations to seek out warmer climes. Other animals on the land and in the sea also adopt this escape strategy. As terrestrial herds of caribou, the American name for reindeer, head south, aquatic narwhals escape the Arctic's bitterly freezing winters by migrating through channels in the sea ice far out to sea where the water will be warmer. These, sometimes arduous, journeys are necessary for the survival of the flock, herd, shoal or swarm.

The winter palette

Winter's sketchbook is full of cool colours, from silvery greys to icy blue. The pure, brilliant white of snow and the charcoal black of rocks peeping through. Deciduous trees are now bare umber branches, while conifers remain dark green. Another evergreen makes an appearance as a Christmas decoration – holly's waxy serrated leaves and blood-red berries. Try mixing five colours that capture the atmosphere of a winter's day.

Winter's tree

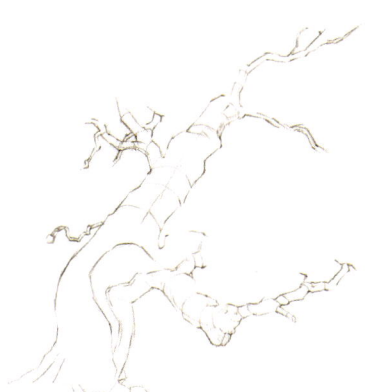

1   *Start your sketch of a winter tree with the trunk.*

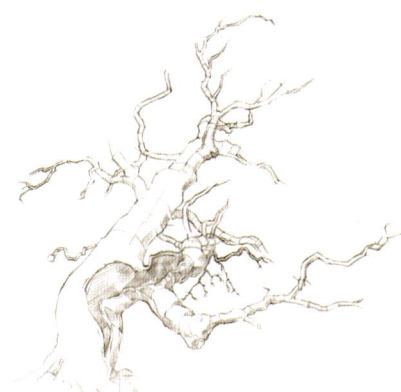

2   *Continue to draw by following the way the tree grows – adding the branches and working your way out to the little twigs.*

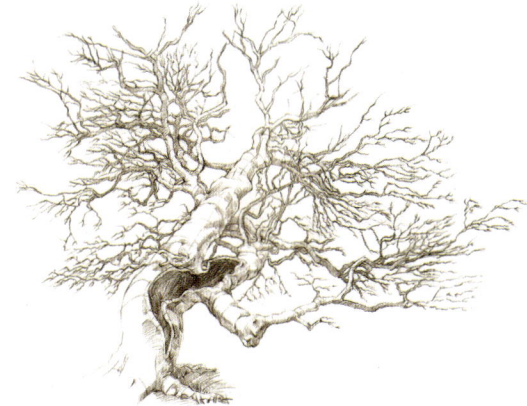

3   *It is important to remember that with such a complex subject you are creating an interpretation – you don't need to draw every twig.*

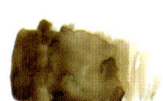

Raw Umber   **French Ultramarine**

4   *When the sketch is ready, add varying quantities of Raw Umber and French Ultramarine with a small chisel brush.*

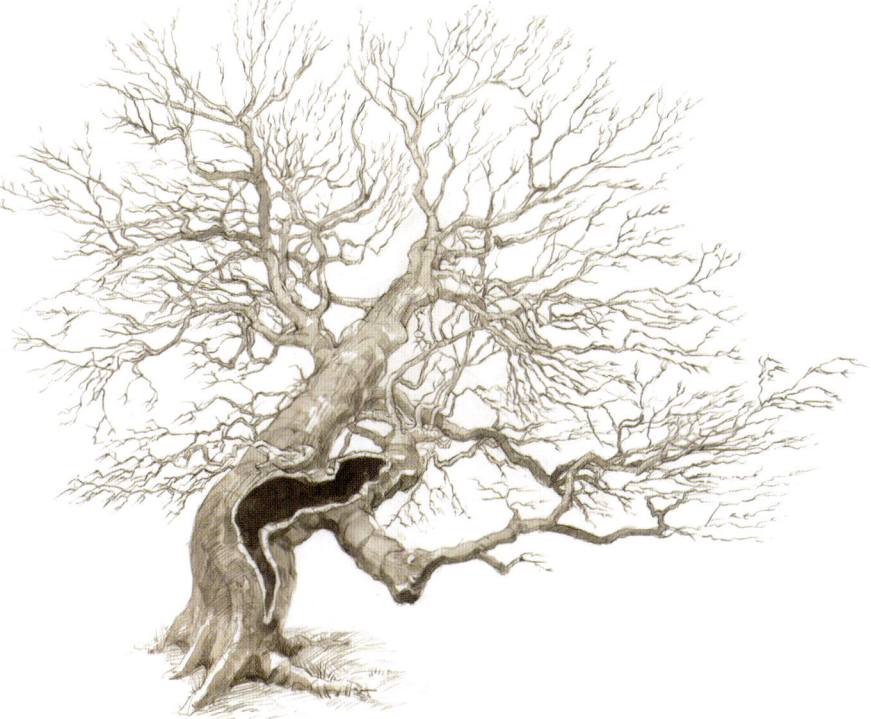

Coniferous Forests

In most temperate coniferous forests, conifers predominate. Their needle-like leaves can survive extreme frozen winters, are resilient to strong winds, bright sunshine, prolonged rainfall, and are tough to eat.

The success of this simple leaf strategy has aided certain species, such as the giant redwood, to become the tallest in the world. Coast redwoods or sequoias are among the oldest living organisms in the world. They can live for more than 3,000 years and grow up to 275ft (84m).

The story of the conifer begins some 250 million years ago when the Earth's climate was becoming colder and drier. Plants needed new tactics to survive. Conifers, or cone-bearing trees, evolved to have needles that retain more water and seeds that could hang on until there was enough moisture to germinate. The needles perform the same function as leaves, creating oxygen through photosynthesis. Needles have a thick, waxy coating that retains more water than a regular leaf and have lower wind resistance than big, flat leaves, so they're less likely to make the tree fall over during a big storm.

In evergreen environments, a variety of food options are somewhat limited. Apart from insects, few animals eat the conifer needles, which are hard to digest, and instead, herbivores concentrate on seeds, buds and berries. Some animals have adapted to eat whatever is available, making them omnivorous. Wolverines are cunning predators but will also eat plants and berries. They have also been known to drag away carrion for consumption, such as a caribou head or carcass, making the most of any food available to them.

Brown bears, another carnivore, follow a similar strategy and eat what they can find, mostly on the ground. The coniferous forest offers protection from the fierce winter blizzards for the Alaskan moose and other hoofed mammals.

Camouflage and colour change

Some animals in coniferous forests change the colour of their pelt or feathers with the changing of the seasons. For example, during the warmer months the snowshoe hare has brown fur, which camouflages it with leaf litter and a thick layer of dead needles on the forest floor. In the winter months, the hare's pelt changes to a snowy white. A similar strategy can also be found in coniferous forest ground-dwelling birds such as the ptarmigan. One of the most fascinating animals that thrive in the coniferous forest environment is the beaver – it has the incredible superpower of being able to cut down conifers wider than a fully grown man's shoulders with its teeth to create a home.

▶ **Atlas cedar**
Atlas cedars are large evergreen conifers, with a conical base growing into a broad crown. They have spreading branches bearing silvery blue-green needles. These cedars can grow over 39ft (12m) and are native to the Atlas Mountains of Morocco and Algeria.

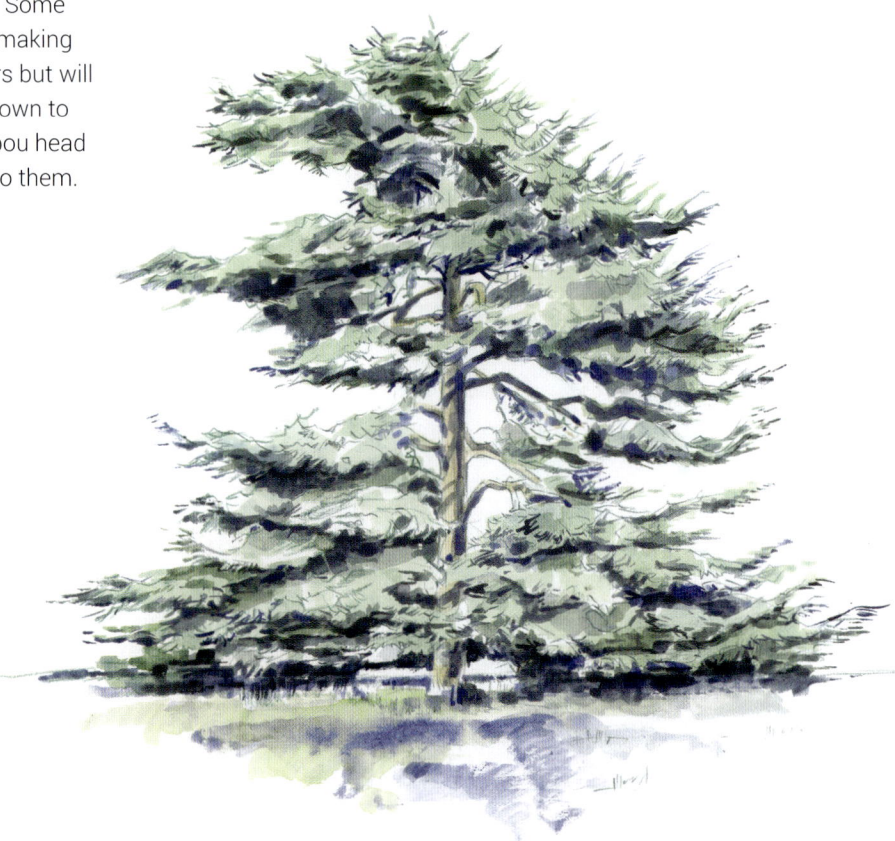

Tutorial: *Conifer Tree*

Conifers are trees with a lot of detail. With such complexity before your eyes, it is essential to remember that you are creating an impression rather than an identical copy. A good trick when painting conifers is to think of the branches as arms with a feathery claw at the end.

Tip
If you just draw the side fronds, your conifer will look flat. To help create the illusion of form, try to capture the foreshortened branches coming towards you.

1 *Start by sketching a light armature. Create a vertical line in the first instance. A few further sketch lines will help you work out the overall shape so that you know you can fit the subject on the page. Try to get the proportions accurate. How tall is the tree to its width?*

2 *Break the tree down into clumps of light and shade rather than trying to sketch every needle, which would be an impossible task. I find squinting helps to work out the main areas of light and shade, as it reduces detail.*

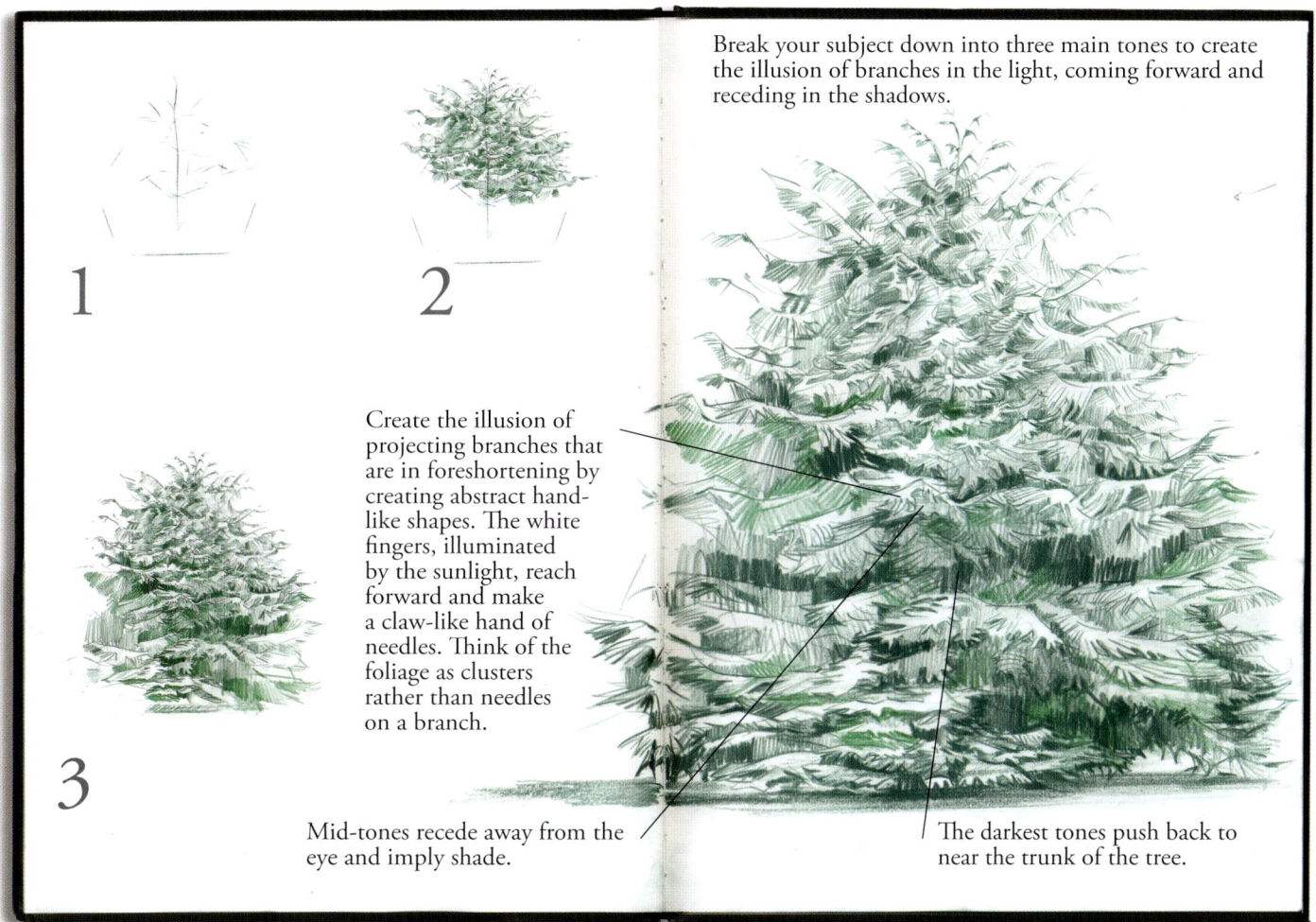

1

2

3

Break your subject down into three main tones to create the illusion of branches in the light, coming forward and receding in the shadows.

Create the illusion of projecting branches that are in foreshortening by creating abstract hand-like shapes. The white fingers, illuminated by the sunlight, reach forward and make a claw-like hand of needles. Think of the foliage as clusters rather than needles on a branch.

Mid-tones recede away from the eye and imply shade.

The darkest tones push back to near the trunk of the tree.

3 *Navigate from shape to shape, massing in the foliage and working your way from the top of the tree to the base. Try to create marks that capture the needles on the spindly branches.*

Study Sheet: *Grizzly Bear*

A mighty apex predator, the grizzly bear, also known as the North American brown bear or simply 'grizzly', is a population or subspecies of the brown bear inhabiting North America. Grizzlies are typically brown, though their fur can appear white-tipped or grizzled, giving them their name. Although they are not fussy eaters, much of their diet consists of nuts, berries, fruit, leaves and roots. They also feast on salmon, which provide them with valuable nutrition to sustain them through the long winter ahead. Dramatic gatherings of dozens of grizzly bears can be seen at Alaskan waterfalls when the salmon leap upstream for summer spawning.

Anatomy
Knowing a little about the anatomy can help you understand what you are looking at and inform your painting.

Bones
Knowing the bones can give your drawing structure and the feeling that the legs are supporting weight.

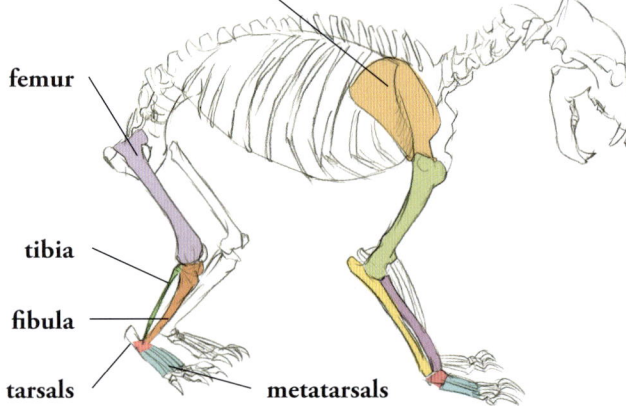

scapula
massive scapula for powerful muscle attachments

femur

tibia

fibula

tarsals   metatarsals

Muscles
Grizzlies are so hairy that you can't see the muscles, but some knowledge can help with bulking out your painting.

Shoulder hump
Grizzly bears have well-developed shoulder muscles for digging and turning over rocks. These muscles appear as a prominent shoulder hump between the front shoulders, which is visible in profile.

Head
Capturing the barrelled nose with a slightly upturned snout is key in expressing the 'beariness' of the bear. The head is large with disc-like shapes with small eyes and ears.

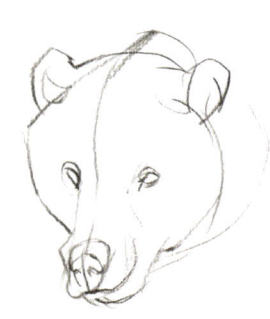 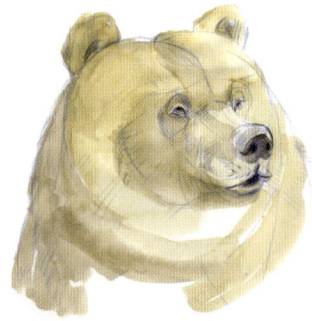

Paws
There are five digits on each limb with long, curved, non-retractable claws.

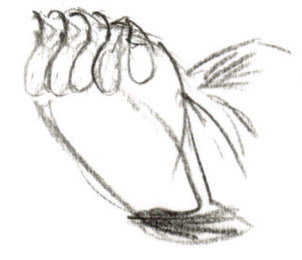 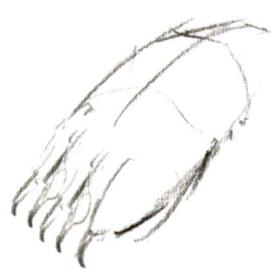

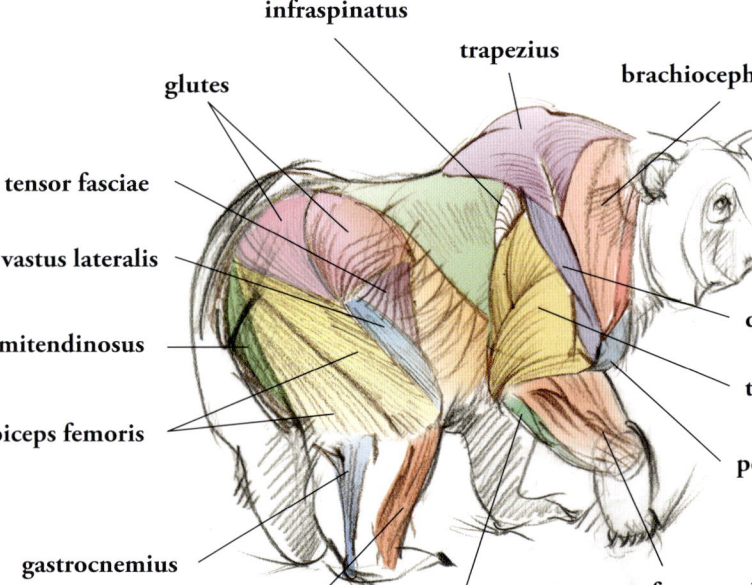

infraspinatus

trapezius

brachiocephalicus

glutes

tensor fasciae

vastus lateralis

semitendinosus

biceps femoris

gastrocnemius

deltoid

triceps

pectorals

extensors of paw and wrist

extensors of foot   flexors of paw and wrist

Different gaits

Terrestrial mammals are classified into three groups depending on their walking stance and the arrangement of bones in their limbs.

Plantigrade stance

Bear's hind feet are plantigrade, which is similar to those of humans with the heel planted on the ground. Cats and dogs are digitigrade, as are many mammal predators (although not all). Think of the stance as walking on tiptoes to quietly sneak up on someone. Ungulates are animals that walk on toenails. Think of a blade runner with an explosive spring of escape.

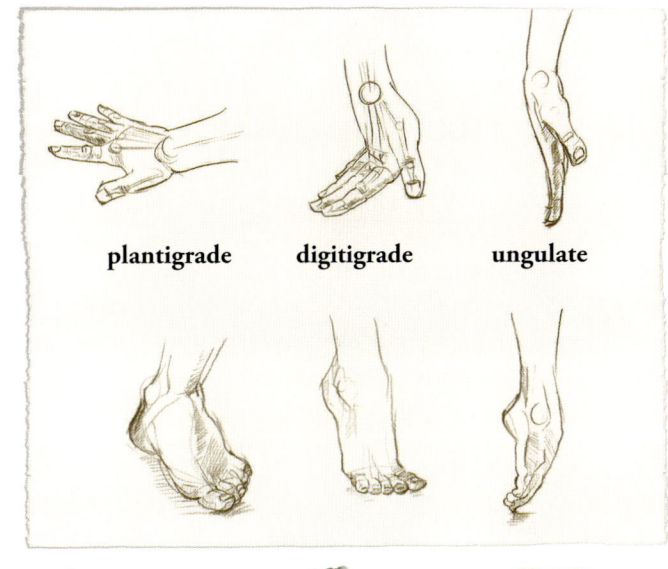

plantigrade　　**digitigrade**　　**ungulate**

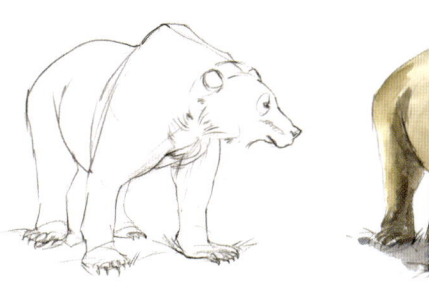 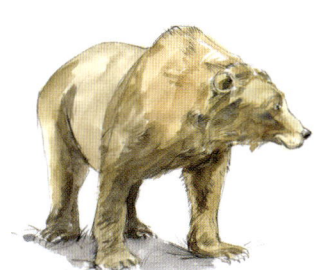

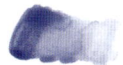 **French Ultramarine**　　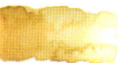 **Payne's Grey**　　**Yellow Ochre**

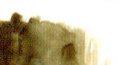 **Burnt Umber**　　**Raw Umber**

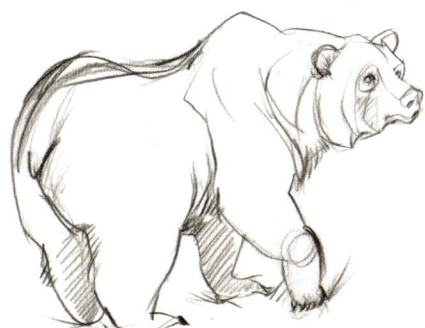 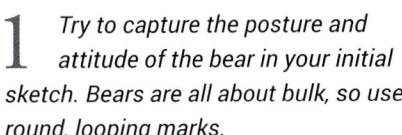 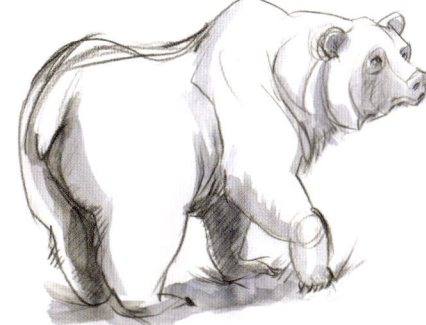 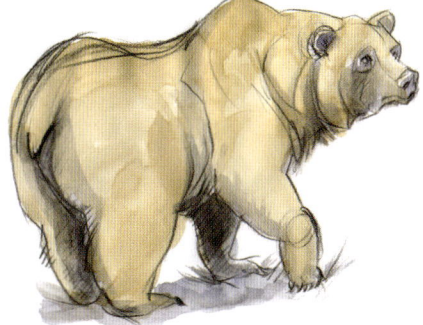

1 *Try to capture the posture and attitude of the bear in your initial sketch. Bears are all about bulk, so use round, looping marks.*

2 *Next, create a blue grey underpainting with a combination of French Ultramarine and Payne's Grey.*

3 *A variety of combinations of Yellow Ochre, Raw Umber and Burnt Umber can be used to create slight modulations of warmer and cooler shades of colour across the pelt.*

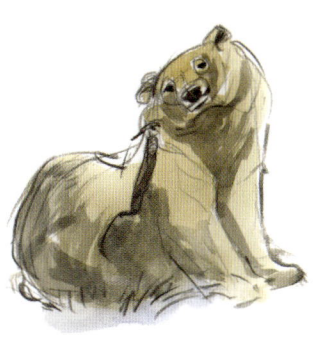 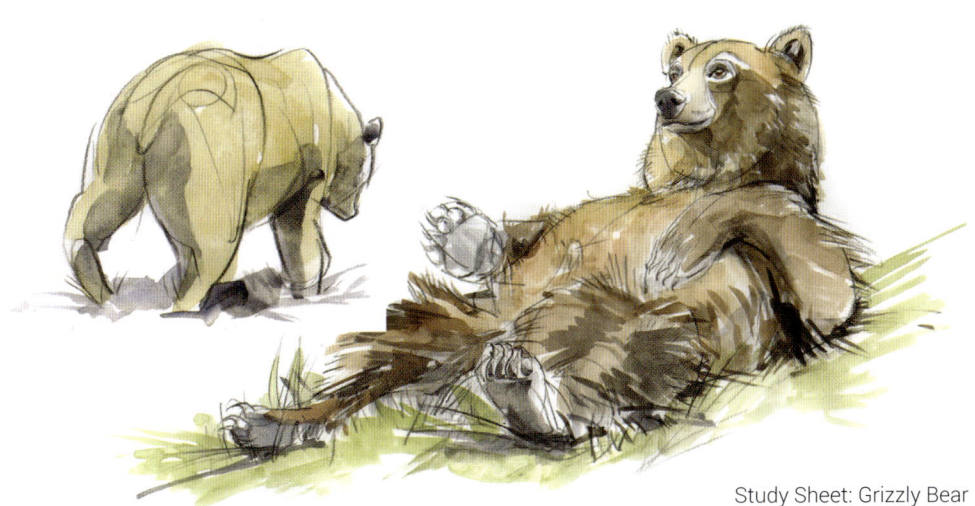

British Deciduous Woodlands

Deciduous woodlands, full of broad-leafed oaks, beech trees and elms, occur in areas with plenty of annual rainfall. These woodlands, some of which are ancient, are places where we can take time to regenerate and immerse ourselves in a green world bursting with scents and sounds. The wolves have long gone, but many British forests still have a sense of the 'wildwood' that stirs the imagination.

As with any forest, the vegetation is layered. Above your head, the branches of tall trees reach to the sunlight creating a canopy layer. To your side is the shrub layer made up of smaller trees including ash, hazel and holly. Beneath your feet is the ground layer, which can be a bracken, grass or a bright-blue bed of bluebells in spring. Deeper down is fertile rich brown earth that is replenished annually with the fall of autumnal leaves that decompose with the help of insects and are mixed into the soil by earthworms.

In woodlands, as with every other place on Earth, no one organism lives in isolation – each is dependent on countless relationships. All this life evolved together over millions of years creating stable natural communities. These communities act as a trading cycle of nutrients – something not needed by one species becomes food for the next, creating a waste-free circular cycle. Insects create the foundations of this ecosystem. They recycle dead leaves, turning them into vital nutrients for plants. Insects also pollinate flowers and they are at the bottom of the food chain.

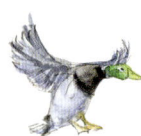

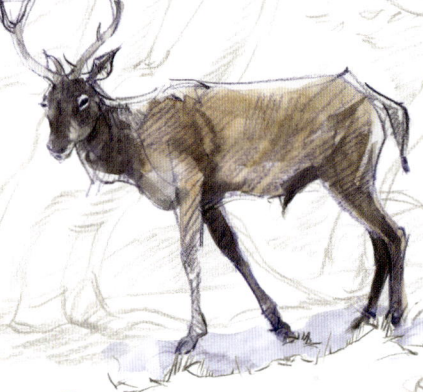

▶ Red deer
In woodland, red deer are largely solitary or occur as mother-and-calf groups. Traditionally, these large herbivores provided sustenance for larger predators such as wolves. Only the male has horns.

▶ Red squirrel
Grey squirrels were introduced to the UK from North America by the Victorians. The first record of them escaping and establishing a wild population is 1876. From then on, they have taken over the red squirrels' niche, forcing them to the country's margins. They are both small arboreal mammals that feed on seeds, nuts, berries and fungi and spread their seeds and spores.

▲ Mallard
Mallards play a key role in keeping wetland plant communities diverse and healthy.

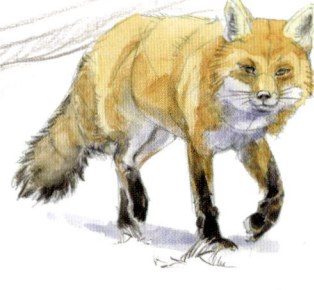

▲ Red fox
Foxes have a unique way of hunting mice. They stand motionless, listening and watching intently, then leap high and bring their forelimbs straight down, pinning the mouse to the ground.

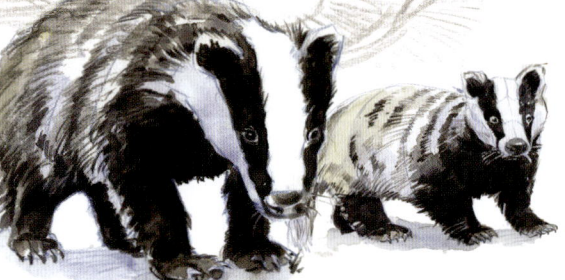

▲ Badger
Badgers are essential apex predators, uniquely adapted to digging, which helps them find and eat burrowing mammals, thereby controlling the number of rodents and protecting the ecosystem from being overrun.

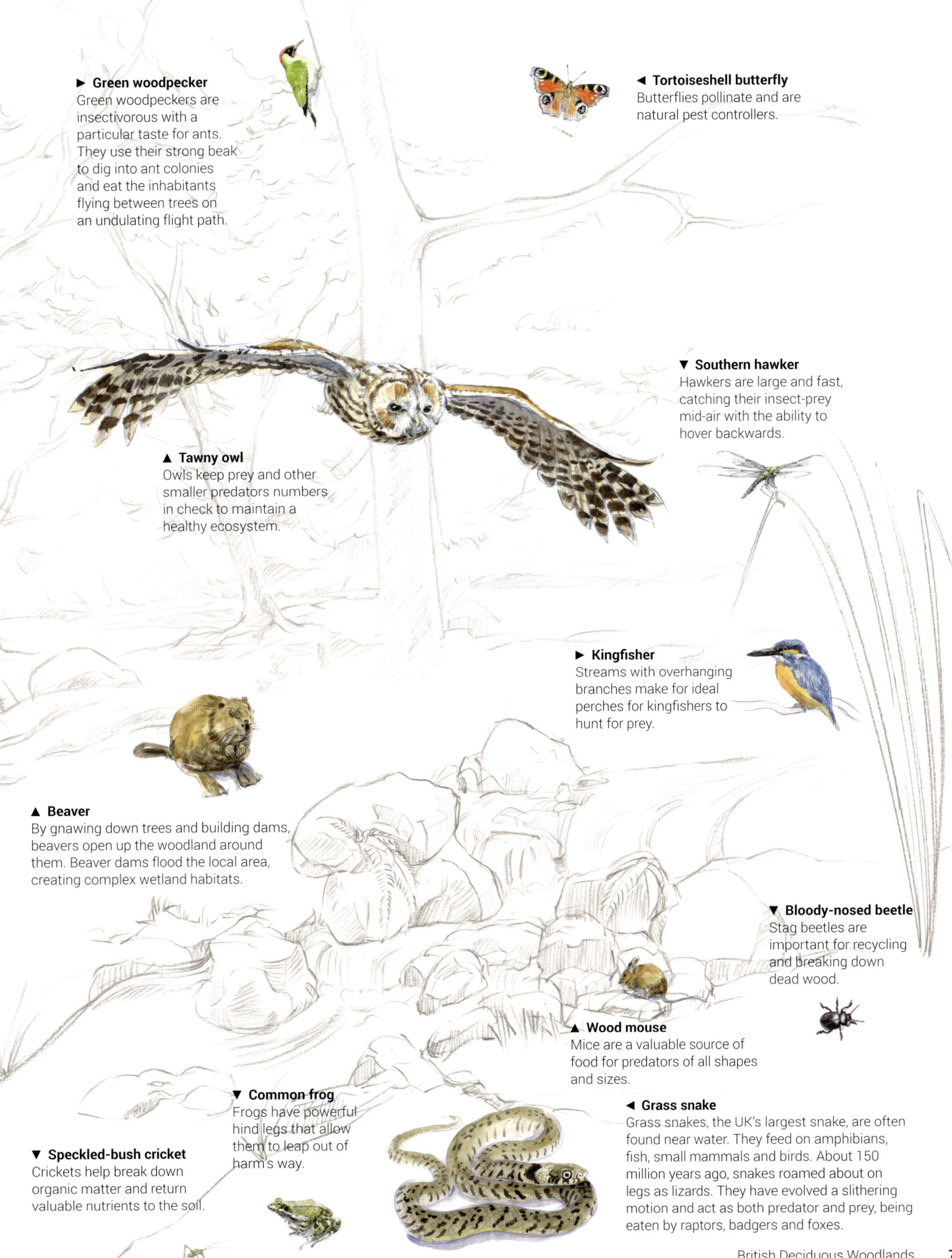

► Green woodpecker
Green woodpeckers are insectivorous with a particular taste for ants. They use their strong beak to dig into ant colonies and eat the inhabitants flying between trees on an undulating flight path.

◄ Tortoiseshell butterfly
Butterflies pollinate and are natural pest controllers.

▼ Southern hawker
Hawkers are large and fast, catching their insect-prey mid-air with the ability to hover backwards.

▲ Tawny owl
Owls keep prey and other smaller predators numbers in check to maintain a healthy ecosystem.

► Kingfisher
Streams with overhanging branches make for ideal perches for kingfishers to hunt for prey.

▲ Beaver
By gnawing down trees and building dams, beavers open up the woodland around them. Beaver dams flood the local area, creating complex wetland habitats.

▼ Bloody-nosed beetle
Stag beetles are important for recycling and breaking down dead wood.

▲ Wood mouse
Mice are a valuable source of food for predators of all shapes and sizes.

◄ Grass snake
Grass snakes, the UK's largest snake, are often found near water. They feed on amphibians, fish, small mammals and birds. About 150 million years ago, snakes roamed about on legs as lizards. They have evolved a slithering motion and act as both predator and prey, being eaten by raptors, badgers and foxes.

▼ Common frog
Frogs have powerful hind legs that allow them to leap out of harm's way.

▼ Speckled-bush cricket
Crickets help break down organic matter and return valuable nutrients to the soil.

Tutorial: *Deciduous Trees*

Every species of tree has distinct physical features which create a presence in the countryside that can not only be seen but also felt. The oak is full of muscular, angular, elbow branches that are bestowed with large clumps of lobed leaves in summer, while the silver birch is tall and elegant with delicate leaves and a silvery-white trunk. All deciduous trees support plants, such as moss and fungi, and thousands of animals living in a myriad of microhabitats from their roots to their twigs.

Activity
Pick a tree and observe it through the seasons, from the bare branches of winter to the leafy canopy of summer.

Essentially, the shape of all trees can be viewed as a series of cylinders joined together, a bit like plumbing. The trunk forms the core, providing a vertical armature for the reaching branches. Seeing the tree in this manner encourages the artist to volumize the form. Wrapping the abstract pattern of shadows around the branches helps suggest their physicality. I really enjoy the imperfections, the cracks and cavities, which give additional information that can help sculpt the tree.

Tree widget

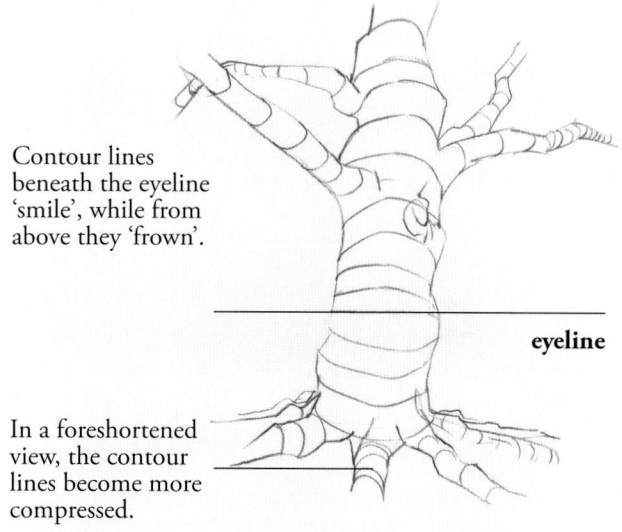

Contour lines beneath the eyeline 'smile', while from above they 'frown'.

eyeline

In a foreshortened view, the contour lines become more compressed.

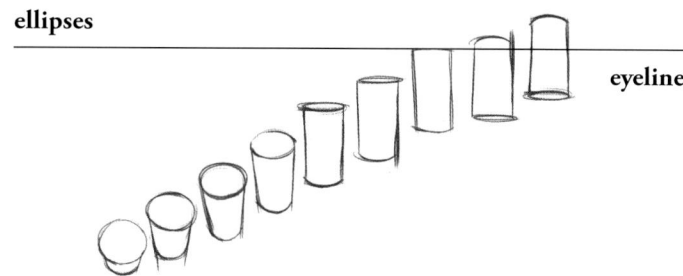

ellipses

eyeline

▲ Understanding ellipses
Experiment with a cylinder shape, such as a paper cup, and lift it above and below your eye level. You should notice that the ellipse becomes rounder and broader the further above and below it is. Beneath the eyeline, you can look into the cup; from above, you see the base; at eye level, the ellipse becomes a flat line. When creating ellipses, practise drawing smooth circular shapes in the air, ghosting the mark before committing to the paper.

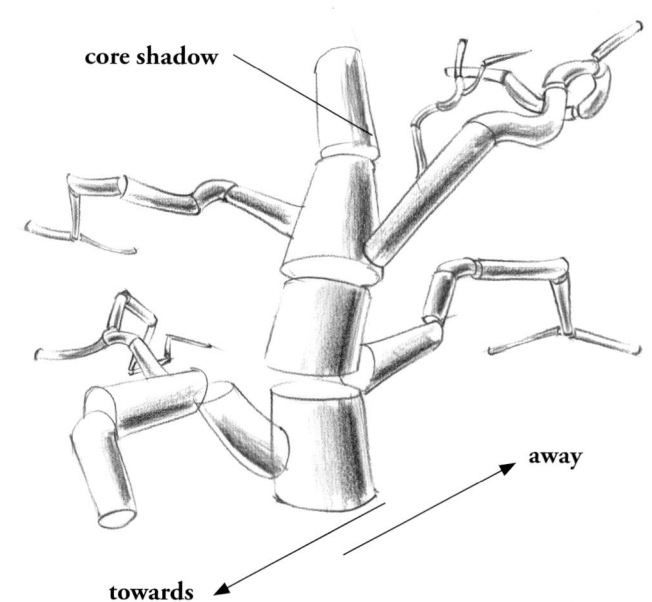

core shadow

away

towards

▲ Branching out
Branches are full of dynamic bends and angles. Use overlapping lines to create the illusion that one branch is in front of another. Try to capture foreshortened, compressed branches coming towards you and moving away, so your tree does not look too flat.

Tip
Faraway trees tend to appear flattened. Their twigs and branches can be suggested in a minimal shorthand sketching style, reducing the intense visual noise to a few marks. Experiment and simplify by creating twig marks that give the impression of visual complexity.

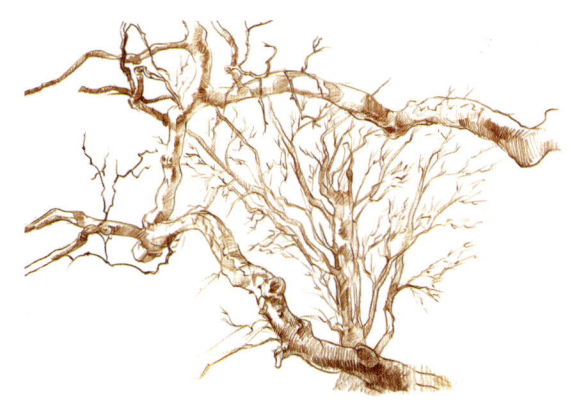

▶ Spring shadows

In spring, trees are fledged with infant leaves allowing the artist to see the branches. Shadows cast on the cylindrical forms warp and wrap around the structure of the interweaving branches. They merge with the shadow of form, which is on the opposite side of the light source. Start by creating the outline of the foremost branches. Vary your marking and imagine that your pencil is touching the tree. Try to sculpt the branch forms on the paper, carving them out with shading. Do not overlook the core shadow from light reflected on the ground, particularly if there is snow when there is a lot of reflected light.

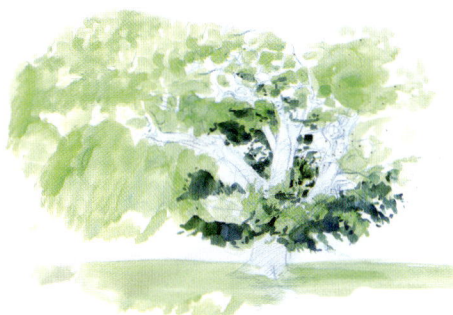

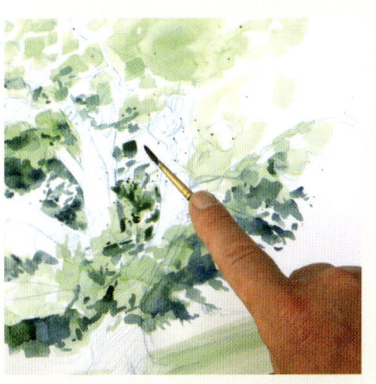

1 *Find a focal point on the trunk to begin and create a loose sketch. Look at the negative shapes of leaf windows between the branches to navigate the tree and let your drawing grow shape to shape.*

2 *Break your subject down into three main tones. Rather than drawing every leaf, try instead to create an impression of the large clumps of leaves by using loose, characterful brush marks. Squint to reduce visual noise and see abstract patches of light and dark. The dark notes will recede and give depth to your study. Look for windows of light between the branches where the leaves are often in silhouette. Pushing the contrast of these values helps denote a feeling of light.*

Splatter

Spattering the paint by giving the brush a tap helps create the impression of the thousands of leaves. I tend to do this limitedly, as overdoing it can look like a swarm of flies. The tiny spatters help to provide a sense of scale, emboldening the branches into thick pillars.

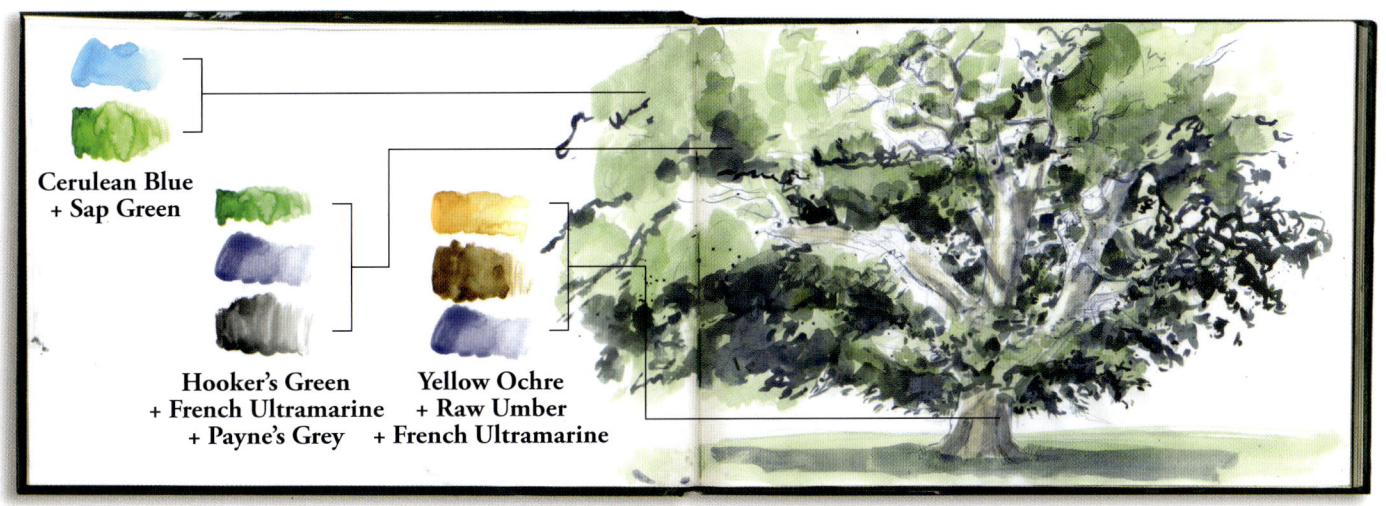

Cerulean Blue + Sap Green

Hooker's Green + French Ultramarine + Payne's Grey

Yellow Ochre + Raw Umber + French Ultramarine

Tutorial: *Oak Sprig*

Use this tutorial to learn to capture the lovely undulating form of the waxy oak leaf, the roundness of the acorns and mix the deep warm green shade of their leaves in this step-by-step tutorial. One of the objectives of this exercise is to create overlapping lines that enable the viewer to see that one leaf is in front of the other.

Leaf gizmo
Visualize the leaves piled up like a dishevelled stack of cards.

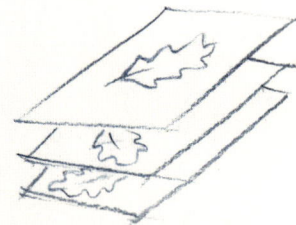

Tip
For best results, work on a thick, smooth cartridge paper 220gsm, stretched to prevent buckling (see pages 10–11).

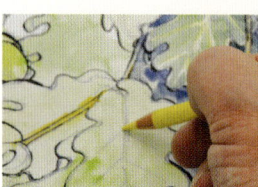

Tip
To help with the fiddly job of capturing thin veins, use a waxy colouring pencil with a sharp tip to create a slight wax resist. A wash of dark green leaf colour can then be gently worked towards this impression.

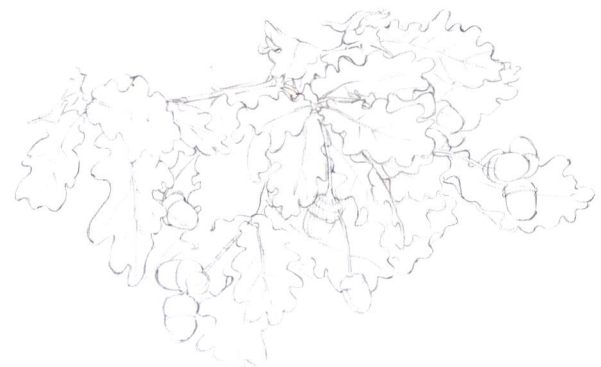

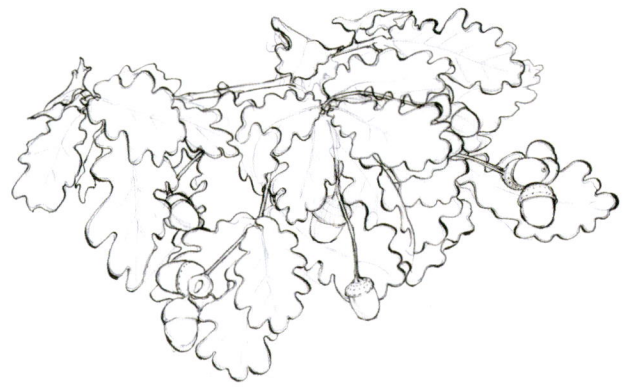

1 *Place your sprig in front of you on a table and sit close to your subject. Focus your eye on a starting point, a single leaf, and let your drawing grow from leaf to leaf as you navigate your way across the foliage using both positive and negative shapes (see page 42). Capture the characteristic dog-eared shapes of the leaves with flowing arabesque lines. Try to simplify the intricate detail into the main leaf and twig shapes. Envisage your twig in three levels. Sketch the top storey first, gradually working your way down through the layers using overlapping lines to create the impression that one leaf is in front of the other. Start roughing-out lightly to establish the main shapes and change the proportions before committing to darker lines. Overlapping lines create the convention that one leaf is in front of the other. Play with this illusion to make the impression of various levels of leaves.*

2 *Redraw, still looking intently at the sprig; don't merely trace over the initial sketch. The light sketch acts as a loose armature for the more exacting ink line. Imagine the tip of your dip pen or pencil touching the contours of the oak leaves and take your line for a walk, like a bug, around the shapes, observing every nook and cranny. Guide your line, looking more at the subject than the paper. Capture the character of the forms with an accurate line that bites into the edge of the form. Notice imperfections, interesting broken bits and insect bite marks. Not all the lines you create are on the edge of the form; perhaps there are marks such as the central vein that runs the length of the leaf, and the branching veins can be delineated with a lighter pencil stroke. The exercise should be done slowly and with conviction. Vary the thickness of your line from thin to thick by varying the pressure. The leaves nearest to you can be delineated with a thicker line to pull them forward on the page.*

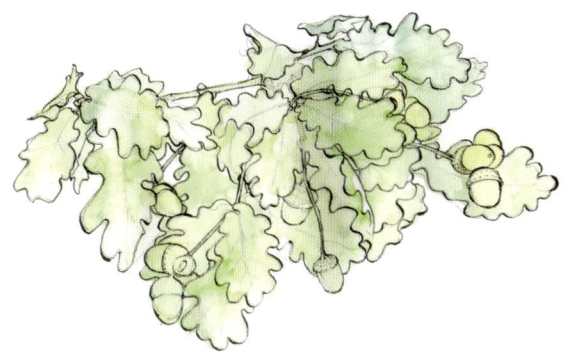

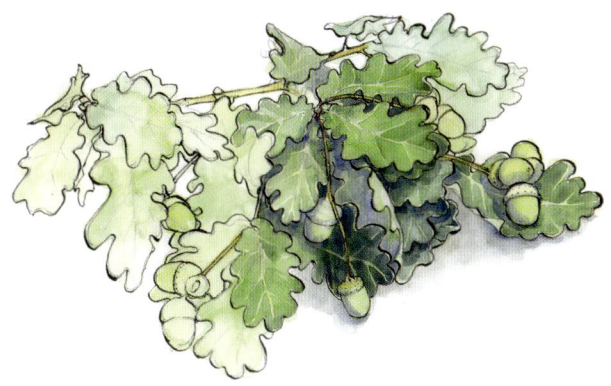

3 Before you start to add watercolour, identify your light source and keep this consistent. The veins of my oak leaf and acorns are yellow-green; this is the lightest and brightest colour and the first that I put down on paper. I break off a leaf and place it by the palette to achieve an accurate mix. I begin lightly with watery transparent washes that stain the ink line drawing. The selection of colours I use is only a recommendation; experiment with your paintbox to discover your way of interpreting the colours. Modulate by graduating different shades wet into wet (see page 27) to reflect the way the colour varies across the sprig. Cooler colours will tend to recede, while warmer colours project forward. This convention can be played with to enhance depth further.

4 Now you can paint in the body colour of the leaves. Try to mix a natural green body colour of the oak leaf. Experiment with different combinations. I create little colour daubs on a separate scrap of paper to test the colour match. I spend longer mixing the colour than applying. Keep modifying your mix until you feel confident that your shade captures the warm oak green. Most pure green pigments will need adapting to create an appropriate shade. The veins create a slight dip in the leaf, which makes a small shadow of form. Add a small quantity of French Ultramarine to the body colour of the leaf. French Ultramarine with a slight touch of Payne's Grey creates a cast shadow colour that stops the sprig from floating in space and sits the study on the white paper.

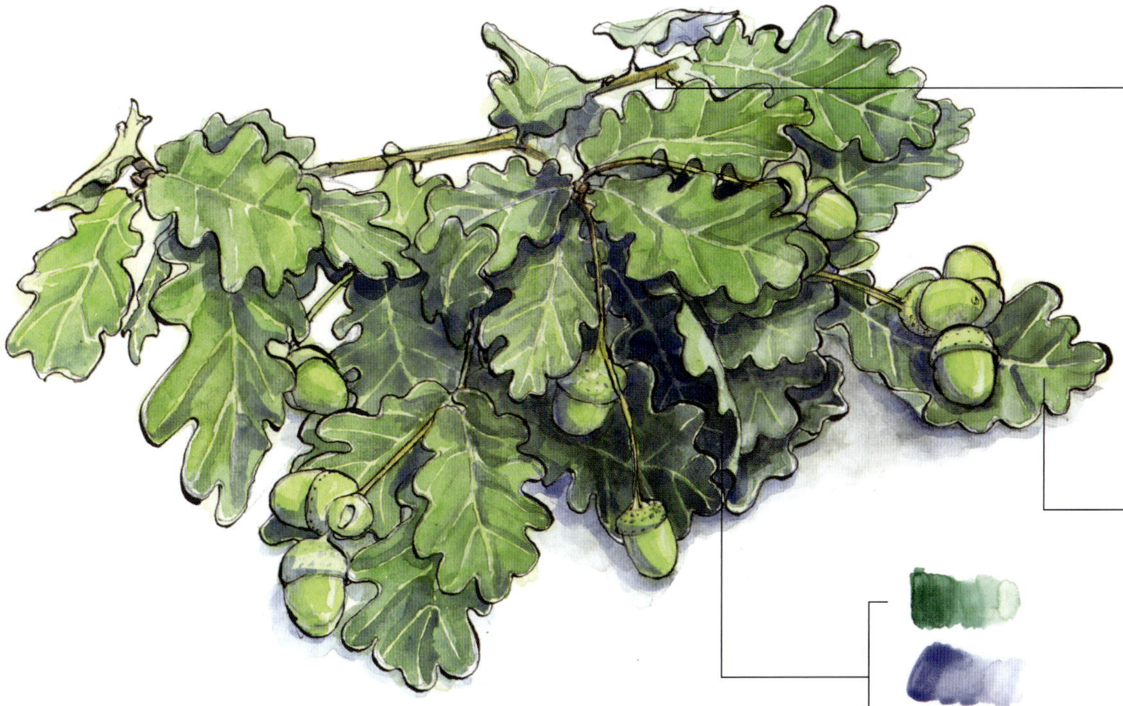

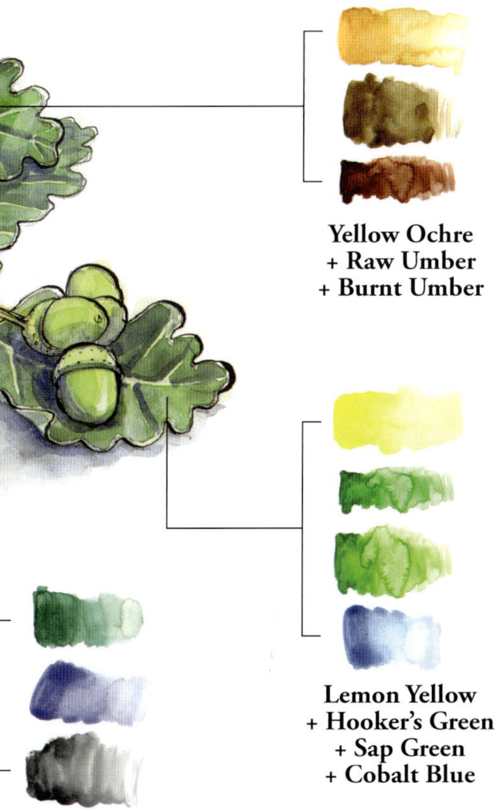

Yellow Ochre + Raw Umber + Burnt Umber

Lemon Yellow + Hooker's Green + Sap Green + Cobalt Blue

Viridian Green + French Ultramarine + Payne's Grey

5 To help emphasize the stacked impression that one leaf is on top of the other, apply a cast shadow lip of darker blue-green. As the green darkens in the shadows add an increased amount of French Ultramarine.

Study Sheet: *Woodland Insects*

There are some 950 thousand different kinds of living insects known in the world. They inhabit every single continent from the hot to the cold. If backboned animals disappeared overnight, the natural world would survive. However, it would be a different story if insects disappeared, so crucial is their role in providing the foundations on which ecosystems depend.

Insects act as pollinators, pollinating flowers to bring us nutritious fruit and vegetables. They tirelessly work behind the scenes, even while we sleep. They also provide food for birds, bats and small mammals. Importantly, insects replenish the soils, enabling plants to grow and keep pest numbers in check. Scavenger insects, such as the dung beetle – a waste disposer, clean up and protect us from disease.

In all continents of the world, even Antarctica, insects have found a place and have evolved into a marvellous array of different appearances. Their quick reproduction lifespan means that adaptations have happened more quickly. Some of these are beyond the imagination, such as the dead leaf butterfly that has adapted fantastic camouflage and falling leaf behaviour to hide from predators.

The latest research shows that insects evolved simultaneously with the earliest plants on the land about 480 million years ago and took to the air some 80 million years later. They were one of the first animals on land, crawling up as sea arthropods (meaning 'jointed leg') from the sea when early plants such as horsetails and ferns created a habitat for insects to dwell within.

One of the best ways to draw insects is by breaking their body down into segments, which is easy to learn. All insects follow the same body plan – an archetype of simple units that join together.

Anatomy

Knowing a little about the anatomy can help you understand what you are looking at and inform your painting.

Speckled bush-cricket

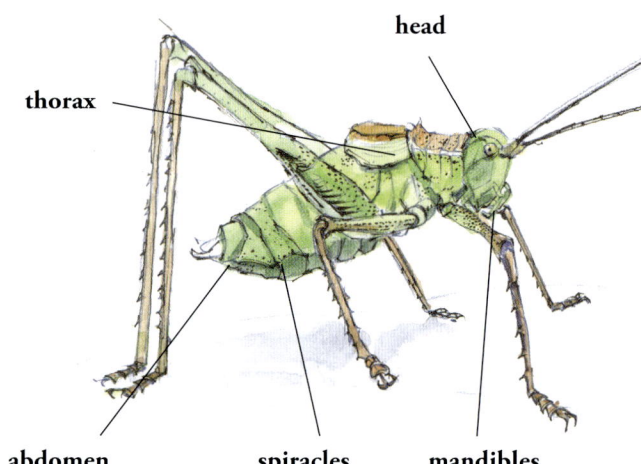

thorax

head

multi-segmented antennae

abdomen   spiracles   mandibles

Head
This is where the antennae, compound eyes and mandibles attach. Some species also have a head horn for defence and impressive weapons.

Spiracles
Insects breathe through tiny holes along the side of the thorax and abdomen called spiracles.

Thorax
The thorax is full of muscles and is the central machine area for both walking and flight. Both the wings and the legs attach to it.

Abdomen
The abdomen retains the segmented division of its earlier worm-like ancestors and contains the heart, reproductive organs and digestive organs.

Claw
The claw is used for hooking and holding the light insect on a variety of surfaces. A water strider has a single hook with lots of hairs that helps it balance on the water.

► Compound eye
To imagine how a compound eye works, think of lots of little eyes on a dome shape. This hemispheric shape gives all-round vision, which is good at detecting motion and spotting a predator approaching, even from behind.

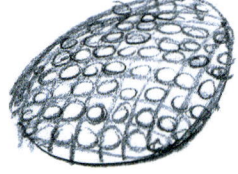

Legs

All insects have six legs. While butterflies in the nymphalidae family may appear to have four legs, they do in fact have two tiny front legs tucked up so that you can't see them. The coxa joins the thorax, then the trochanter, femur, tibia, tarsus and claw. The proportions, shape and number of tarsus vary widely.

Exoskeleton

The exoskeleton is created from a strong substance called chitin and can be thought of as a suit of armour. As with the insect's ancestors, the sea arthropods, to grow means shedding the case. Some bugs, such as stag beetles, have really sharp angular planes, and it helps to keep your pencil sharp to describe the crystal-like structures. I enjoy attempting to emphasize the shininess by leaving white gaps and allowing the watercolour to bleed. There are always interesting alien shapes and components coming from a seemingly other world to explore. I always look out for pie-crust edges of the carapaces.

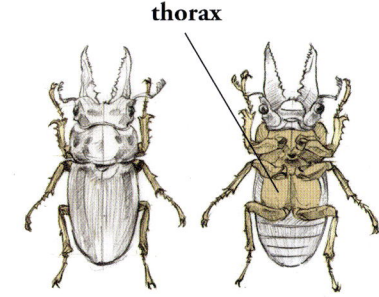

lines can be sketched around the form to help express its volume

coxa

defensive spikes

femur

tarsus

tibia

claw

trochanter – equivalent to the ball and socket joint in your hips

thorax

▶ **Elytra**
The elytra are the beetle's modified, hardened forewings, which serve as a protective wing-case for the gossamer hindwings underneath.

elytra

▲ **Insect archetype leg**
The back legs can appear to join the abdomen. However, this is misleading as the thorax tends to be longer on the underside of the insect.

A view from above

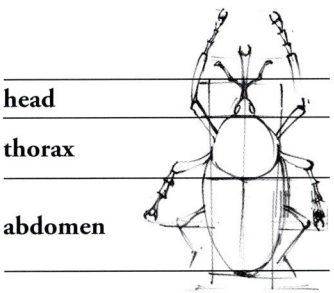

head

thorax

abdomen

▲ Front legs tend to face forward. A light directional armature can be sketched before fleshing out and adding thickness to the leg.

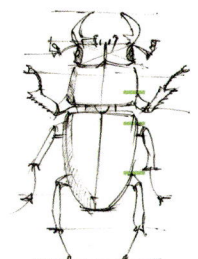

▲ Use light horizontal lines to judge the length of the legs. Ensure they line up on either side of the body. Note from beneath which body part they emerge.

A dynamic viewpoint

abdomen
thorax
head

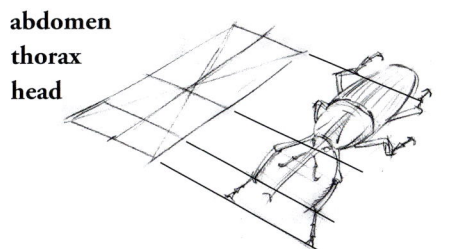

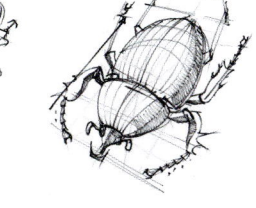

▲ Directional shading sculpts the form.

▲ Use sharp concave marks to create defensive spikes. Count the number of tarsus.

Build up the paint in stages from light to dark

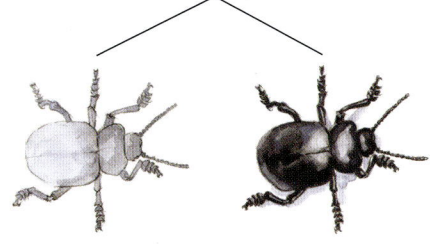

◀ **Bloody-nosed beetle**
Capture the shiny carapace by leaving white patches of bare paper in carefully observed shapes. A light stipple at the edge of these patches captures the pitted texture found on some beetles.

▶ **Stag beetle**
When sketching insects, try to create the impression that the thin tubes of the chitin legs are supporting the weight of the body.

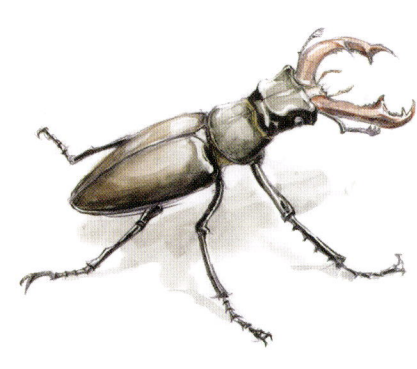

Tutorial: *Seven-Spot Ladybird*

The seven-spot ladybird is the UK's most recognizable species of ladybird. They are often found overwintering indoors or in dry, sheltered crevices such as beneath tree bark. As a voracious predator of aphids, they are an excellent natural pest controller. Painting these bulbous little bugs from a three-quarter view beneath the eyeline helps express the three-dimensional qualities of their form.

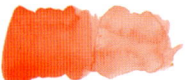
Cadmium Red

Cadmium Orange

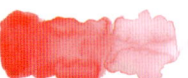
Alizarin Crimson

French Ultramarine

White Gouache

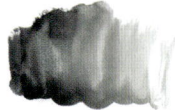
Payne's Grey

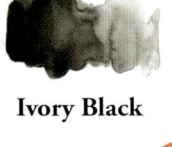
Ivory Black

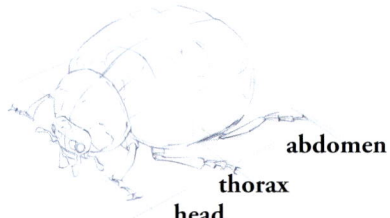
abdomen
thorax
head

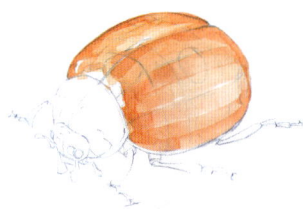

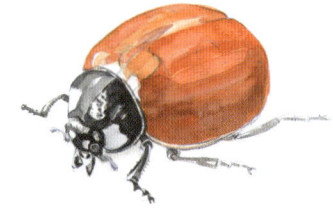

1 *Sketch the body's three main segments and the bilateral line of symmetry. Note where the legs emerge from beneath the body. Name the leg segments in your mind as you draw them and count the number of tarsus. Create light, round lines around the abdomen to start coaxing the form from the paper.*

2 *In the light, the ladybird's elytra become more orange; in the shade it takes on a cooler tone. Use Cadmium Red as the base and graduate by adding Cadmium Orange and Alizarin Crimson. Notice the light ridges and paint around the form.*

3 *Now increase the mid-tones, placing the white eye patch and nearside elytra in the shade by using French Ultramarine in the mix. The head, legs and distinctive black spots are created with a pure Ivory Black in various diluted washes.*

Ladybird widget

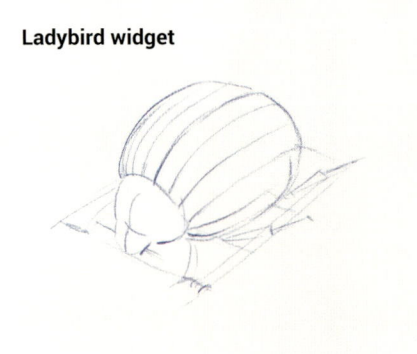

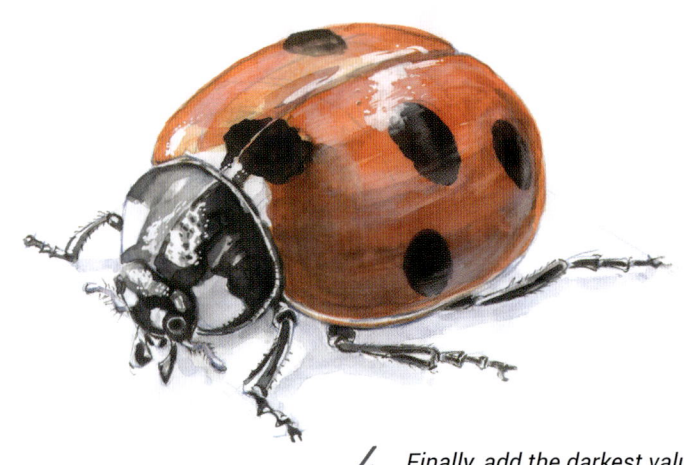

4 *Finally, add the darkest values and highlights with White Gouache. The drop shadow is created by a mixture of French Ultramarine and Payne's Grey.*

Tutorial: *Butterfly*

Butterflies are a beautiful and essential part of wildlife. They are highly sensitive indicators of the environment's health, play crucial roles in the food chain and are pollinators. The iridescent colour of the wings is not created by pigment alone; the nanostructure of the chitin, or wing scale, affects how light is reflected, creating brilliant colours that can only be captured in watercolour by keeping your water clean and pigments bright.

As a butterfly emerges from its chrysalis, it pumps fluid into veins that unfold the wing. These veins give structure to the wing. Both the upper and lower wings have discal cells, which I find really useful for navigating the wing. You will see this with some variation in most butterflies and moths.

White Gouache

Lemon Yellow

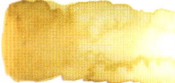
Yellow Ochre

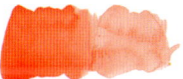
Cadmium Yellow

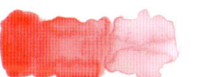

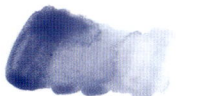
Cadmium Red

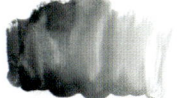
Alizarin Crimson

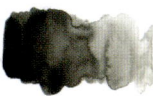
Cobalt Blue

French Ultramarine   **Payne's Grey**   **Ivory Black**

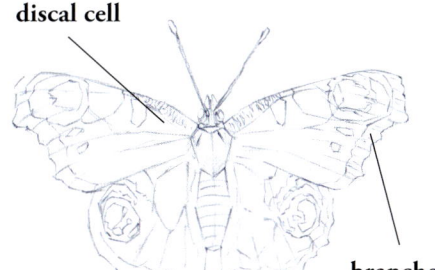

discal cell

branches

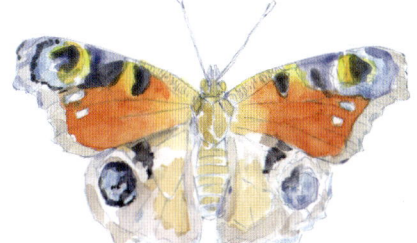

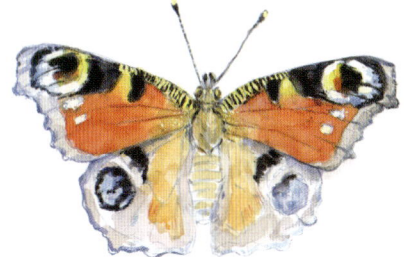

1 *In your initial sketch, try to get down all the information you want to show through the translucent washes of watercolour. Indicate the discal cells and the branches you can see, as well as outlining the markings. Note that the lower wings are beneath the upper wings.*

2 *Now paint in the lightest and brightest colours. Use wet into wet techniques and graduate your washes (see page 27), letting one colour bloom into another.*

3 *Work broadly at first, then work towards the detail, gradually using smaller and smaller brushes until you start speckling in fine dots with a rigger brush, using a mixture of White Gouache and Lemon Yellow.*

Butterflies in flight gizmo

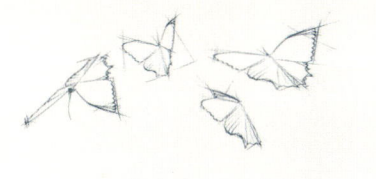

4 *Add a drop shadow beneath the top wing to emphasize that they are in front and use a watercolour pencil to highlight the branches and create the texture of fine hairs on the thorax.*

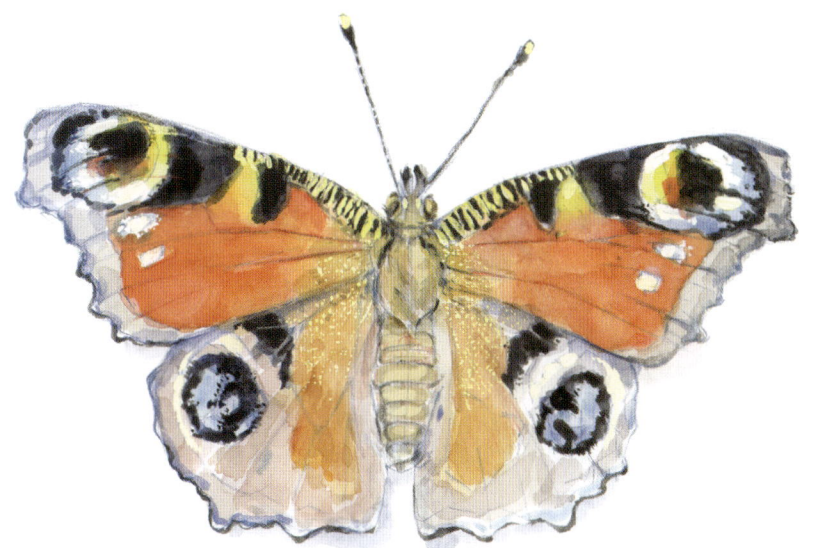

Grasslands

Grasses started to make an appearance on the Earth around the end of the Cretaceous period, between 70 and 55 million years ago. At first, they were a small group of plants that lived in the shade on the edge of forests. As the Earth warmed and its climate became drier, these grassland habitats opened up and spread to every continent except Antarctica, and they now make up around one-fifth of the Earth's surface.

Grasses grow near the ground and are not harmed from having the tips of their stem cut off by animals eating them – in fact they thrive from being grazed. Grazing animals help the grass maintain dominance by eating the competing plants that do not recover as well. Almost all hoofed mammals are grazers, a word that means 'grass-eaters'. Grazers and browsers include horses, cows, sheep, buffalo, deer, horses, zebras and kangaroos, to name but a few. Most of these species have digestive systems primarily evolved for processing grass, which forms a significant portion of their diet. Some of them chew the cud, have fermenting stomachs and grinding molars to process this sturdy fibrous plant material.

Almost all wild grazers are prey animals and share these wide-open spaces with their fearsome predators. Some grassland mammals herd, as it can pay to stay together if you want to go far. Zebra and kangaroos can be seen travelling in large groups, and of course there is the spectacular great wildebeest migration in Africa, which traverses the nations of Tanzania and Kenya. I was once fortunate enough to witness this incredible event, more than 1.5 million wildebeests migrating in a large loop every year in the search for greener pastures.

With little shelter, grassland offers few hiding places, and life becomes a daily battle for survival for both predator and prey. 'Disruptive colouration' is one of nature's strategies frequently used in grasslands by both prey and predator. Zebras have black-and-white stripes to break up the outline of their body. Cheetahs have spots to help them blend in seamlessly in dappled shade and long grass.

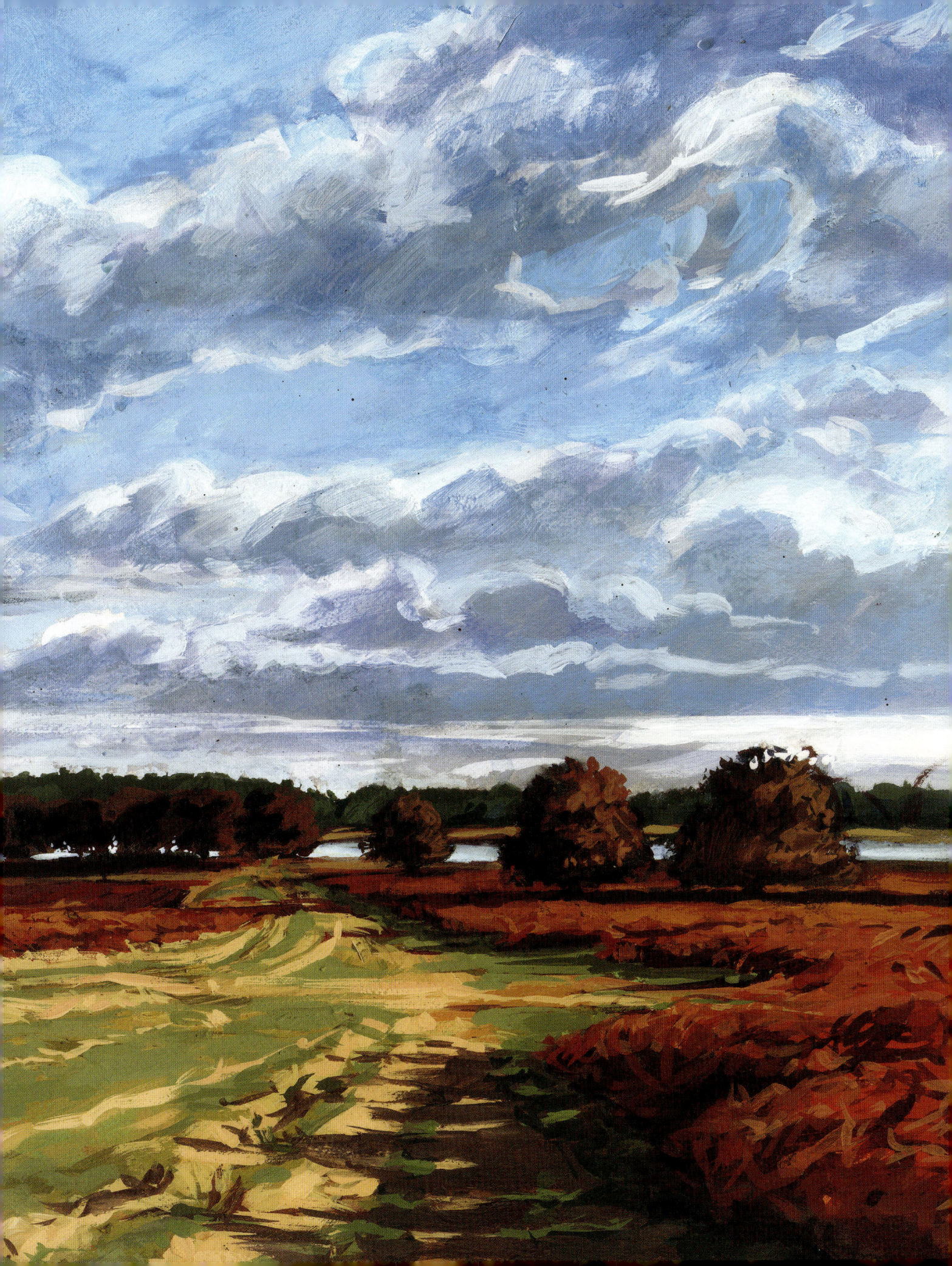

The African Savannah

The tropical grasslands of Africa are open spaces. There is not enough annual rainfall in tropical regions to support dense tropical forests and the grasses have taken over. These are landscapes with dramatic seasonal change. They provide habitats for some of the most amazing life forms on the planet and are witness to the spectacular daily battle for life between hunter and prey.

Nowhere is the circle of life and death played out more intensely than on the tropical grassland. Every day is an intense and brutal battle for survival for both predator and prey.

The lack of overhead branches allows giraffes to graze, gives cheetahs the free space to run, and enables wildebeest to migrate. The African plains are peppered with umbrella acacia trees that provide shelter from the sun in the dry season for leopards.

Tropical grasslands lie close to the equator globally, primarily to the north and south of the tropical rainforests. There are tropical grasslands in Australia, India and South America, but Africa houses the largest of them and is full of some of the most vibrant diversity of life found anywhere on the planet.

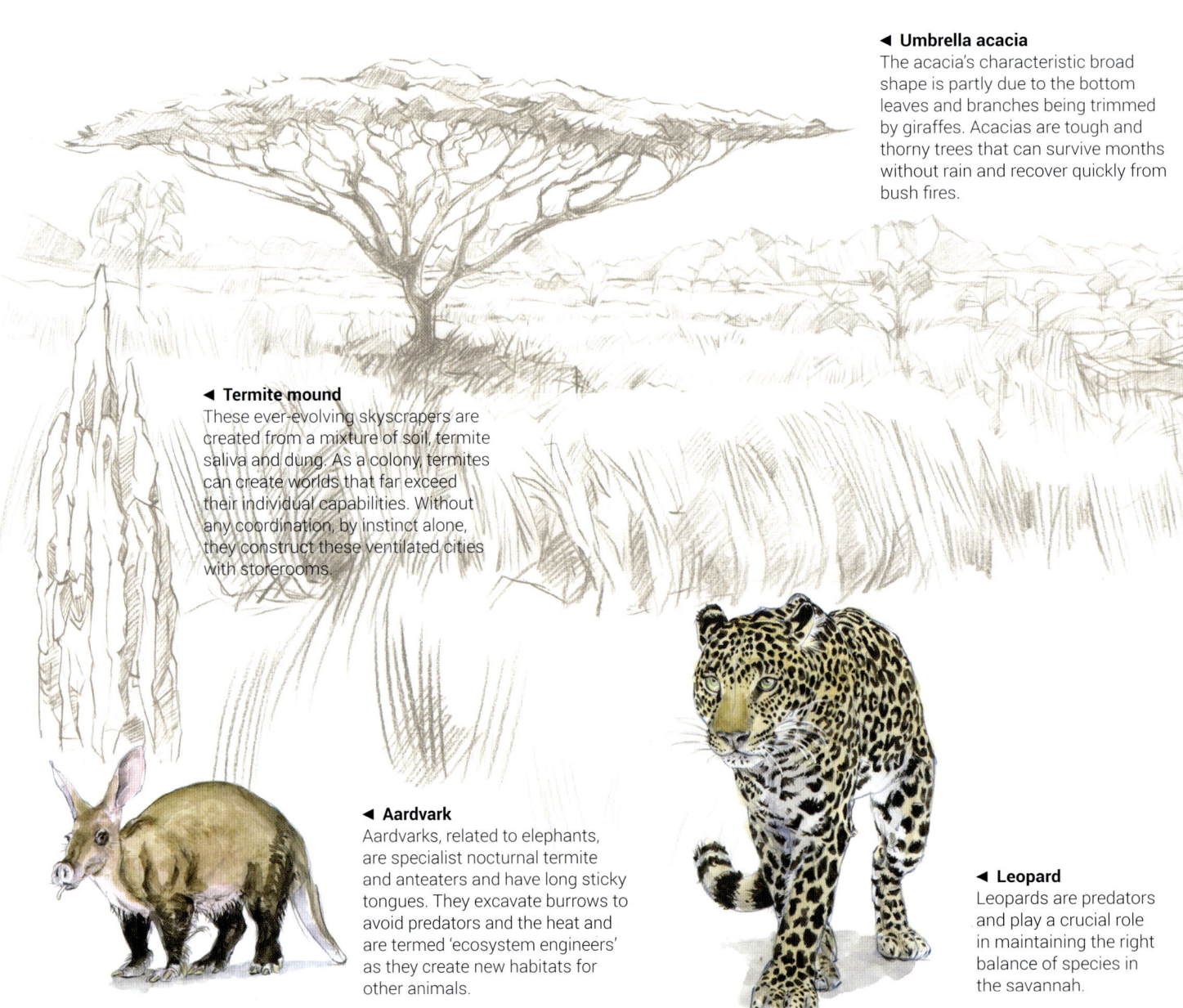

◄ Umbrella acacia
The acacia's characteristic broad shape is partly due to the bottom leaves and branches being trimmed by giraffes. Acacias are tough and thorny trees that can survive months without rain and recover quickly from bush fires.

◄ Termite mound
These ever-evolving skyscrapers are created from a mixture of soil, termite saliva and dung. As a colony, termites can create worlds that far exceed their individual capabilities. Without any coordination, by instinct alone, they construct these ventilated cities with storerooms.

◄ Aardvark
Aardvarks, related to elephants, are specialist nocturnal termite and anteaters and have long sticky tongues. They excavate burrows to avoid predators and the heat and are termed 'ecosystem engineers' as they create new habitats for other animals.

◄ Leopard
Leopards are predators and play a crucial role in maintaining the right balance of species in the savannah.

▶ White-backed vulture

These African vultures play the crucially important role of removing dead animals and thus disease, acting as the cleanser of the savannah and making sure that no food goes to waste, picking a carcass to the bone.

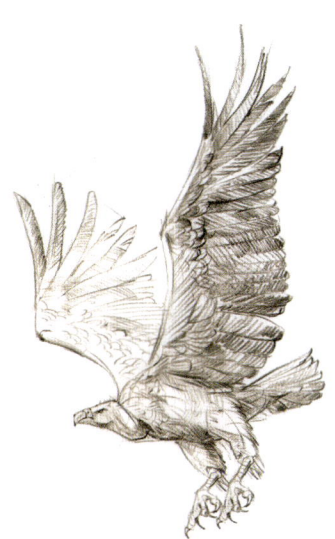

▼ Giraffe

The long necks of giraffes help them to eat leaves, flowers and fruit higher than other grazers can reach. Giraffe's lives are closely intertwined with acacia trees, and some species of acacia only germinate after the seeds pass through a giraffe's digestive system.

▼ Elephants

On the savannahs, elephants feed on tree sprouts and shrubs to help to keep the plains open. In the dry season, they use their tusks to dig for water and create temporary watering holes. Elephants are the constant gardeners of the savannah; their dung is full of seeds from the many plants they eat. These seeds germinate into new grasses, bushes and trees.

▲ A dazzle of zebras

Zebras group into herds for protection. There is a phrase, 'If you want to go further, go together!' Disruptive colouration breaks up the shape of the animal and helps them escape predators.

▲ Nile crocodile

Nile crocodiles are ancient apex predators, evolving 200 million years ago in the days of the dinosaurs. They deter fish and animals from overcrowding and degrading the ecosystem. They are not fussy eaters, although they mainly eat fish. They will attack almost anything unfortunate enough to cross their path, including zebra, small hippos, wildebeest, birds and even other crocodiles. They will also scavenge carrion.

◀ Lilac-breasted roller

Rollers are an indicator species and would be the first to be affected by changes in the air quality because of their delicate lungs.

Study Sheet: *Thomson's Gazelle*

Capturing action poses is an essential tool for any artist. Knowing the skeletal system and the pivot points will significantly benefit your sketching ability. Imagine how it would feel if your body was in the posture you are sketching, how the body stretches or compresses. Feel the flow of movement through the whole body of the animal. Lines should convey the rhythm and grace of the animal's movement, making the drawing look like it was created with ease and in sympathy with the subject.

Anatomy
Knowing a little about the anatomy can help you understand what you are looking at and inform your painting.

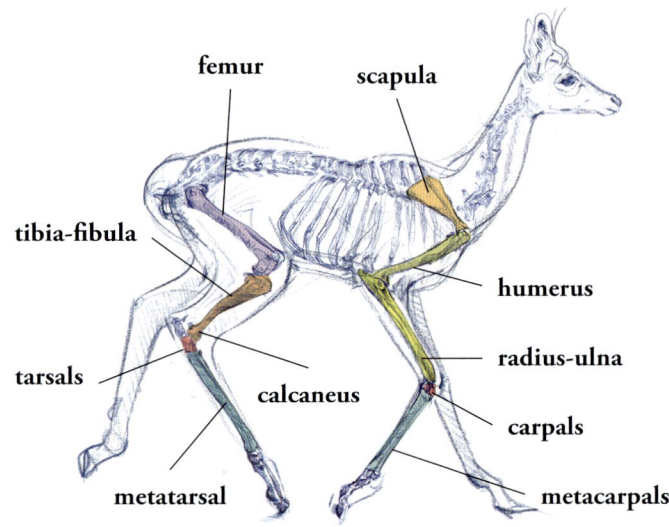

femur

scapula

tibia-fibula

humerus

radius-ulna

tarsals

calcaneus

carpals

metatarsal

metacarpals

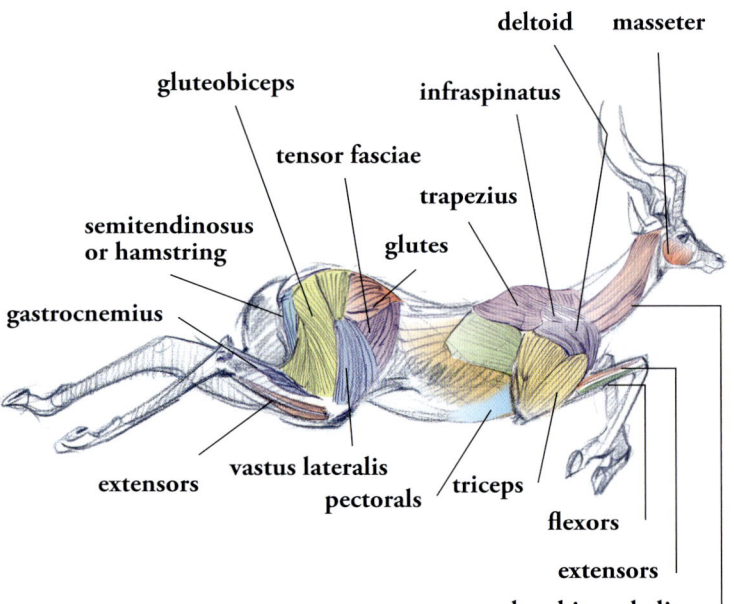

deltoid masseter

gluteobiceps

infraspinatus

tensor fasciae

trapezius

semitendinosus or hamstring

glutes

gastrocnemius

extensors

vastus lateralis
pectorals

triceps

flexors

extensors

brachiocephalicus

Bones
Knowing the bones can give your drawing structure and the feeling that the legs are supporting weight.

Muscles
Recognizing a few key muscles can help model the form and make sense of the lumps and bumps.

Legs

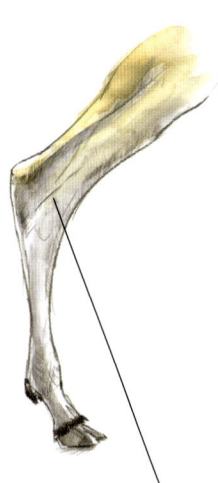

The gazelle's legs' length has evolved into long poles with the radius and ulna and the tibia and fibula fusing for strength, losing their rotational ability in the process for the payoff of an explosive escape. The back leg in repose can be thought of as a cocked spring. Capture the dynamic angle of the heel. Enjoy capturing the knobbly calcaneus, (heel bone) and the pronounced Achilles tendon, which attaches from the heel to the gastrocnemius.

There is a gap between the tendon and the bone where the long calcaneus acts as a lever.

Ears
The ears of ungulates are directional cones, twitching forward and back. Be decisive in which way they face.

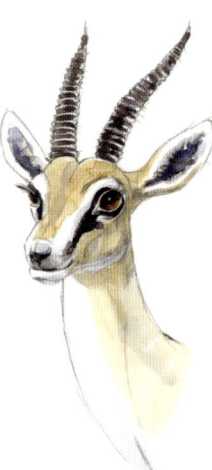

Evasive manoeuvres
Cheetahs are the major predators of Thomson's gazelles. If a gazelle catches a glimpse of the cheetah, it alerts the others by starting to run in bounding leaps. The herd move together, keeping the cheetah at a safe distance, zigging and zagging left to right, but not yet running at full speed, looking for a scrub of trees in the grassland to use as a ploy for an explosive escape. They would not stand a chance if they ran in a straight line as the cheetah has a roughly 20 percent speed advantage – a Thomson's might make a 40mph (64km/h) dash compared with a cheetah's 65mph (105km/h) – however, gazelles can turn more quickly than cheetahs, hence their zigzagging movement.

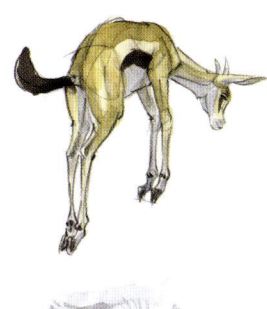

◄ Pronking
A noticeable behaviour of Thomson's gazelles is their bounding leap, known as stotting or pronking, used to startle predators and display strength.

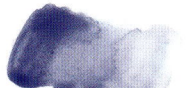
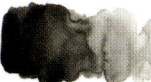

French Ultramarine   **Ivory Black**

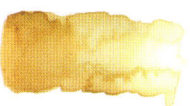
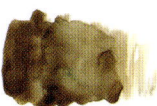

Yellow Ochre   **Raw Umber**

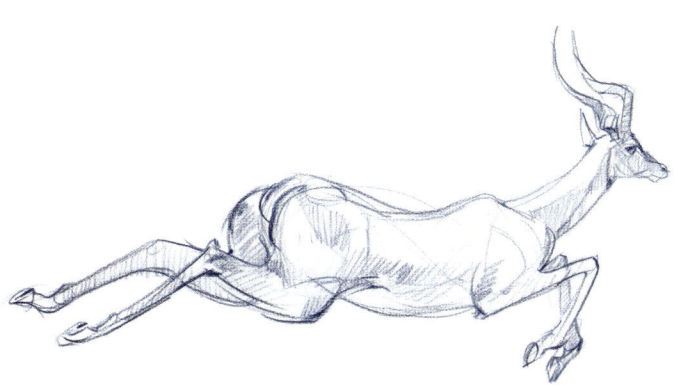

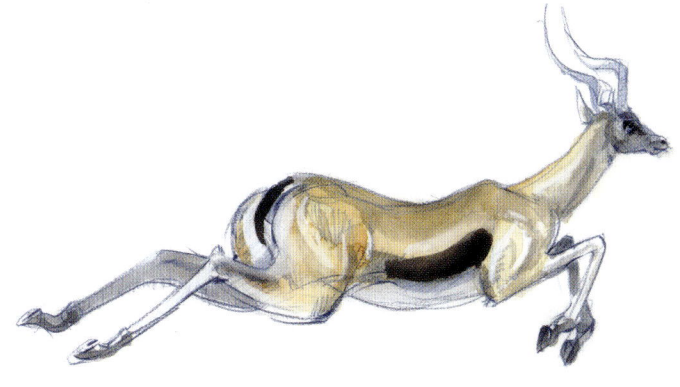

1 *Begin with an outline sketch, followed by a tonal underpainting in French Ultramarine and Ivory Black.*

2 *Yellow Ochre is used to colour the pelt. When this layer is dry, the muscles are modelled with darker shades of Raw Umber and the distinctive markings are created with a combination of Raw Umber and Ivory Black.*

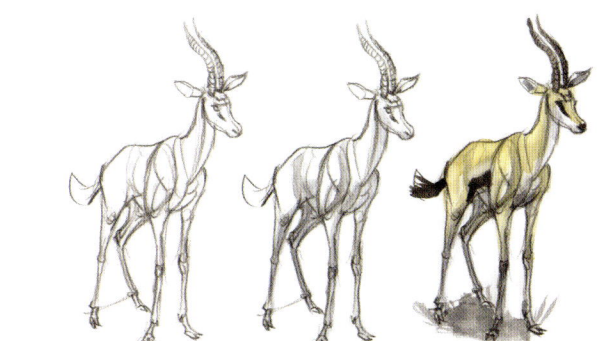

Feel the power and force of the animal with your whole body to get it down on the paper.

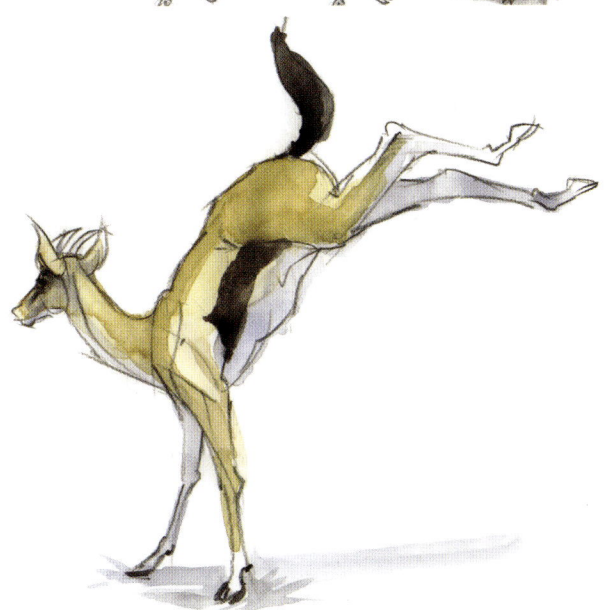

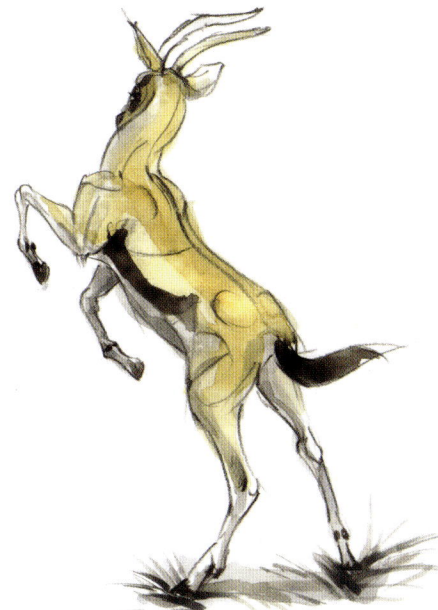

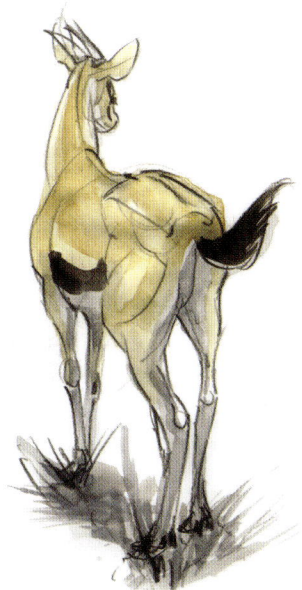

Study Sheet: *Giraffe*

Giraffes are majestic animals that oversee the plains of Africa. They weigh up to two tonnes (2,000kg) and are the tallest living mammal in the world. Their extraordinary adaptations function remarkably in the habitat of the savannahs. Their long necks enable them to graze from the tough leaves of acacia trees with a powerful black sunproof tongue that measures 18−20in (45−50cm).

They are one of the most enchanting animals to sketch because of their beautiful shapes and character. They move gently and with grace, which makes them a fantastic animal to start drawing from life. They have feminine eyelashes; a black line around their eye makes them look like they have been outlined with mascara. The arabesque shape of their head and long neck gives them a unique and iconic look. Besides being beautiful to draw, their long leg bones are also a fearsome weapon that can kick out at lions and other predators and knock them out dead.

Anatomy

Knowing a little about the anatomy can help you understand what you are looking at and inform your painting.

Hooves

Cloven hooves equip giraffes with good balance on uneven terrain. Only three ungulates (meaning 'walking on your toe') have a single hoof: the horse, donkey and zebra.

Muscles

Recognizing a few key muscles can help model the form and make sense of the lumps and bumps.

Bones

Knowing the bones can give your drawing structure and the feeling that the legs are supporting weight.

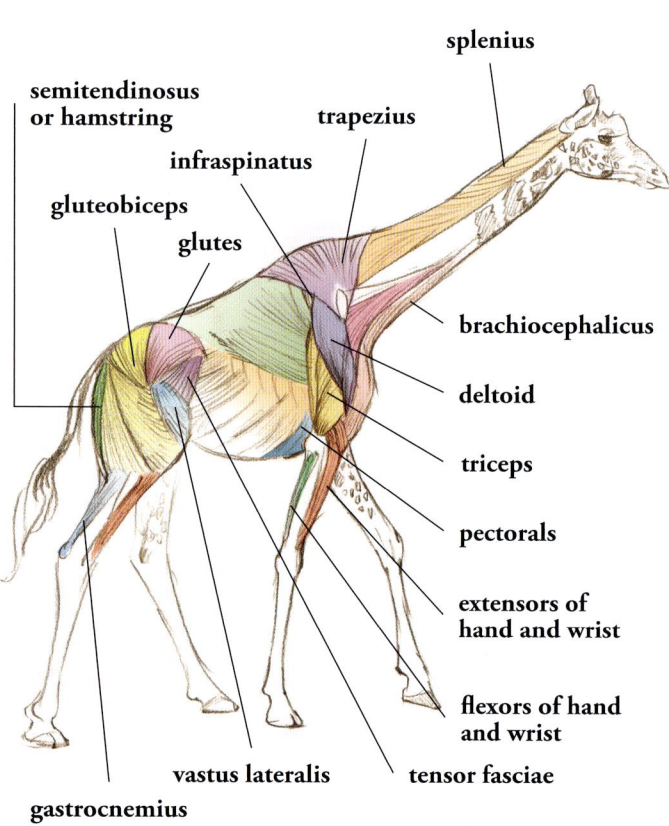

thoracic vertebrae
thoracic vertebrae are higher than the scapula, creating a stiff mound shape on the upper back. Powerful muscles and ligaments attach here to help lift the heavy head and neck and keep the head steady when running

ossicones
these residual horns are normally tufty in females; males tend to be bald through sparring

splenius

semitendinosus or hamstring

trapezius

infraspinatus

gluteobiceps

glutes

brachiocephalicus

deltoid

triceps

pectorals

extensors of hand and wrist

flexors of hand and wrist

vastus lateralis

tensor fasciae

gastrocnemius

median lump
median lump is larger in males and is created by calcium deposits as the skull ages

scapula

humerus

carpals or wrist

metacarpals

patella
where there is a patella, there is a knee

radius and ulna
these are fused to create a powerful long pole for explosive running

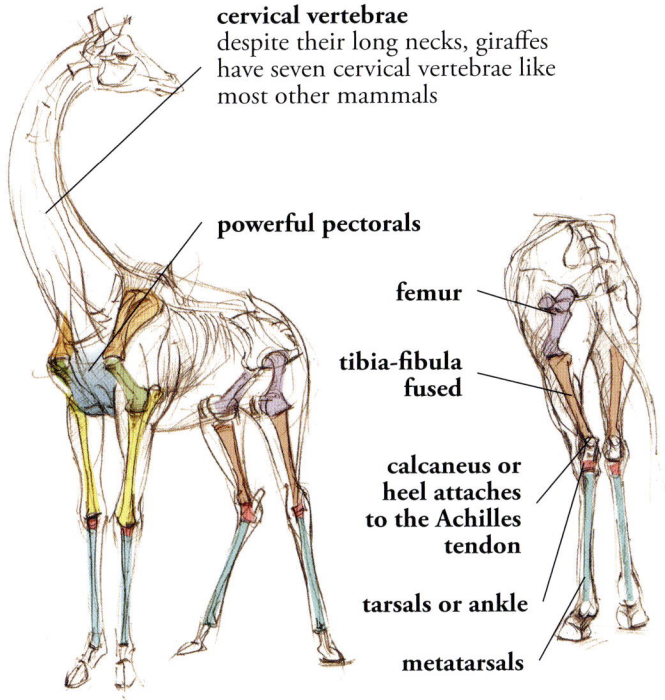

cervical vertebrae
despite their long necks, giraffes have seven cervical vertebrae like most other mammals

powerful pectorals

femur

tibia-fibula fused

calcaneus or heel attaches to the Achilles tendon

tarsals or ankle

metatarsals

qualities by drawing the giraffe, its silhouette shape and inner contours. Vary the pressure of your drawing implement, change the lightness and darkness, and the thinness or fatness of your line for visual interest. Where the form is supported, such as beneath the hooves, I create a darker mark for emphasis.

Take a line for a walk

A giraffe's character is full of arabesque shapes. Without looking at your paper, practise capturing characteristic lines of the animal by starting at the top of the head with the ossicones. This warm-up exercise will not result in a recognizable drawing but an abstract set of overlapping giraffe-like lines. Try to imagine that the tip of your pencil is touching the animal rather than the paper, as if a bug is walking around the contour and then travelling along the inner contours of the legs and folds in the skin. If you feel the form going away from you, ease off the pencil; press down on your pencil where you feel the weight is being supported. You are involved in the process of learning to look without the idea of making a perfect drawing. Fight the desire to look at your paper; instead immerse yourself in the discipline of this exercise.

Warm-up exercises
Lines inspired by the character of the animal

The objective of this drawing exercise is to warm up your hand-eye coordination. The quality of line you create is as personal as handwriting and relates to the feeling you have for the subject. This exercise explores the linear

Get in the flow with a study sheet

Spend a few hours at a giraffe enclosure and really get to know the animals. Watercolour pencil is an excellent way of getting the colour down. It can be left dry, or water can be added to transform it into paint.

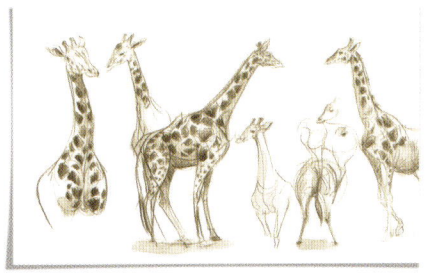

▲ **Monochrome study**
Zoological Society of London, Whipsnade Zoo, UK.

Facial details
Notice the long face and soft, flexible lips with the top lip overhanging the bottom. Capture the beautiful shape of the eyes.

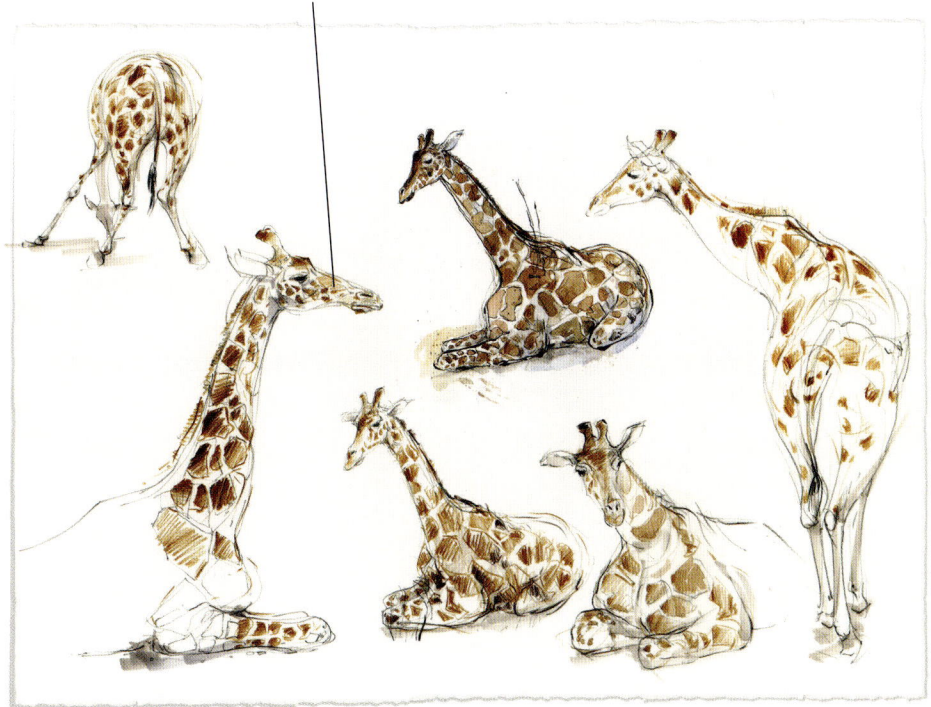

▶ **Reticulated giraffe**
Zoological Society of London, Whipsnade Zoo, UK.

Study Sheet: *Mara*

Mara are long-legged relatives of guinea pigs. The eye and muzzle of the head are deer-like and they have long legs, which are great for explosive escapes. The unassuming rodents represent 40 per cent of all mammal species and are a highly successful and adaptable order. The mara is monogamous, but often breeds in warrens that are shared by several pairs.

There are two extant mara species. The Chacoan mara (*Dolichotis salinicola*) is found in southern Bolivia, western Paraguay and north-western Argentina. The Patagonian mara (*Dolichotis patagonum*) that I painted is common throughout central Argentina. Maras are herbivores, and the central parts of the Patagonian steppe are dominated by shrubby and herbaceous plant species, while to the west, where precipitation is higher, bushes are replaced by grasses.

Mara are excellent subjects to sketch from life, particularly on a sunny day when they will sit and bask in the sun. They will allow you to sit quite close, and in some zoos the animals are free-roaming, so it is a good idea to have a sketching stool with you to sit on. These are fantastic animals to get your hand and eye warmed up and coordinated at the start of the day. At first, simply watch them and wait patiently until they are settled and comfortable with your proximity. Your calmness is essential to develop some trust between yourself and them.

Anatomy

Where animals have a thick pelt, it's not so helpful to know about their muscles because they're not visible. For this reason, I haven't included a muscle chart, which appears on some other pages. However, knowing where the pivots are, the arrangement of leg bones and the number of toes is beneficial.

Feet

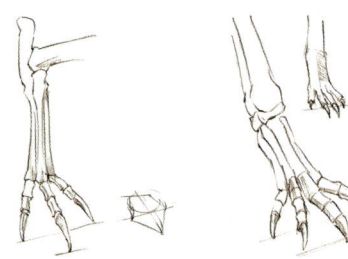

The hind foot has three toes.

The front paw has four toes.

Head

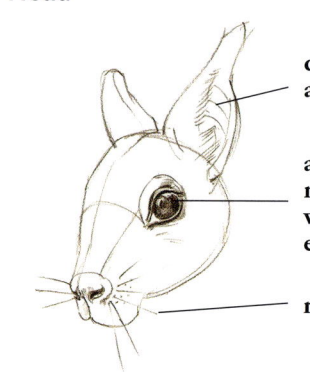

distinctive-looking long ears, a bit like a jackrabbit

a dark ring around the eye like mascara – leave a lip of light where the skin overlaps the eyeball at the base.

radiating whiskers

Bones

Knowing the bones can give your drawing structure and the feeling that the legs are supporting weight.

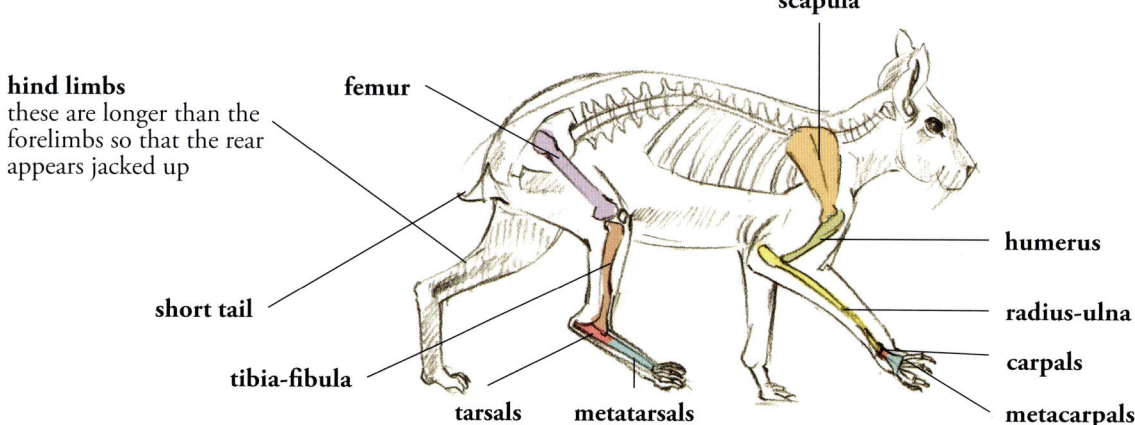

scapula

hind limbs
these are longer than the forelimbs so that the rear appears jacked up

femur

humerus

radius-ulna

carpals

metacarpals

short tail

tibia-fibula

tarsals

metatarsals

Warm-up exercise
Outside and inside contours

Imagine that your pencil, rather than touching the paper, is touching the mara. The marks you create are attempting to capture the posture and pose of the mara, from the character of the head to its short stubby tail. The closer you can get your lines to bite into the shape of the form, the closer you will get to capturing the character or 'maraness' of the mara. Not all the contours lie on the outer edge of the mara. For example, from a frontal viewpoint, the mara's body is compressed in a foreshortened position. I use overlapping lines to help create the illusion that the nose is in front of the shoulders and the shoulders are in front of the belly and back legs.

Get in the flow with a study sheet

In this study, I worked on a 16½ x 23⅜in (A2 size) sheet of 110lb (200gsm) cartridge. I sketched the mara in a number of positions, including a back view and loop shapes to try to capture their orb-like bottom, and observed behaviours such as preening. I selected a colour that is similar to the pelt – a Faber Castell Polychromos Walnut Brown.

The initial sketch is only a guide for the following stages to come. It does not create a set of shapes that simply need to be filled in, but a working drawing that should be modified and adjusted as the painting journey begins. As the Earth turns, the direction of the sun changes and is different from when you started your sketch. As the sun sinks in the sky, the subject is affected by the changing angle and direction. The shadows move imperceptibly to the eye but are growing longer as evening draws in. Some people are unaware of the sun's position, but for the painter, this is critical.

As I sketched these mara, it was turning towards evening, and I wanted to capture them in sidelight three-quarter light. However, I planned to do this back in the studio, so I took a series of photos as I went along. There is a romance to painting at either end of the day – early morning in high-key tones or during the evening in a low key, when subjects in the landscape carry long shadows and almost melt into their surroundings.

Later, back in the studio, I stretched the drawing by dampening the back of the paper. I then painted a light wash of Yellow Ochre and Sap Green on the taut, stretched paper. Once dry, I applied a darker, more saturated colour, finishing with black mixed with a granulation medium (see page 27) to create a graduated wash over their backs.

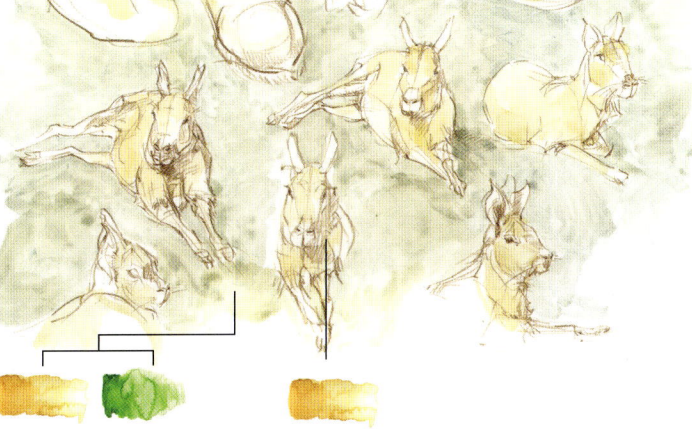

Yellow Ochre +
Sap Green   **Yellow Ochre**

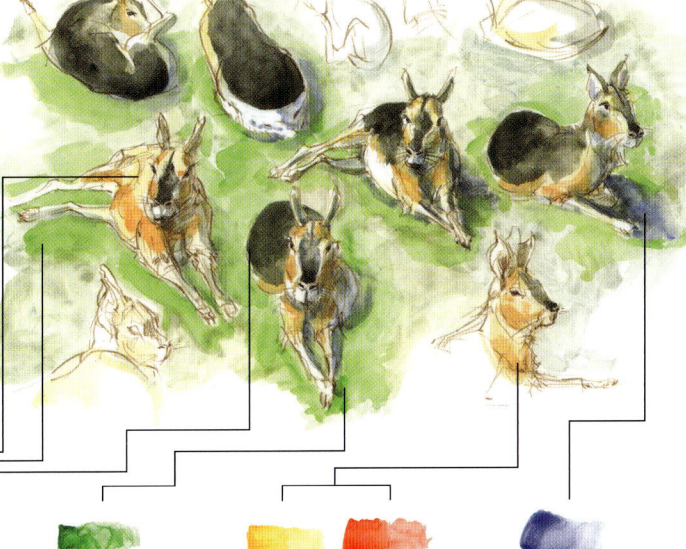

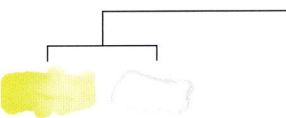 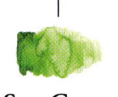 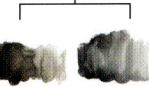 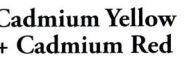

Lemon Yellow +   **Sap Green**   **Payne's Grey +**   **Hooker's Green**   **Cadmium Yellow**   **French Ultramarine**
White Gouache   **Ivory Black**   **+ Cadmium Red**

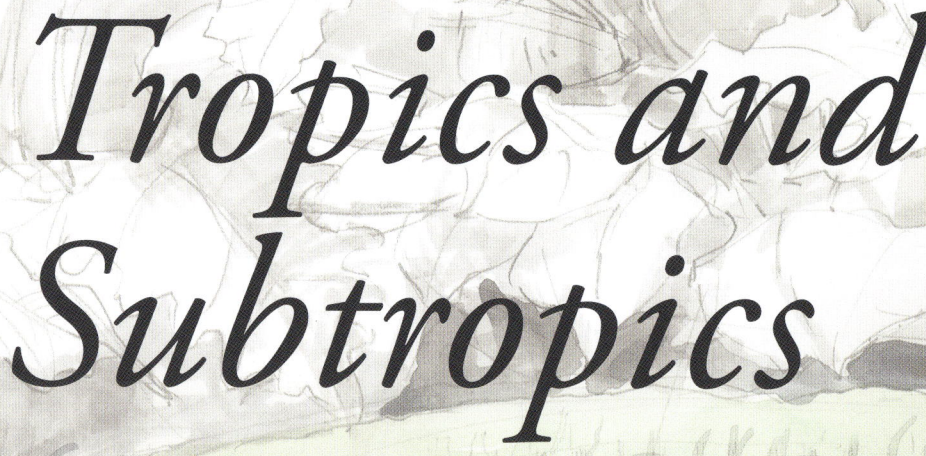

Tropics and Subtropics

The Earth's hottest areas lie on the equator, creating some of the most precious wildlife habitats that teem with every class of animal. Here, plants flourish in the tropical, damp climate, creating a habitat for multi-coloured birds, while the warm waters abound with exotic fish.

The tropical zone is the area around the middle of the Earth, forming a belt between the tropics of Cancer and Capricorn, approximately at latitudes 23 N and S respectively. In this zone, the sun passes directly overhead throughout the year, with little seasonal change. Tropical climates have monthly average temperatures of 64°F (18°C) or higher year-round and have high levels of precipitation.

The subtropics are the region for about 10 degrees latitude N and S of the tropical zone. Here the sun is never directly overhead but summer days are longer, so weather can be even hotter. Significant portions of the world's sandy deserts are to be discovered in the subtropics.

The tropics are notable for their rainforests, which cover only six percent of the world's surface but make up 50 percent of species and play a vital role in sustaining life on Earth. Large leaves allow tropical plants to capture more sunlight energy, and a ready supply of water can convert this energy into food for growth. It is a race to the light between the plants, relying on capturing unpredictable shafts of sunlight, known as sunflecks, breaking through the canopy. Very little light falls on the forest floor, so plants here have vast leaves to capture as much sunlight as possible. Many plants have waxy leaves that help repel the rain.

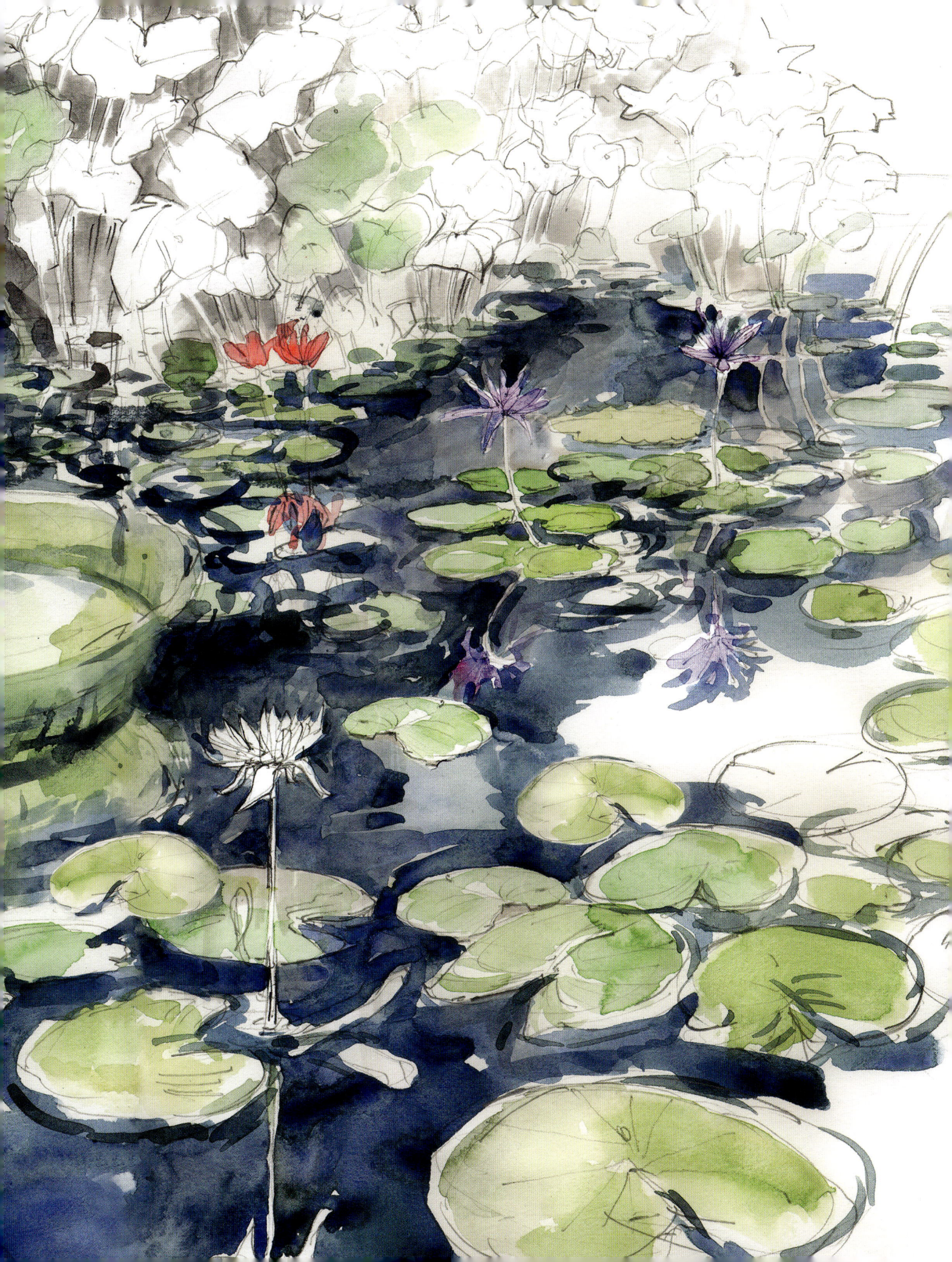

Tropical Rainforests

Rainforests are essential for the Earth; they remove carbon from the atmosphere and produce oxygen. But due to deforestation, they're disappearing faster than anywhere else on the planet. They are wonderful and unique habitats that are a cradle of biodiversity and are vital to preserve.

Life in tropical rainforests exists in abundance. Despite covering less than six percent of the Earth's surface, it is home to half of all the animals and plants on land. Its richness in water, light and nutrients creates a recipe for a spellbinding ecology of diversity.

The plants here have evolved into spectacular lush vegetation with large leaves to harvest the sun's energy in the race for light where only two percent of the sun's rays reach the ground.

Up to 90 percent of the animals spend their lives up in the trees and have adaptations to enable them to move around. Animals such as the spider monkey have evolved specialist limbs, hands and even a prehensile tail to swing through the trees. They thrive in a complex three-dimensional environment with these adaptations that allow them to climb and survive, for their lifestyle depends on their ability to climb.

Multi-storey ecosystems

All woodlands and forests can be considered multi-storey ecosystems with a variety of different living spaces. These are niche environments to which animals have adapted, from crocodilians in the rivers to golden lion tamarins running along the intricate lattice of branches overhead.

They can be broken down into four essential storeys. While most animals tend to stay in their preferred storey, some venture between the different layers. Here, to illustrate the various niches that animals have adapted to, I have selected several species from rainforests around the world; for example, the role of the tiger as an apex predator in Asia is taken up by a jaguar in the Amazon.

The emergent

Rising above the canopy, where the tallest trees protrude, is the zone called the emergent. This averages in staggering heights of some 245ft (75m). These tree giants provide nesting sites for predatory birds and roosts for bats. There is little protection or shade to be found, and it is generally very sunny.

The canopy

The canopy also refers to the upper layer or habitat zone formed by mature tree crowns. This zone is the home for flying and climbing animals such as birds, monkeys and butterflies. During the day, the canopy is drier and hotter than other parts of the forest. The foliage is dense, making it difficult to see, so many canopy animals rely on loud calls or lyrical songs for communication. Gaps between trees mean that some canopy animals fly, glide, swing or jump spectacularly to move about in the treetops.

The understorey

The understorey, just beneath the canopy, is an additional layer of growth primarily made up of vines, palms and ferns. It is a warm and sheltered area beneath the dense roof of leaves. Raindrops seem to continually drip through, and rays of light pass through the smaller trees and large-leaf shrubs growing towards the light. Here there is the largest concentration of insects.

The forest floor

The forest floor is the darkest layer, where it is always hot and damp. Incredibly, only two percent of sunlight reaches the ground. In the patches of sunlight that make it through, large-leaf shrubs and saplings grow. Covered with fallen plant debris and leaf litter, the forest floor is a haven for beetles and bugs.

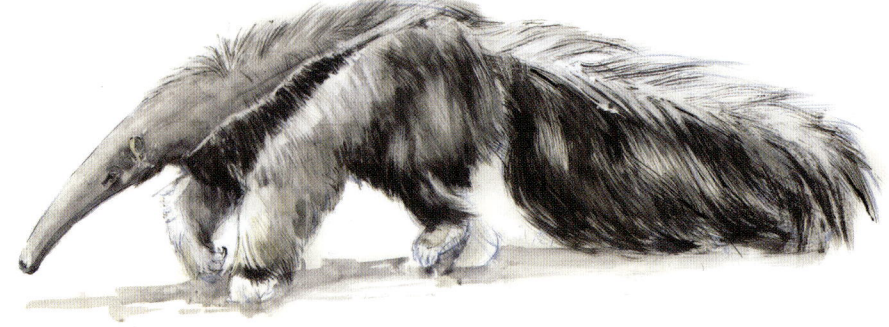

▶ Giant anteater
The giant anteater is found in multiple habitats, including grassland and rainforest. It has no teeth; instead, it has a long sticky tongue to eat up to 30,000 ants a day. It walks on the knuckles of its front feet so that its claws stay sharp.

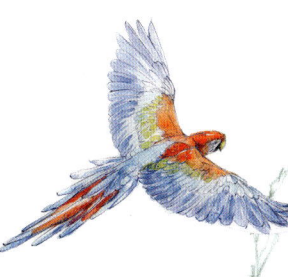

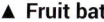

▲ Scarlet macaw
These birds live high up in the emergents and canopy. They feed on jungle fruits and nuts with mighty nut-cracking beaks. Their scaly tongues are dry and contain bone, which is most frequently used for pulling the nut from its kernel. These are social birds, usually seen travelling in flocks in sizes of 10 to 30.

▲ Fruit bat
These are the largest class of bats and they inhabit all the world's rainforests. They spend the day sleeping high up in the trees.

▶ Sloth
Sloths live high up in the trees in the American rainforests, spending most of their time curled up. Their hands and feet have evolved into hooked claws from which they suspend themselves beneath the branches to live life upside down. They are the only mammal to appear green; this camouflaged colour is created by algae that grow in its fur.

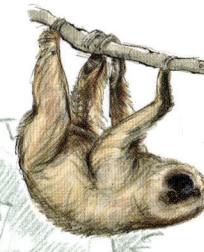

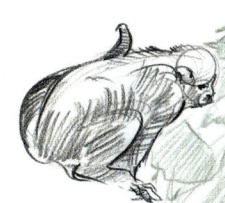

▲ Black-capped squirrel monkey
Rarely going to ground level, black-capped squirrel monkeys spend most of their time in the middle-to-high canopy layer.

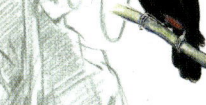

▲ Keel-billed toucan
The keel-billed toucan regulates its body temperature by emitting heat from its large beak during the day and using it as a hot water bottle beneath its wings at night in the canopy.

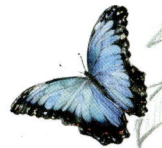

▲ Blue morpho butterfly
A blue morpho butterfly uses an iridescent blue to find a mate in the dense jungle.

▲ Ant
Ants are found all over the rainforest from the floor to the highest treetop.

▼ Soil
Rotting foliage breaks down into nutrients and minerals to revitalize the soil to support abundant plant growth. The earth is the home to such animals as worms and herbivorous rodents who live in burrows.

▼ Stick insect
Rainforests contain many insects that engage in mimicry, the art of disguise. Some look like living or dead leaves, even with splotches and leaf holes. Only the best disguise survives!

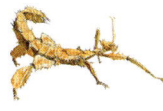

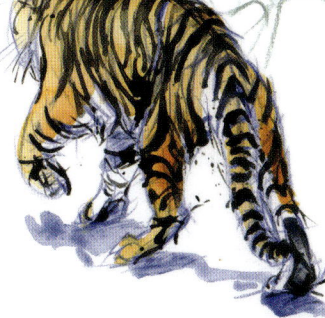

◀ Tiger
Serving as apex predators, tigers are the largest carnivore in their ecosystem. They control natural prey populations. This, in turn, controls the amount of vegetation eaten by tiger prey.

Tutorial: *Rainforest Plants*

In the rainforest setting, the artist needs to be able to see through all the visual noise. Remember, you are creating an interpretation of what you are seeing; you are not a camera. Plant structures can be slightly forgiving in that the proportions can't be tested by the viewer. Pick a focal point as a starting point at the core of the plant's stem and let your drawing grow, working shape to shape, navigating your way to the outer branches and leaves.

Activity
Travel with your sketchbook to the depths of the rainforest by visiting your local botanical gardens and enter the Palm House, where the air is heavy, hot and humid, and the lush vegetation has grown to giant proportions.

Swiss cheese plants

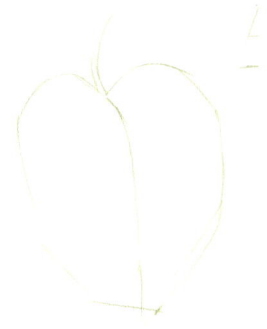

1 *Start lightly capturing the leaf shape and midvein.*

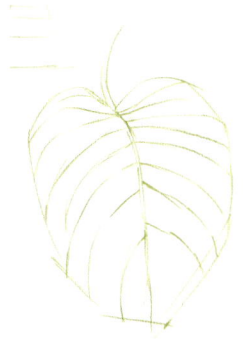

2 *Put in the branching veins. The veins nearer to you should be wider.*

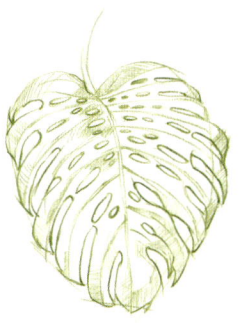

3 *Now draw the serrations or dog-eared shapes and the elliptical holes.*

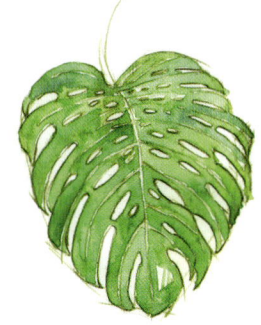

4 *Paint a base coat of the lightest and brightest shade of green.*

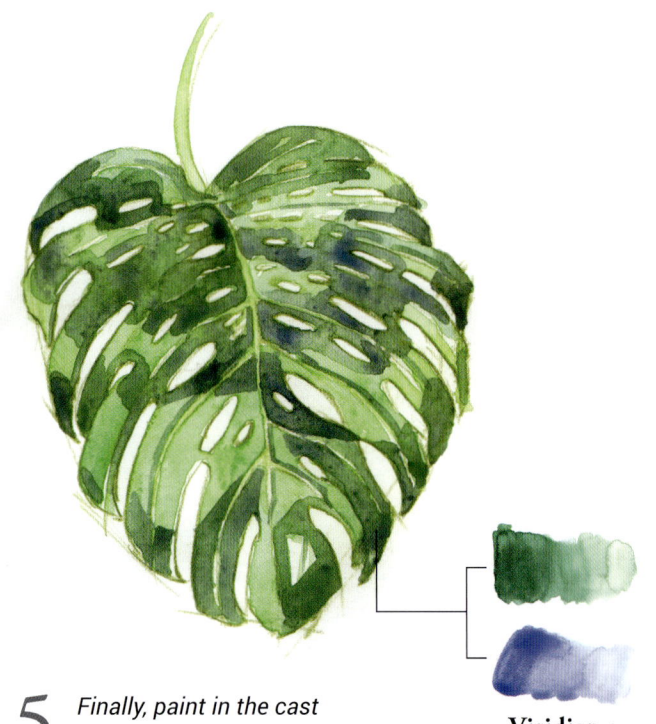

5 *Finally, paint in the cast shadow colour, which is both bluer and darker.*

Viridian + French Ultramarine

Foreshortened leaves

Explore creating curling and foreshortened (see pages 19–20) leaves. Think of each leaf as a flat elastic shape that can bend and wave in the wind. Pick up a single leaf and rotate it in front of your eyes. Try to capture the side and compressed view. Observe how the midline moves smoothly from the underside view to the topside.

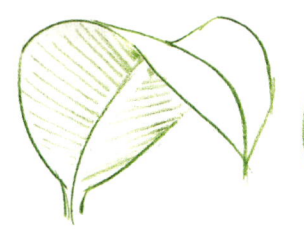

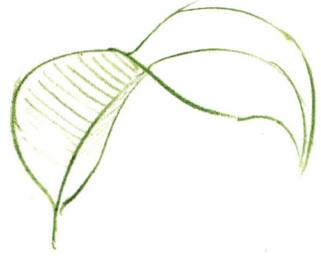

Capturing a jungle scene

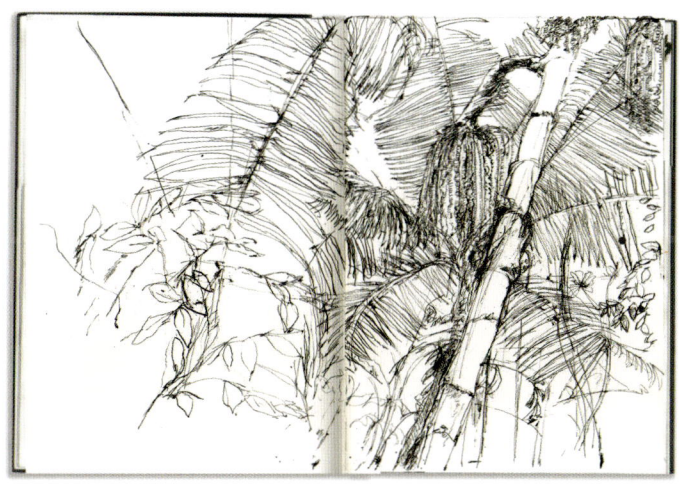

Leave a light edge where the trunk picks up reflected light.

1 *Working with a dip pen and ink, create a linear sketch, making marks that reflect the different textures.*

2 *When the ink is fully dry, wash in the exotic greens, light to dark.*

Fan palm

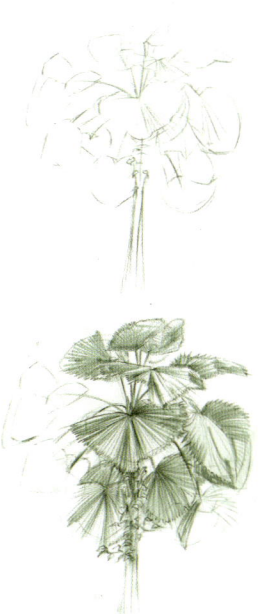

Bulk out in clumps, as areas of light and shade. The underside is typically in shadow.

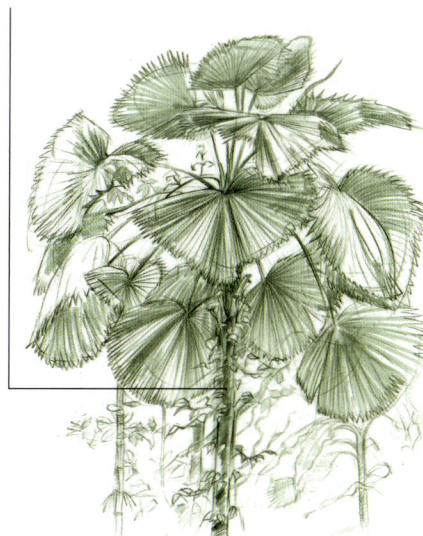

Look for leaves in the light and those in silhouette and the interplay between the two.

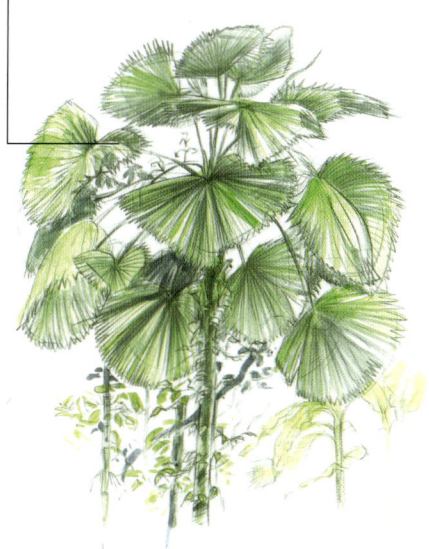

1 *Begin by creating very light construction lines. Try to establish the main shapes and proportions. I envisage the trunk as a central pole with radiating branches.*

2 *With a thin brush No. 2 and Terre Verte, create a light underpainting with swift strokes, capturing the crinkles in the leaves, regularly swapping between the brush and pencil.*

3 *Once the underpainting is dry, add a splash of Sap Green, painting along the leaf crinkles.*

Terre Verte

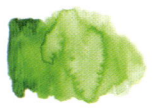

Sap Green

Deserts

A desert is a place that receives almost no rain (less than 10in [25cm] per year) or snow. We often think of a desert as hot and sandy, but there are cold deserts too. The largest hot desert in the world is the Sahara, with blistering temperatures of up to 122°F (50°C) during the day, dropping dramatically to below freezing at night. Cold deserts tend to have hot summers and freezing winters. Primarily these deserts appear in high, flat areas, called plateaus, or mountainous areas in temperate regions of the world, such as the Gobi Desert. The most significant cold deserts are the polar regions of the Arctic and Antarctic.

For animals and plants, the harsh sandy desert environment is a challenging place to live. The baking temperatures during the day with little or no shade and freezing temperatures at night has meant they have had to adapt. Some of the plants have evolved into cacti, which become storage devices for water. Cacti have spines instead of leaves, which minimize the surface area and reduce water loss. The needles also protect the cacti from animals that might eat them, making them something like the equivalent plant version of the sea urchin.

For animals, too, life in the arid and empty sandy desert regions is partly about water management to survive. Reptiles' scaled skin, rather than the membranous skin of the amphibians, is better suited to prevent dehydration, and this allowed them to pioneer these hostile environments. Equipped with eggs that have breathable yet hard shells, reptiles were able to cut their reproductive ties with water. Lizards and snakes in particular have discovered niches in these desolate places and evolved specific features. Both are 'cold-blooded'; this means their internal body temperature varies with that of their environment. The Namaqua chameleon, found in southern Africa, has a unique way of regulating its temperature. In the morning, it flattens its body like a solar panel and angles its dark-coloured body towards the sun to warm up. But as the sun grows higher and hotter in the day, the Namaqua goes through a colour transformation, with the side of its body facing the sun becoming white, while the side in the shade remains a dark grey, regulating an equal internal body temperature.

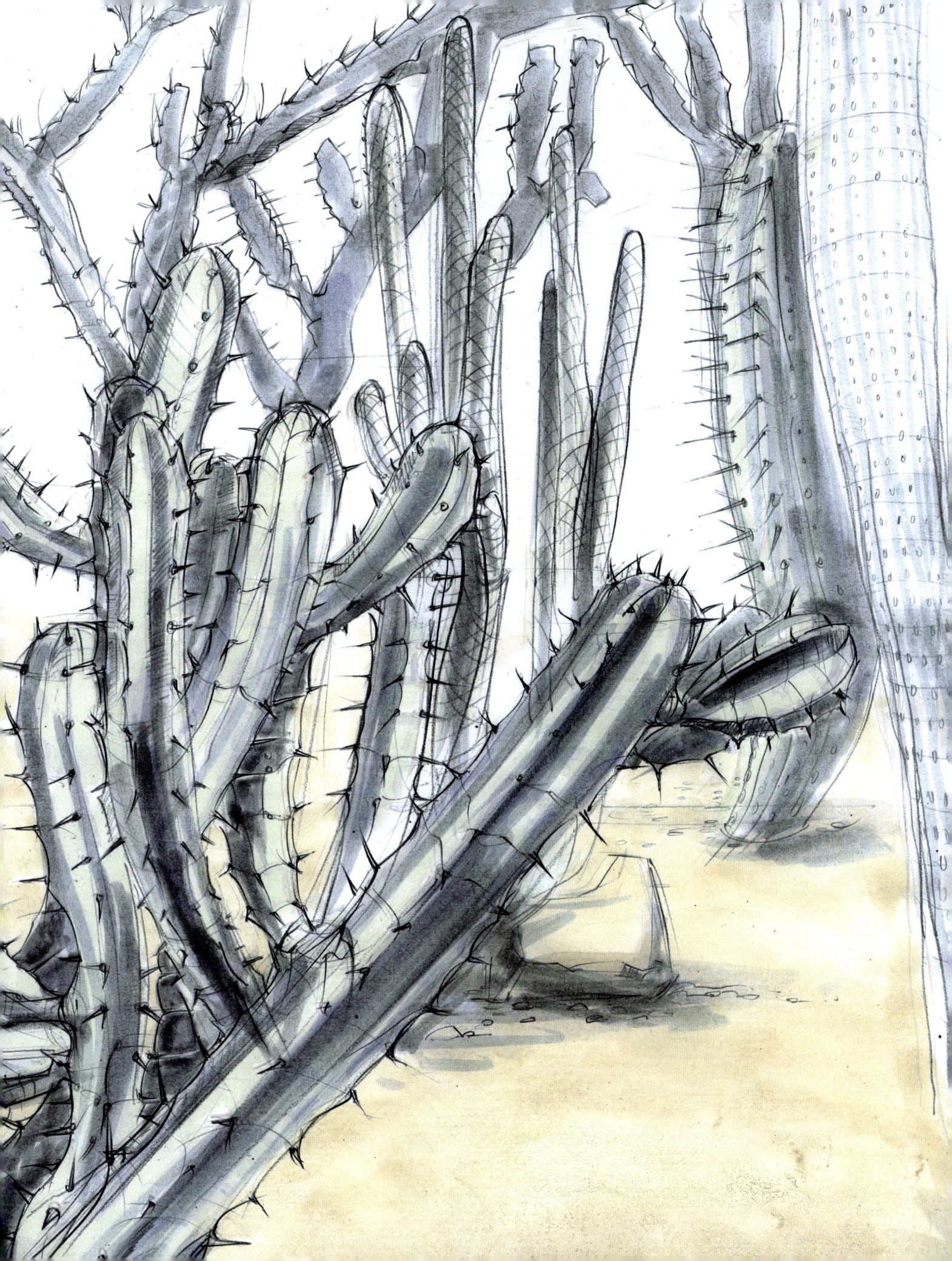

American Sonoran Desert

Deserts are the world's driest habitats and range from freezing polar caps to the Australian outback and the Sahara. They are places with little precipitation, some getting little or no rainfall for years, creating challenging conditions for life to flourish. However, life in the North American Sonoran Desert is one of the world's most diverse ecosystems, receiving regular rainfall and supporting a fascinating range of plants and animals. Rainwater is soaked up by plants and cacti, which provide food for herbivorous animals such as the jackrabbit and kangaroo rat, which in turn become food for the top predators such as the coyote and sidewinder snake.

Prey is scarce in these desert regions, so a lot of predators use venom. Secreting deadly poison into their victim ensures their meal doesn't get away.

▲ Gila woodpeckers
Gila woodpeckers turn a spiky cactus into a home and excavate cavities in cacti as nesting sites.

▶ Saguaro cactus
The saguaro is only found in the Sonoran Desert. Saguaros can live to be 150 to 200 years old and grow to 39−59ft (12−18m) tall, becoming a cactus tree. They take their name from an Indian word and should be pronounced *sah-wah-ro.*

▼ Desert tortoise
Desert tortoises live in burrows to stay cool. As herbivores, they are one of nature's gardeners, dispersing seeds in their dung.

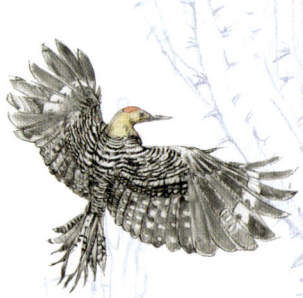

▼ Bark scorpion
Scorpions have changed little in the 350 to 400 million years since their ancestors first climbed from the sea. The bark scorpion is the most venomous in North America.

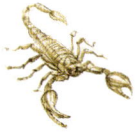

▲ Bighorn sheep
Bighorn males are renowned for their enormous, curled horns that they use to fight for dominance. Bashing into each other at charges of some 20mph (32km/h), creates a resounding clatter that echoes through their rocky habitat. Bighorns have unique rubbery hooves that enable them to climb the steep mountains with agility.

▲ Roadrunner
The legendary roadrunner is quick on its feet and is a predator of rattlesnakes, scorpions and horned lizards. Its long tail helps it stop and turn at high speeds, getting up to 18mph (30km/h).

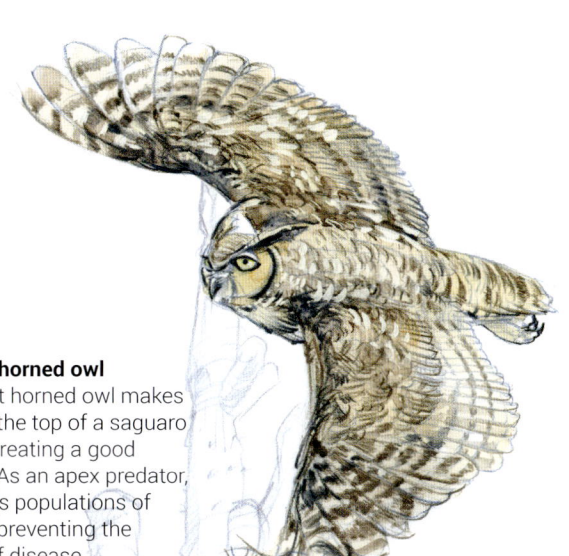

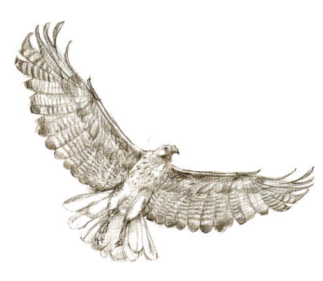

▲ Red-tailed hawk
Red-tailed hawks play an essential role in the Sonoran Desert ecosystem by controlling small mammals, such as rodents, which prevents plants from being over predated.

► Great horned owl
The great horned owl makes nests at the top of a saguaro cactus, creating a good lookout. As an apex predator, it controls populations of species, preventing the spread of disease.

▼ Coyote
Coyotes are a keystone species, meaning that their presence or absence significantly impacts the surrounding biological community. Keystone species like the coyote can have a regulatory effect on smaller predator populations, allowing prey of the smaller predator species to survive. For example, since small predators, especially fox, cats, opossum and raccoons, consume eggs and small or young ground-nesting birds, an increase in the smaller predators can significantly affect bird populations. Coyotes prey on these small predators, keeping the small predator population in check.

▼ Jackrabbit
The long ears of the jackrabbit help it to stay cool in the hot, arid climate. Large, vascular ears enable the jackrabbit to cool down its body temperature and to deflect heat.

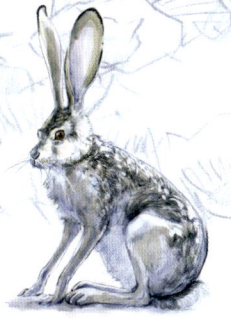

▼ Kangaroo rat
Herbivorous kangaroo rats can get all the water they need from plants and survive without drinking.

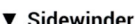

▼ Sidewinder
The sidewinder is so-called because of its unique way of getting around, travelling sideways. They can also bury themselves in soft sand and disappear entirely.

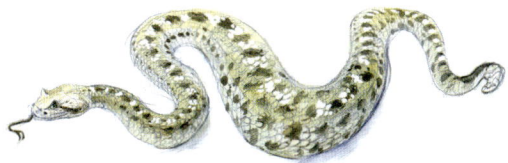

► Scolopendra heros
The giant desert centipede is a nocturnal predator and hunts invertebrates and small vertebrates, including rodents, reptiles and amphibians. The centipede uses its venom to subdue prey and can grow up to 8in (20cm).

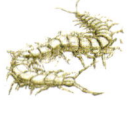

Tutorial: *Succulents*

Succulents have thick, fleshy tissues adapted to water storage. Some succulents, such as cacti, store water only in their stems, while others, such as agaves, store water mainly in their leaves, which are typically sharply spined and in a large rosette formation. Most succulents have deep or broad root systems and are native to either deserts or regions with a semiarid season.

Cacti

Cacti have adapted to arid climates, where there is little rainfall and plenty of sunshine. Their prickles turn them into an unattractive meal for most animals. Their leaves have evolved into spines or hairs for defence and to prevent the loss of moisture. Their stems are green to photosynthesize food for the plant because their spiny leaves can't do that. Cacti stems expand to store water when it rarely rains.

Cacti can appear to be intimidating subjects, while in fact they are quite forgiving in terms of getting the proportions right; the real challenge is to see through the visual complexities to get to the main underlying structure.

I began this sketch by picking a focal area and allowing the drawing to grow from an area I had understood, using both positive and negative shapes to guide me.

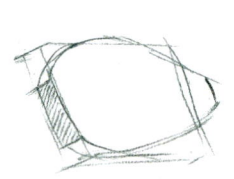 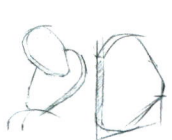

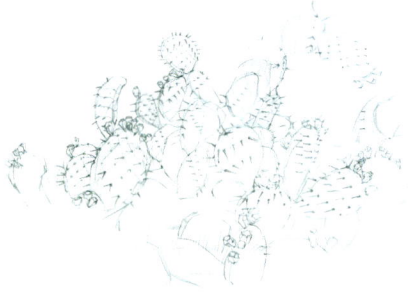

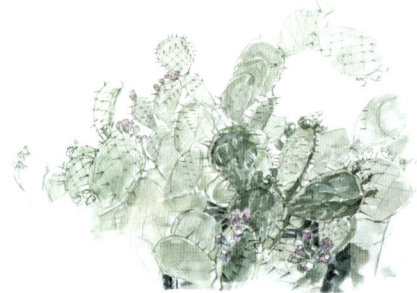

1 *Some of the lobes lay parallel and flat to my view, while others twisted and turned away in perspective. I created book-like frames in all manner of angles to help guide the lobe segments.*

2 *Working from larger to smaller shapes, attach fruit to the ears and their flowers. I noticed that the spines are in rows. So, I wrapped an X-shaped mesh around the lobes and placed a dot at the intersections. On these dots, I drew the spines using a sharpened pencil and a flick of the wrist.*

3 *This cactus is backlit. Backlighting is when the primary source of light is behind the subject. The subject is then placed primarily in silhouette with individual ridges and planes catching the light. To recreate this, mix up a colour for the cactus in the light, and use it all over. Finish by adding French Ultramarine to degrade it for the shadow side.*

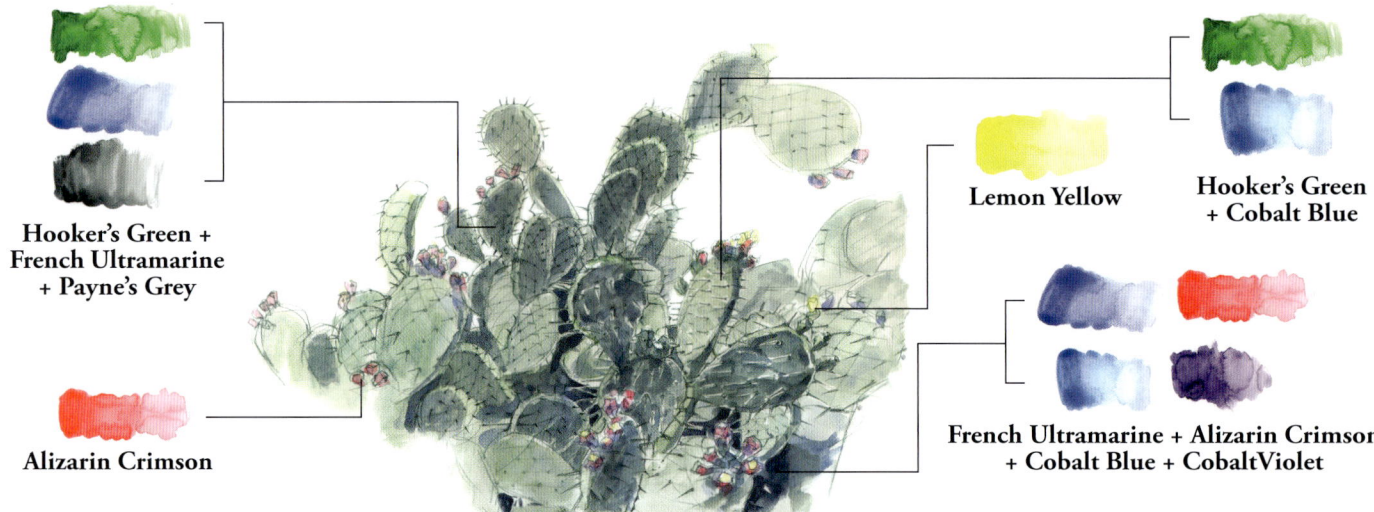

Hooker's Green + French Ultramarine + Payne's Grey

Alizarin Crimson

Lemon Yellow

Hooker's Green + Cobalt Blue

French Ultramarine + Alizarin Crimson + Cobalt Blue + CobaltViolet

Tutorial: *Aloe Vera*

Aloe vera is a succulent with leaves that form a rosette. The leaves range from grey to green and they have white spots on their surfaces. Aloe veras have sharp, pinkish spines along the edges of their bodies to ward off hungry animals.

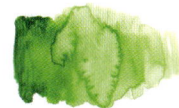

Sap Green

Cerulean Blue

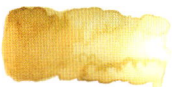

Yellow Ochre

French Ultramarine

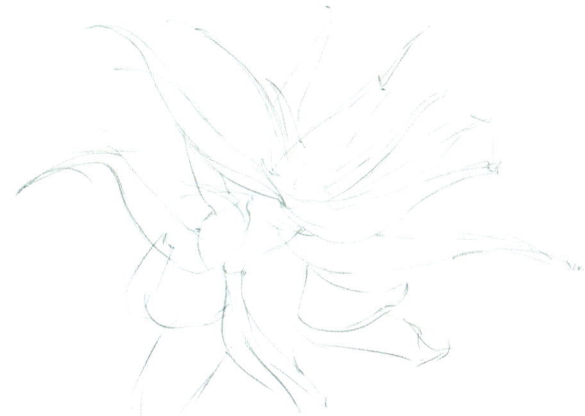

1 *For this sketch, I used a sharpened Cobalt Green Polychromos pencil. First, try to capture the main shapes – the architecture of the plant on which the detail will hang – and keep your lines light and flowing. Periodically, hold up your pencil in the vertical or horizontal position to judge the angles of the blades and look at the relationship between the tips. It doesn't matter if you have several attempts at the line while trying to capture the character of the plant.*

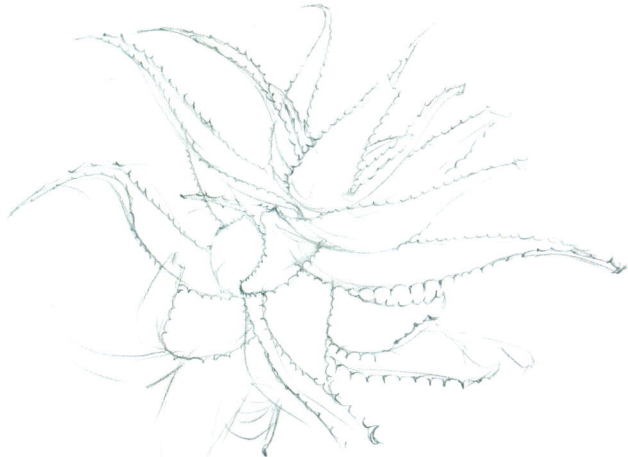

2 *Next, sketch in the sharp protective spines with quick flicks of the wrist. Note that where a blade is compressed in a foreshortened view, projecting towards the eye, the distance between the spikes becomes shorter.*

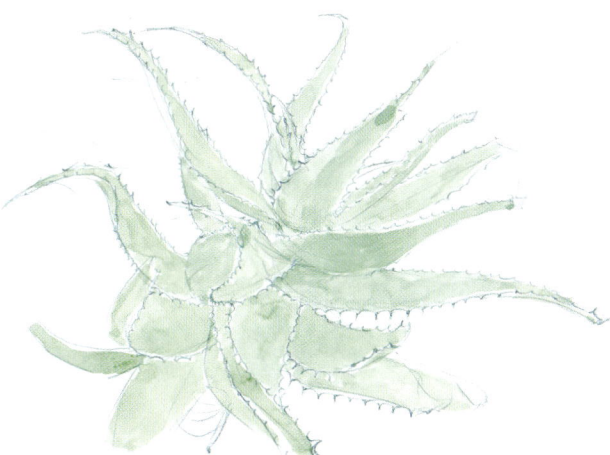

3 *Now is the time to bring in the colour. Begin with a medium brush No. 6. Mix up a quantity of Sap Green, Cerulean Blue and Yellow Ochre. Make swatches on a spare piece of paper and hold them close to the plant to check for colour accuracy.*

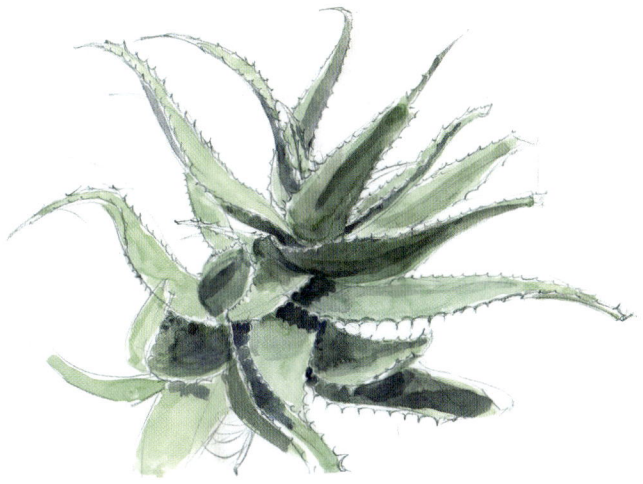

4 *To create the shadow value, add French Ultramarine to the base mix and move to a smaller brush such as No. 4 or No. 2. Typically, I tend to start with the larger brushes and work towards smaller ones to add detail.*

Study Sheet: *Meerkat*

Meerkats live a harsh life in the African deserts and grasslands, constantly threatened by hungry predators, rival gangs of meerkats, drought or burrow-flooding rainstorms. Each morning they emerge from the safety of their burrows for a spot of grooming and basking. The mob will soon head off for a day of foraging for food. Meerkats aren't fussy eaters. Their diet includes insects, lizards, birds and fruit, and they can also handle the odd exotic treat such as a scorpion.

These resilient little characters can be found in most zoos and create a fun yet sometimes frustrating sketching experience with their need to be on a continual lookout in all directions. They will challenge your sketching skills to draw as fast as you possibly can go.

Working directly from an enclosure, create a study sheet of poses and develop a shorthand sketching style to get a multitude of gestural postures. Draw rapidly and continuously and try to capture what the meerkat is doing. Meerkats will move quicker than the time it takes to sketch them. In this situation, it is the actions that you are trying to respond to, rather than creating a photographic likeness. Try to draw the whole body of the animal. Even if many of your sketches just remain as body-less heads, arms and tails floating in space. Begin anywhere, just throwing out a line that responds to the pose you are witnessing. Occasionally, you will find that you have created marks that really capture the character of the animal. These are rewarding moments that are encouraging and motivating to get that sketch finished.

Anatomy

Knowing a little about the anatomy can help you understand what you are looking at and inform your painting.

Paws

Meerkats' front claws are curved and act as shovels. There are four claws on each foot with very sharp, non-retractile nails to dig burrows in the baked earth.

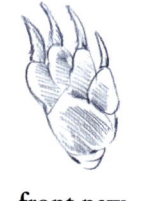 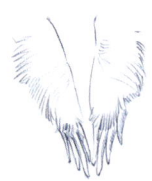 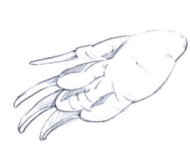

front paw　　**underneath of front paws**　　**back foot, with thick pads**

Meerkat head gizmo

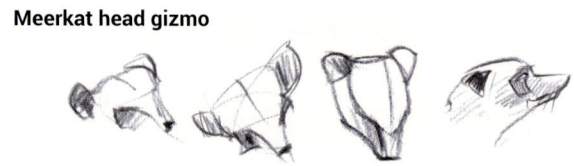

Body

Create a line of symmetry along the spine. Use this as an armature to add the head, legs and tail.

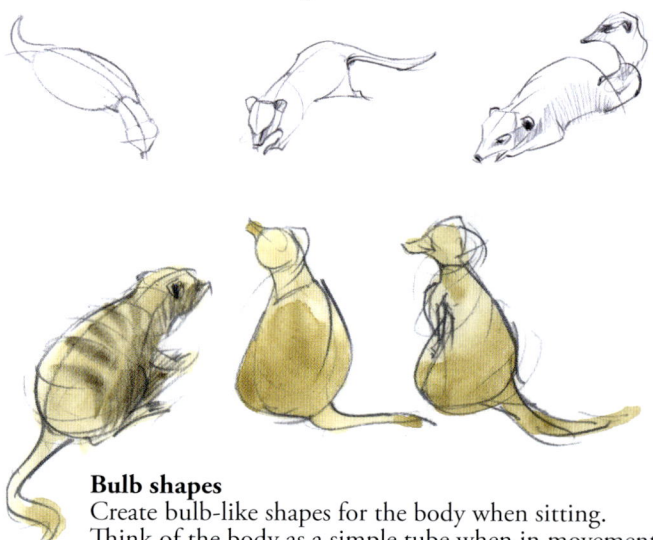

Head

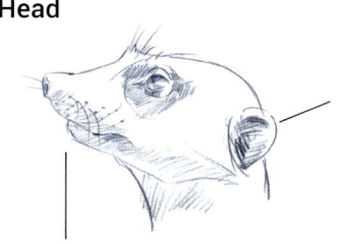

Ears
small ears that can close tightly to keep sand and dirt out

underbite

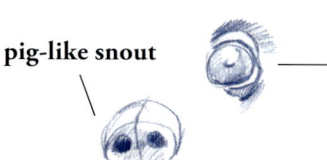

pig-like snout

Eyes
Big eyes with binocular vision have dark patches around them to reduce the glare of the sun. These eyes have a transparent protective membrane that shields them from dirt while digging.

Bulb shapes
Create bulb-like shapes for the body when sitting. Think of the body as a simple tube when in movement.

Bones

Knowing the bones can give your drawing structure and the feeling that the legs are supporting weight.

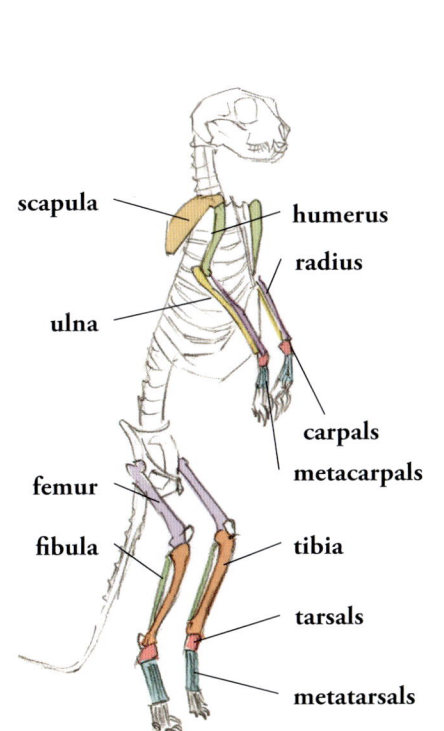

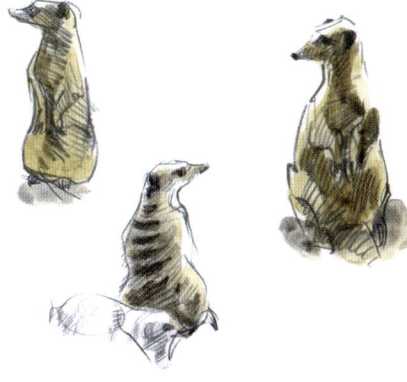

scapula
humerus
radius
ulna
carpals
metacarpals
femur
fibula
tibia
tarsals
metatarsals

Look-out stance
Meerkats perch on their back hind legs using their tail to balance.

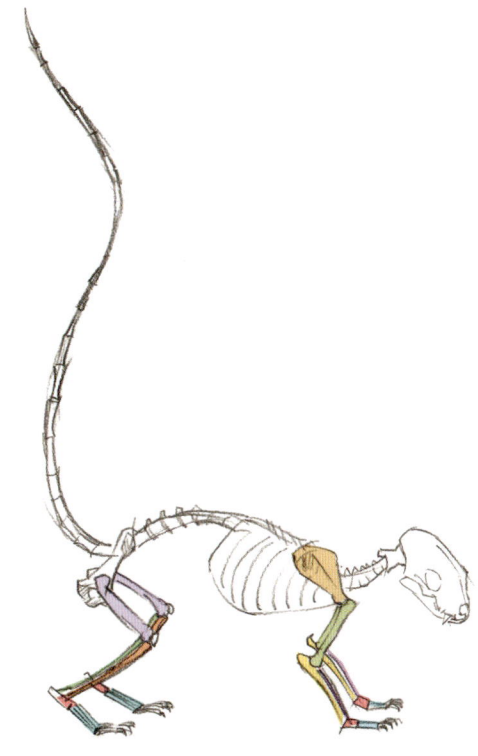

Moving stance
Meerkats' stance is digitigrade, meaning walking on their toes.

▲ Sentry duty
Among all the delightful behaviours you will observe, including scratching, play-fighting and general mongoose mischief, is one particular behaviour – sentry duty. In the wild, while the mob is out foraging for their day's food, a sentry meerkat, or meerkats, stand on their hind legs in a high position, such as up a termite mound, to enable them to scan the sky and landscape for predators such as eagles, hawks and jackals. Meerkats are small and make a perfect meal for such predators. A meerkat on sentry duty, who senses danger, will let out a high-pitched squeal, sending the mob scrambling for cover.

◀ Finishing touches
When you have completed your studies, add touches of watercolour to bring them to life.

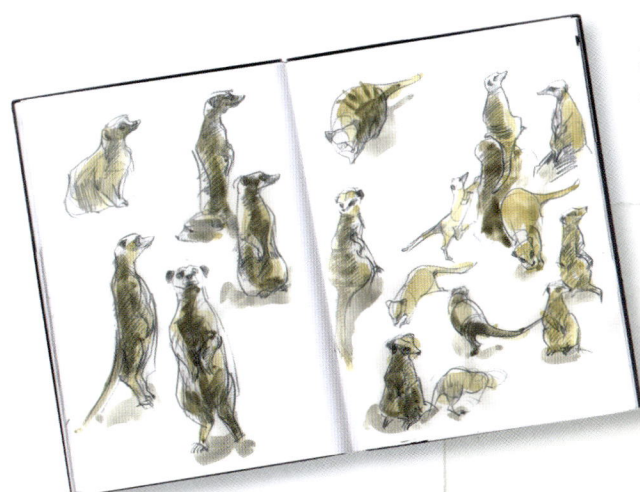

Camouflaged coat
Meerkats have a brindled coat pattern sometimes described as 'tiger-striped', although the brindle pattern is more subtle than that of a tiger's coat. The streaks of colour are irregular and darker than the base colour. This disruptive colouration helps break the body up and camouflage them from predators.

Pelt
Create sharp marks for the nails and softer, suggestive ones for the pelt. Look for the clumps of hair in the meerkat's fur rather than attempting to draw every single hair and explore creating flick hair marks with both pencil and brush.

▶ Meerkats
Zoological Society of London, London Zoo, UK.

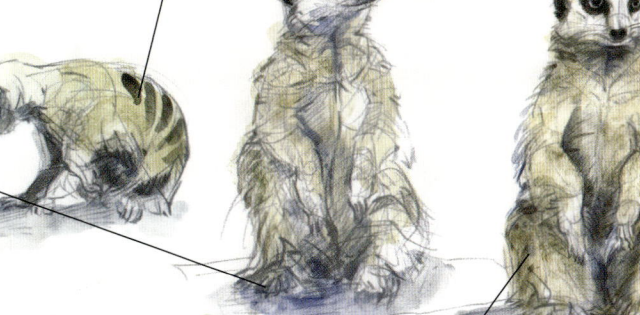

Adding texture
Add granulation medium (see page 27) to help create fur texture.

Study Sheet: *Camelids*

Mammals have adapted to life in the scorching desert climate, and none come better equipped than the six members of the camelid family, including camels and those bred by the Inca in Latin America – the llama and alpaca.

Camels have some specialist adaptations. They have a fleshy pad, which joins together their two toes, very much like a snowshoe, to create wide feet for stability in both sand and snow. They have muscles in their slit-like nostrils to close them tight against sandstorms, and two rows of eyelashes that lock tightly together to prevent sand from entering. A split upper lip with a groove allows water from the nostrils to go straight into the mouth and stops the camel from losing valuable water. The hump on their back is a storage chamber, not of water but of fat, which is like a larder of food that can be carried around and drawn from in the inevitable lean times of desert life. The hump goes floppy when the food is used up. They can, however,

drink an enormous quantity of water. After eight days without drinking, camels can drink 33 gallons (150l) of water in one go.

Camels have long legs and a distinctive gait known as 'pacing', which involves their front and hind legs moving forward and backwards simultaneously, enabling them to walk for great distances. The bactrian camel is an 'Old World' camel living in the wild between western China and Mongolia and can be identified by its two humps. The other camel is the dromedary, or Arabian, which has a single hump. Both have thicker fur on the top of the body for shelter and a thinner coat elsewhere, such as the legs and belly, to allow heat loss.

The dromedary has not occurred naturally in the wild for 2,000 years. The domesticated dromedary is generally found in Africa and the Middle East and a significant feral population occurs in the outback of Australia.

Anatomy
Knowing a little about the anatomy can help you understand what you are looking at and inform your painting.

Head
Use gizmos to help with the complex shape of a camel's head.

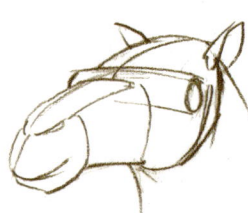

Very soft lips with a droopy mouth.

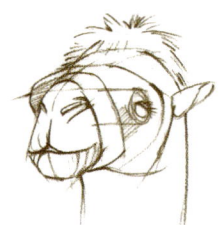

Add a scuba diving mask shape to create bulging eyes.

Feet
Camelids are even-toed ungulates, which means that they walk on their paired toenails. These wide feet are cushioned and splayed with pliable soles to stop them from sinking in the sand.

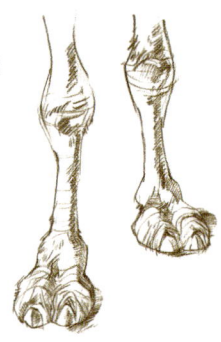

Hump
Dromedary camels are recognizable by their single hump or by placing a D horizontally on its back, and the bactrian, with its two humps, can be remembered by replacing the D with a B.

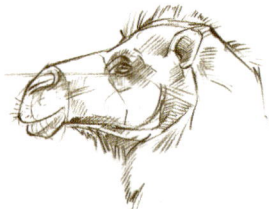

Bottom of the eye is in line with nostril when the head is horizontal.

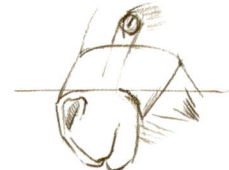

This relationship changes as the head is rotated

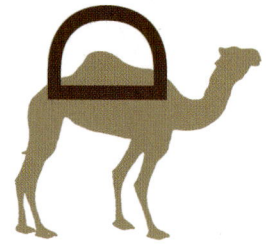

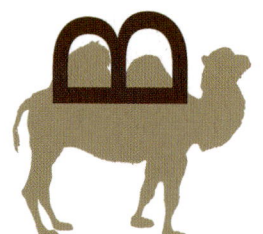

Bones

Knowing the bones can give your drawing structure and the feeling that the legs are supporting weight.

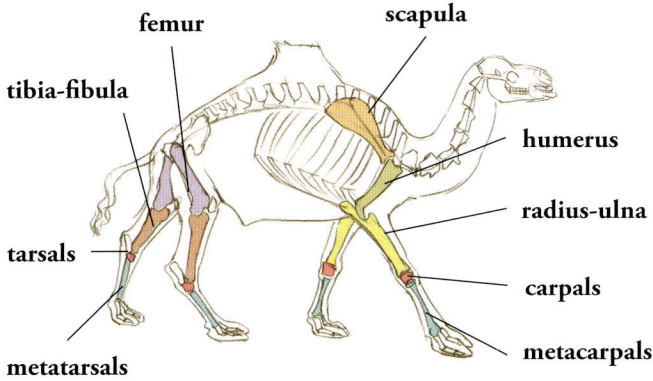

- femur
- scapula
- tibia-fibula
- humerus
- radius-ulna
- tarsals
- carpals
- metatarsals
- metacarpals

Muscles

Recognizing a few key muscles can help model the form and make sense of the lumps and bumps.

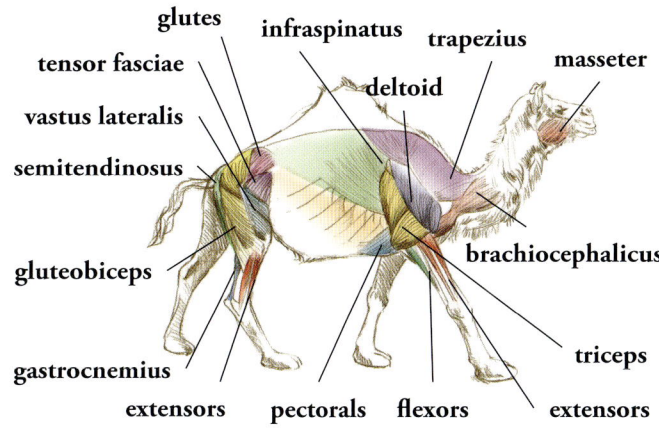

- glutes
- infraspinatus
- trapezius
- tensor fasciae
- deltoid
- masseter
- vastus lateralis
- semitendinosus
- brachiocephalicus
- gluteobiceps
- triceps
- gastrocnemius
- extensors
- pectorals
- flexors
- extensors

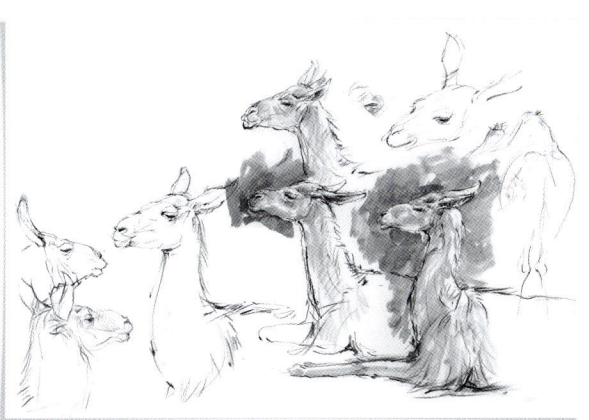

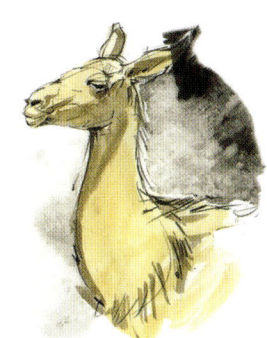

◄ Llama study sheet
Experiment with light and shade relationships to create a sense of falling sunlight. The shade helps to create a sense of light.

hind quarters | body | forequarters

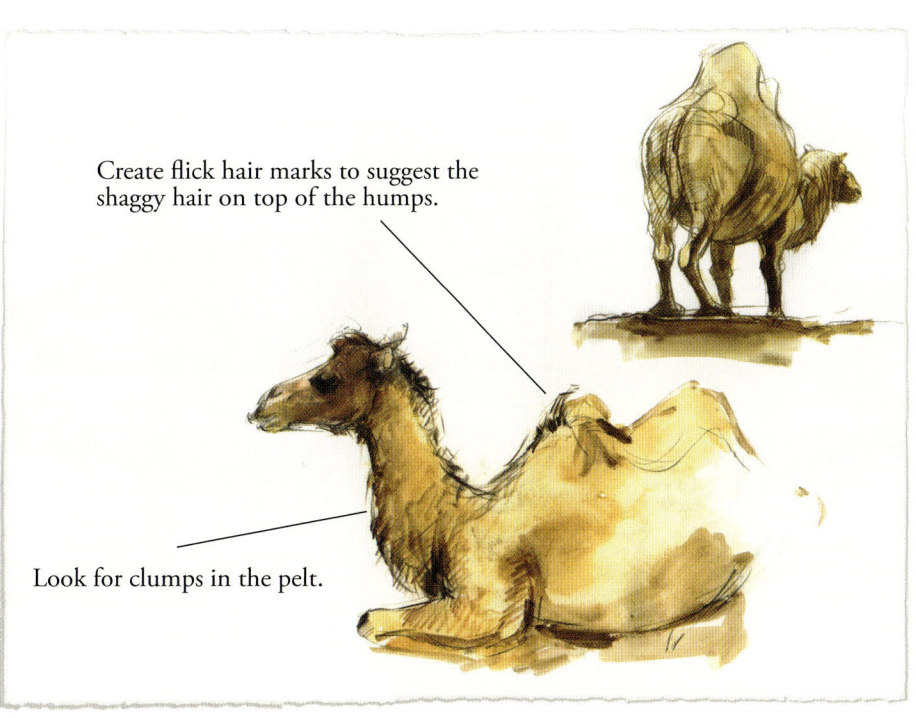

▲ Breaking things down
I always try to break my subject down into manageable body zones. In this sketch of a bactrian camel, I started sketching the zone of the body closest to me, the back legs. I really enjoyed modelling the calcaneus and Achilles tendon, which is attached to the gastrocnemius muscle.

▶ Winter coat
The somewhat scruffy appearance of the bactrian camel at certain times of the year is also an adaptation. It copes with a sudden change in temperature between a freezing winter, followed by the soaring temperatures of spring by moulting a thick winter coat.

Create flick hair marks to suggest the shaggy hair on top of the humps.

Look for clumps in the pelt.

Aquatic Habitats

Aquatic environments are worlds within worlds. Each world supports a host of communities, where every part of nature seems to know its place, individually playing a role to benefit the ecosystem through a complex web of interconnections. From the Mariana Trench and meadows of seagrass and kelp to the village pond, aquatic habitats are the most ancient of all. Life evolved there, with the first multicellular animals appearing about 600 million years ago. Being so old has given evolution time to create some of the weirdest and most wonderful of all the life forms.

Oceans make up the largest of the Earth's continuous habitats for life. It was here that the journey of life began and has adapted to the myriad of diverse habitats that are beneath the sea, from the inshore waters of kelp beds to the coral reefs, open sea and plunging depths, where life still exists, sometimes in bizarre forms, around hydrothermal vents.

In the inshore waters, there is plenty to take inspiration from. Lobsters aren't fussy eaters. They are scavengers of the seabed, crawling along the bottom looking for live or dead prey and tidying up. Some animals, such as the leatherback turtle, use the sea to migrate long distances and have been returning to the same breeding grounds for millennia, pulling themselves up on tropical sandy beaches to lay their eggs. In the open sea, some fish shoal as a form of a coordinated defence mechanism to escape from predators.

Freshwater habitats range from mountain streams to vast rivers and from seasonal ponds to giant lakes. Some plants and animals, such as fish and pondweed, live completely submerged in freshwater. Others, such as hippopotamus and amphibians, share their time between water and land.

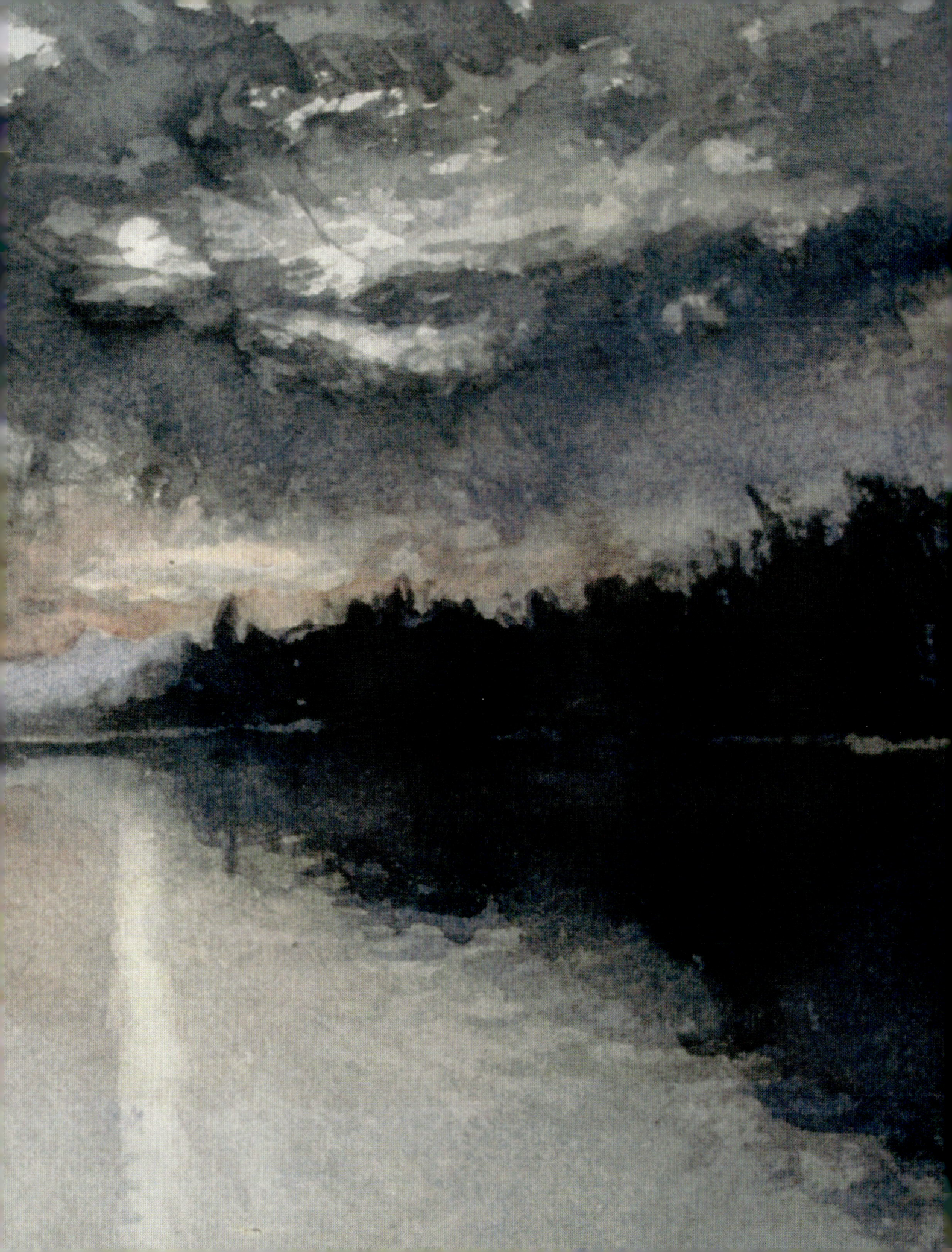

Tutorial: *Waves*

The ocean is a mirror that reflects the colour of the sky. The lapping warm waters are jade green to aquamarine blue in summer, reflecting a cerulean blue sky. In winter, the sea can turn battleship grey, taking on the angry appearance of a gunmetal sky. At night it becomes inky black and can reflect shimmering moonbeams on its surface. Whatever time of year or day, the challenge is to capture the glassy surface to which the transparent qualities of watercolour lend themselves.

Waves have been crashing on shorelines worldwide for an eternity and are most commonly caused by wind. Wind-driven waves, or surface waves, are created by the friction between wind and surface water. As the wind blows across the surface of the ocean, the energy creates a wave crest. The front of the wave is concave and its back is rounded. The base of the sea is level with the horizon.

I created this study with the aid of a photo collage, combining the sandy foreground with a dramatic wave behind it. The photograph freezes a split second into a permanent record, giving the eye time to observe the shape of the lip and all the myriad translucent qualities a wave possesses.

The mobile, advancing peaks and troughs of waves can be captured with gradations of tone. In this scene the wave is slightly backlit by the overhead sun, throwing cast shadow beneath the lip. The foam also blocks some light, so the sand colour beneath it is darkened with a touch of complementary colour to degrade its vibrancy and darken its tonality.

Sand colours in the light

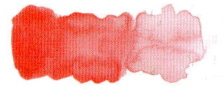 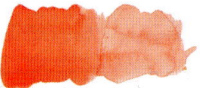 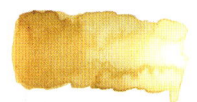

Alizarin Crimson   **Cadmium Red**   **Yellow Ochre**

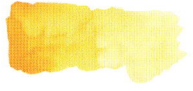 

Cadmium Yellow   **Lemon Yellow**

Ocean and sky colours in the light

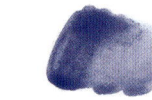  

French Ultramarine   **Cobalt Blue**   **Cerulean Blue**

 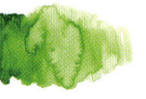

Hooker's Green   **Sap Green**   **Payne's Grey**

Sand colours in the in the shade

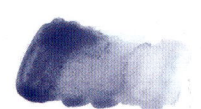 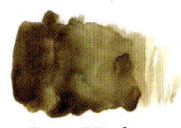

French Ultramarine   **Raw Umber**

Ocean and sky colours in the shade

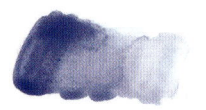 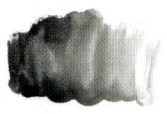

French Ultramarine   **Payne's Grey**

Tip
A Posca pen allows you to draw with an opaque water-based paint, in fine or broad lines, making it perfect for painting and drawing. To ensure a consistent texture from beginning to end, a little ball is placed inside the marker to mix the paint and the marker needs to be shaken before use.

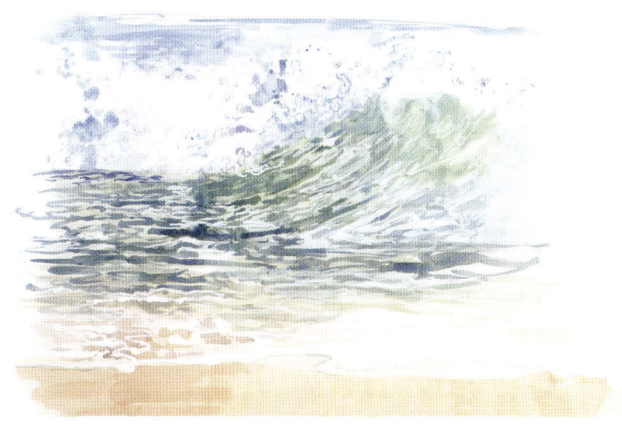

1 *Begin with suggestive loose washes. Try to get the wave to emerge, just like an image in a photographic tray, with watery abstract glazes that overlap. Avoid hard lines and keep everything soft. In the foreground, lay in a light wash of salmon pink sand.*

2 *Create a paper aperture to focus on a small area to cut down the visual complexity and capture the abstract pattern of swirls.*

Dark horizon
As the Earth turns away from the eye, a greater concentration of particles makes the dark band on the horizon.

Foam
The crashing waves create foam, which are tiny bubbles of aerated water. To depict these, I used a small natural sponge and White Gouache to dab, as well as drag, the brush around the curve of the lip. To create the shadow of the froth, I added a glaze of pure French Ultramarine. A final spatter of White Gouache, created by flicking the brush, denotes the spray, giving the impression of dynamism and drama. These tiny specks also help to give a sense of the enormity of the wave. The accidental little white dot on the horizon created a focal point.

Sand in shadow
The pink sand gradually transitions to the colours of the ocean as the water deepens. The pink sand appears darker under the water, where the foam obscures some of the sunlight.

Sea foam tendrils
The foam settles and is pulled by the movement of the water, drawing the froth out into elongated stripes. It swirls and moves around and helps describe the surface of the water. I use a Posca marker and White Gouache with a brush with gestural movements from the wrist.

Ripples
Light comes through the back of the waves and catches the surface of the sea, creating ripples of light and shade.

The interior of the wave
Skilled surfers get barrelled in the tube of large waves, and small waves share similar characteristics. The lip of the wave curls above the base, sucking up water in its path and creating a shadowy interior. Light falling on the back of the wave can shine through the wall of water.

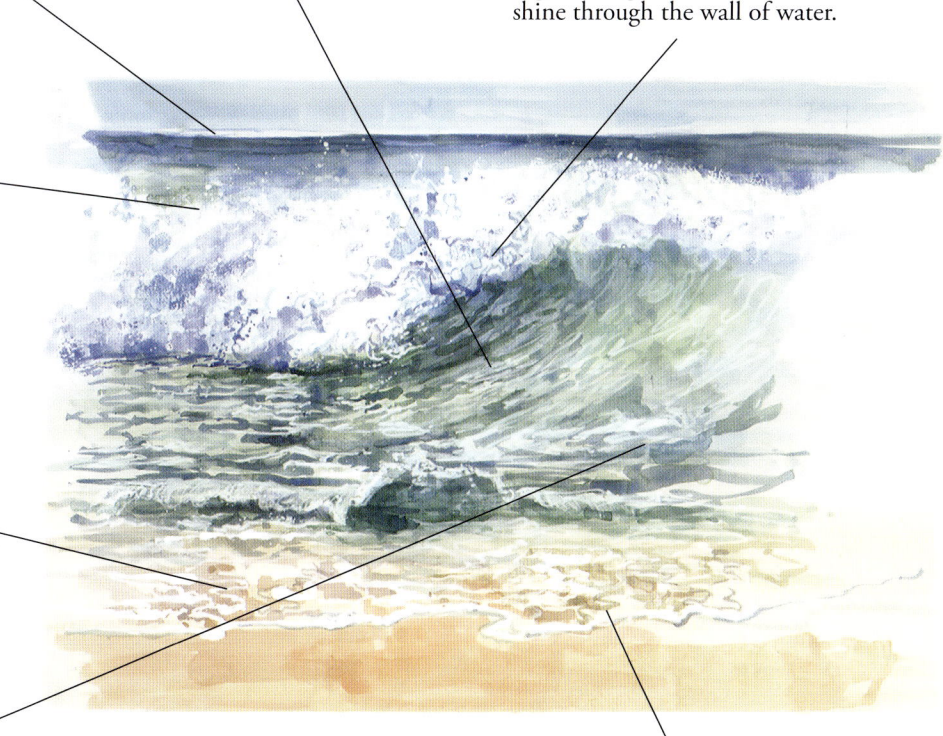

3 *Observe the image carefully and gradually build up the details.*

Backlighting
Finally, I created a delicate lip of shadow on the leading edge of the foam with French Ultramarine.

Shorelines

The meeting place between the land and the sea is a dynamic and inspirational place to sketch. It is a place of continual change, with the smells of seaweed, the cries of sea birds and the sound of the sea breaking on the shore.

Shoreline animals and plants have an ever-changing habitat in an area above the water at low tide and below it at high tide. Powered by the moon's gravitational pull, they must adapt to the twice-daily occurrence of the tide, along with the continual crashing of waves and the rhythmic movement of the tidal current.

This is a place that I never wanted to leave as a child, lifting pebbles in wonderment with a net and bucket in hand. And remains to this day one of my favourite places to sketch in watercolour.

Intertidal zones

There are a great variety of intertidal zones that range from sandy beaches and mudflats to rocky reefs. Each of these is unique and allows the development of a wide variety of plant and animal communities. Intertidal zones are essential habitats for migratory birds, nesting sea turtles and seals taking a break from the ocean. Smaller creatures take refuge in the temporary puddles of rockpools. Starfish live alongside sponges, sea slugs and beautifully coloured sea anemones, their tentacles wavering in the marine currents. Limpets and seaweed attach themselves firmly to the rocks.

An intertidal zone can be broken down into four main parts:

Spray zone

The first section is nearest to the land. It is submerged only during rare, very high tides or severe storms. It is an area where plants need to tolerate the salty sea spray, and scavenging crabs take advantage of the feeding opportunities on dry land.

High-tide zone

The high intertidal is submerged only during the peaks of once or twice daily high tide. Animals and plants have to be able to survive submerged and out of the water.

Mid-tide zone

The middle zone is primarily submerged. Like the high-tide zone, it means that animals and plants have to exist in both wet and dry conditions. Animals such as limpets, crabs, mussels and starfish have successfully adapted to these zones.

Low-intertidal zone

The low-intertidal zone is submerged and exposed to the air only during the lowest spring tides. Some birds have particular adaptations for this zone and have specialized long beaks to dip in the water and find food. They have long legs for wading that keep their bodies away from the water and their feathers dry.

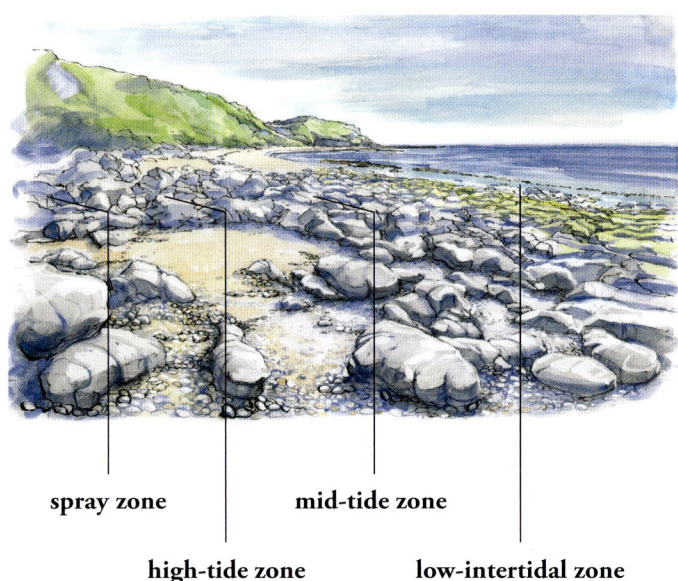

spray zone　　**mid-tide zone**

high-tide zone　　**low-intertidal zone**

Activity
Go to your local beach and create on-the-spot sketches at different times of the day. Observe the same view and capture the morning, afternoon and evening light on the page.

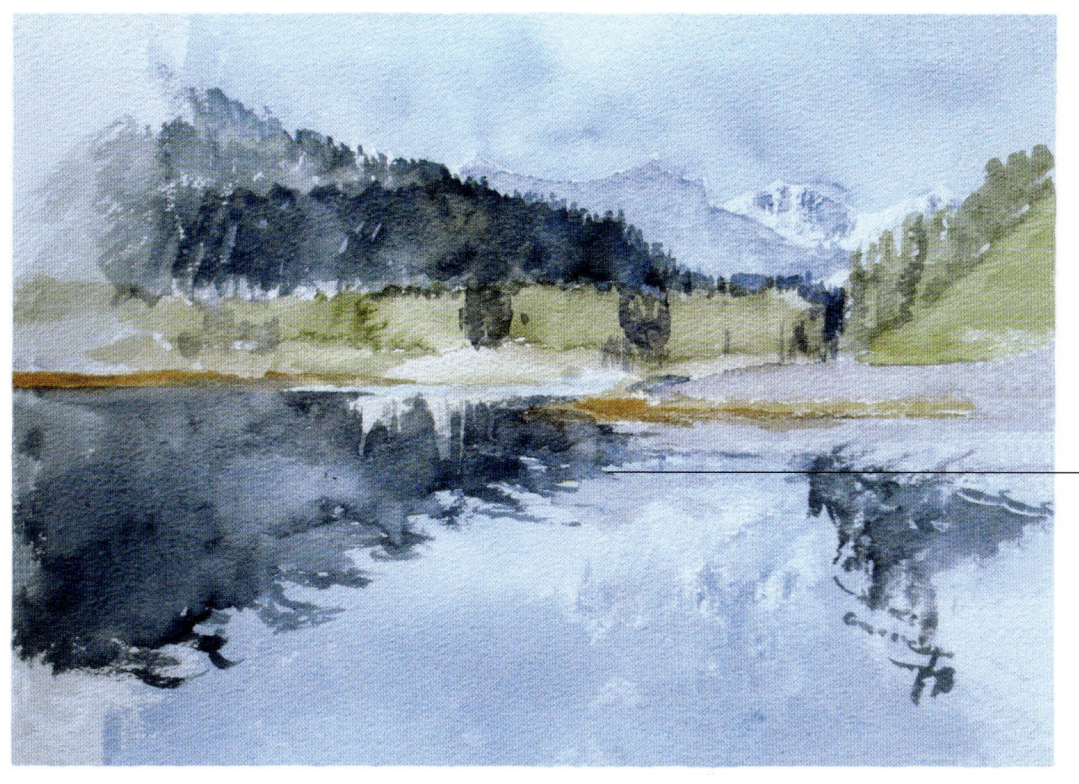

Ripples
Wind creates ripples that disrupt reflections of the landscape. Keep a gestural approach with loose brush marks to keep the feeling of the water's movement.

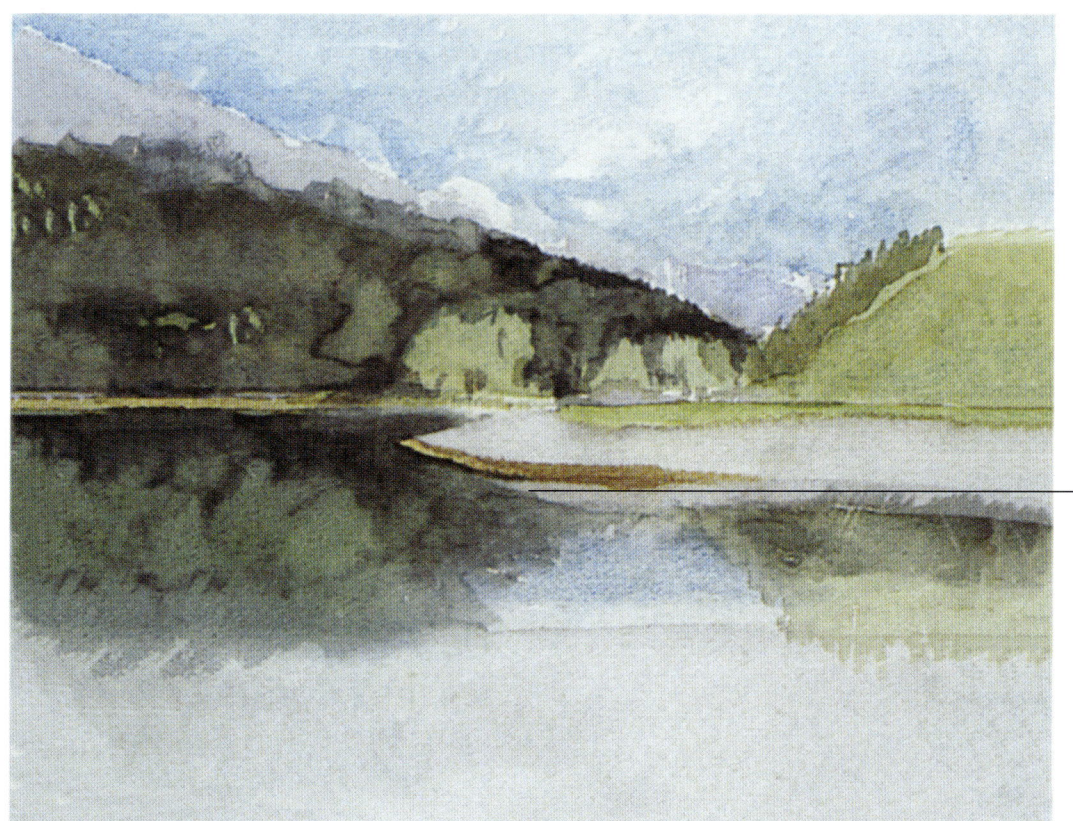

Calm waters
The sea is always in tidal motion. However, when there is little or no wind, the sea can become smooth and oily. The surface of the water can appear as smooth as glass. To achieve this impression, lay watery translucent washes over one another.

Molluscs

Molluscs come in a great diversity of shapes and forms and arguably have the most varied body plans of any invertebrates. As a group, these animals are ancient and evolved some 540 million years ago. They have the unique capability of making their own shells out of a substance called calcium carbonate, the same material as chalk.

They evolved in the ocean and have adapted to life on the land in the form of slugs and snails; these are gastropods, which means having your stomach in your foot. Oysters and clams are bivalves and have a shell consisting of two halves hinged together. Octopus, squid, cuttlefish and nautiluses are part of a group known as the cephalopods, which have tentacles attached to their head. Their tentacles are used to catch prey and transfer it to the mouth or radula. We often think of birds as the only animal with a beak. While theirs is composed of keratin, the cephalopods' beak is primarily made of chitin. Cephalopods have a fascinating way of getting around, that of jet propulsion. They include the fastest and most highly evolved forms of intelligence, the octopus. Even one species of octopus, the female argonaut, can mill its own shell. There are other lesser-known molluscs in the sea, such as tusk shells and chitons and others.

Ammonites and nautiluses

Ammonites thrived in the seas during the time of the dinosaurs and first appeared on the planet some 400 million years ago. They swam much like a nautilus does today and ranged in size from a penny to a large tractor tyre. They went extinct 66 million years ago along with the dinosaurs in the Chicxulub mass extinction event. Fossil records show there to have been more than 10,000 species of ammonite. The ammonites' shells varied greatly in ornamentation. While some were smooth and resembled that of the modern nautilus, others had spines, nodes and bumps, and some, such as the one I am sketching, were ribbed.

Like the ammonite, the shell of the nautilus has many interior chambers or compartments. These chambers have a small central opening, called a siphuncle (think of the word siphon to remember). Through this opening in the septa (which is the dividing wall of the chamber), the nautilus can remove liquid from the partitions and replace it with air, giving the animal the buoyancy that permits it to swim, a bit like the ballast tanks of a submarine. This allows the animal to feed and explore the water column, which it accomplishes by ejecting water through a funnel.

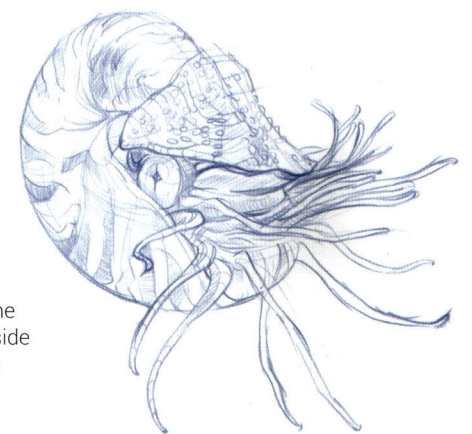

▶ **Nautilus**
Once upon a time, the nautilus lived alongside the ammonite in the open sea.

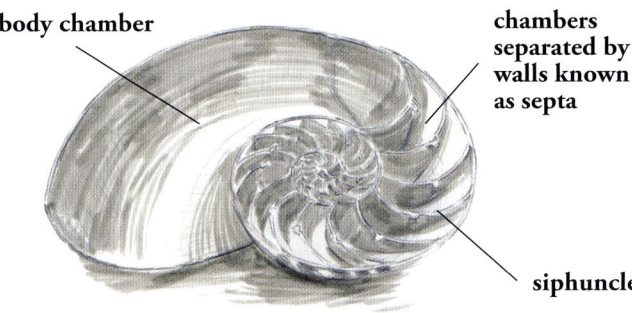

body chamber

chambers separated by walls known as septa

siphuncle

▲ **Shell structure**
The nautilus shell comprises two layers: a matte white outer layer with disruptive brown stripes, a bit like a zebra and a white bottom, which, when upright in the water, acts as countershading. This contrasts with a striking white pearlescent inner layer. Ammonites shared a similar body plan with nautiluses. Like the nautilus, they lived in the last chamber of their shell, which is also the largest and newest chamber.

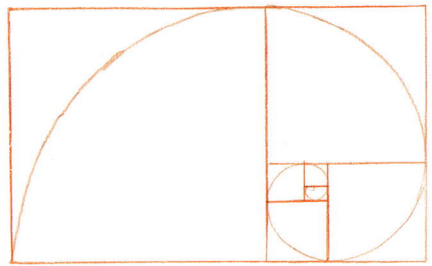

◀ **Logarithmic spirals in nature**
The ammonite and nautilus shells present some of the most beautiful natural examples of a logarithmic spiral. This spiral of growth was first described by Descartes in 1638. The logarithmic spiral can be found in the arms of spiral galaxies, the way a moth will approach a flame and the curvature of a ram's horn.

Activity
Take time out for a bit of fossil hunting. Bring it home, place it under a lamp or in direct sunlight and get ready to sketch.

Tutorial: *Ammonite*

Here we explore how to make a monochrome chiaroscuro study of an ammonite, but you could use any fossil.

Place an ammonite on a piece of white paper in direct sunlight or under a lamp and compare what you can see with the illustration below. Observe how the light sculpts the form, helping to express the volume of the ammonite. Next, follow the steps below to sketch and paint it.

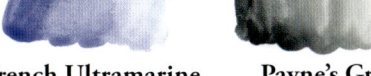
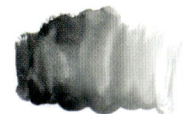

French Ultramarine   **Payne's Grey**

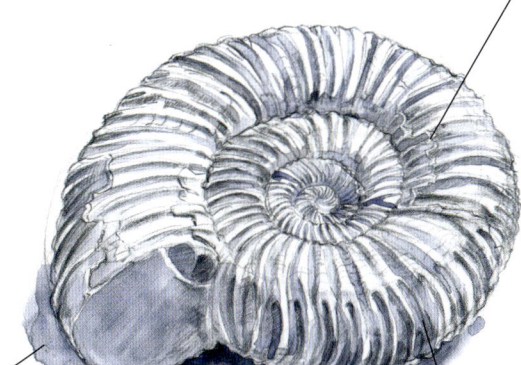

Highlights
Light catches the lip of the fossilized shell.

Cast shadow
This brings drama to your illustration and helps anchor the ammonite so that it doesn't feel that it is floating in space.

Core shadow
Light is reflected off the surface of the white paper beneath, meaning that the darkest part of your shading is not on the far edge but a band just above.

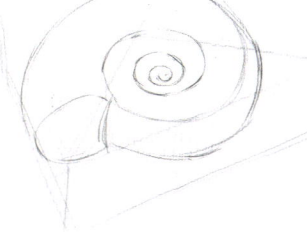
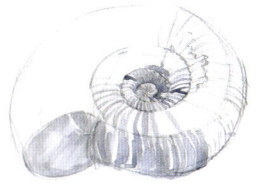
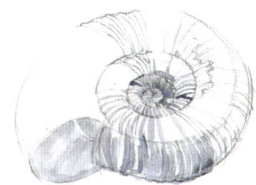

1 *You can start your artwork by lightly sketching a frame. For the underlying drawing, I used a Faber Castell Polychromos in Delft Blue.*

2 *Each complete 360-degree coil is called a whorl. The whorls of the shell get bigger and fatter as the ammonite grows, which means that the centre is not exactly in the middle.*

3 *Once you have sketched a light line you can establish the proportions. Shading can be added using a diluted mixture of French Ultramarine and Payne's Grey.*

4 *Ammonites have a ribbed shell. Remember to leave white gaps for the ridges and let the paper do the work for you.*

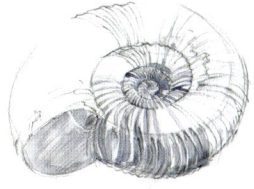
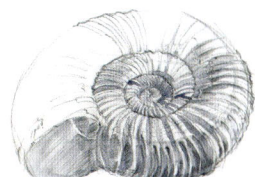
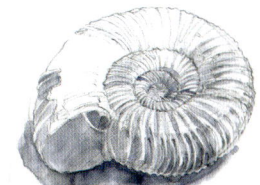
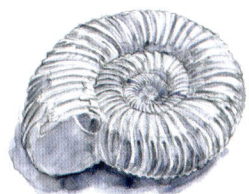

5 *Progressively build up your washes with a higher concentrated wash of colour.*

Tutorial: *Venus Comb Murex*

The Murex or Muricidae is an extensive family of seashells that are predators. Typically, they tend to have heavy or elongated shells that are elaborately spined or frilled, making them a fascinating and challenging subject to sketch. The family occurs throughout the world, but primarily they enjoy the warm waters of the tropics. The venus comb murex is an Indo-Pacific species.

While we don't often think of sea snails as predators, the members of the Murex family feed by drilling a hole through the shell of other molluscs, then, by inserting their long proboscis into the hole, Murex molluscs ingest their prey. Drill-hole marks appear in many shells of their prey that litter the seabed and shore.

The sharp spikes of the venus comb protect from predation, transforming the shell into an impregnable fortress protected by over a hundred spines from all angles. The needles on the base also lift the body from the seabed and prevent the snail from sinking in the soft mud. They are relatively small, and typically grow to 4–6 in (10–15cm).

Before sketching this tropical shell, ask yourself the following questions: What is the best version of this subject I can do? What angle creates visual interest? How can lighting, under a lamp or on a sunlit shelf, help express the volume of form?

Shell gizmo
A shell gizmo gives you an understanding of the fundamentals of geometric form.

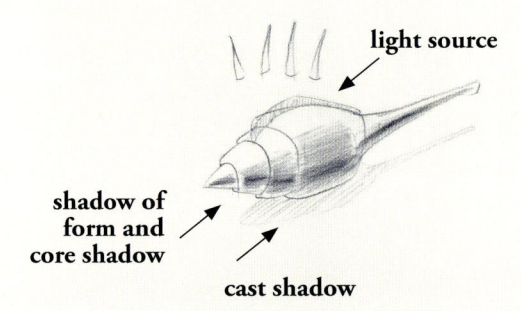

light source

shadow of form and core shadow

cast shadow

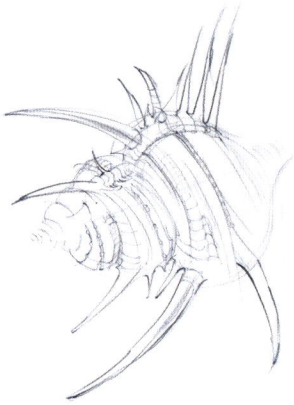

2 *Build along the armature of the axis, drawing around the form, sculpting it from your paper. Flick marks from your wrist can help express the sharpness of the spines.*

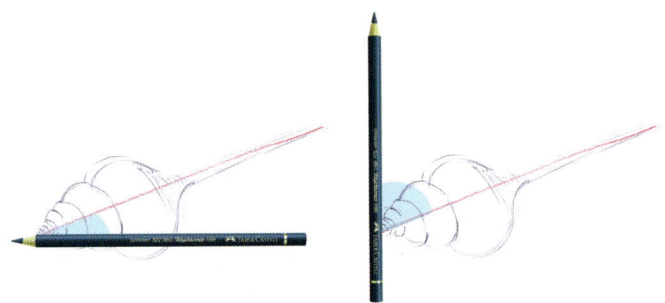

holding up a horizontal　　**holding up a vertical**

1 *Humans tend to enjoy the simplicity of having the object placed on the horizontal, making the study flat to the eye. However, setting your specimen at a three-quarter angle below the eyeline will create a visual drama to this exotic shell study. You might have wondered what artists are doing when they hold a pencil up at arm's length and shut one eye. Imagine a protractor attached to the top of the pencil and establish the angle of the central axis.*

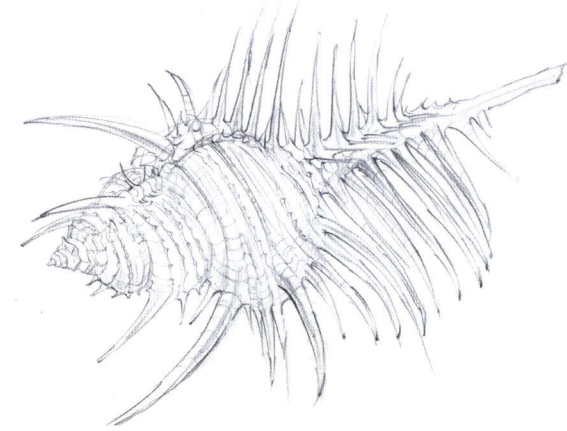

3 *Finalize the pencil sketch. Try to get down as much information as you can.*

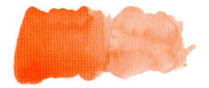
Cadmium Red

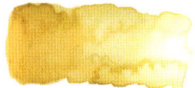
Yellow Ochre

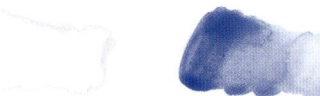
White Gouache

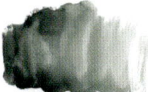
French Ultramarine

Payne's Grey

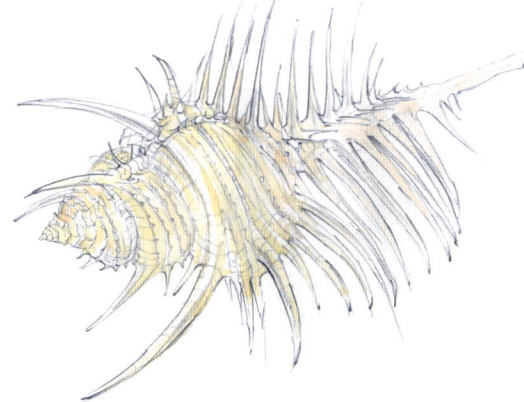

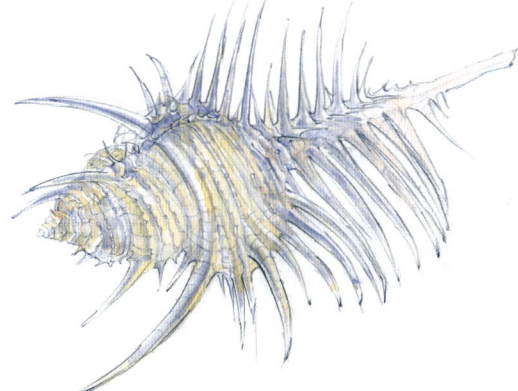

4 *Paint in your lightest and brightest colours first. Ask yourself: Which are the lightest colours and how could I mix them? A little bit of White Gouache has been added to Cadmium Red and Yellow Ochre to create the pearlescent pastel shades.*

5 *Use a combination of French Ultramarine and Payne's Grey to build on your modelling. By squinting at your subject, you can reduce the detail down and see the main areas of light and shade.*

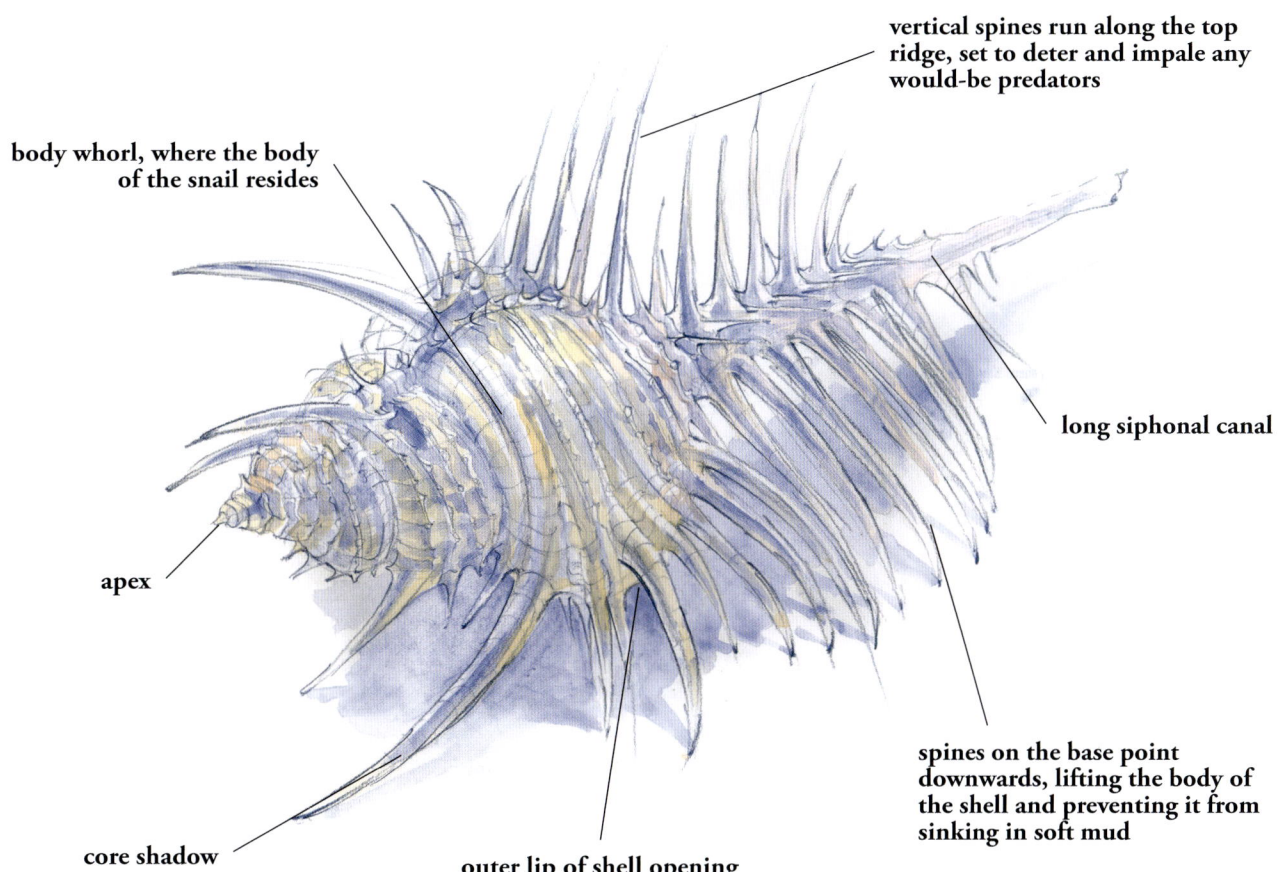

vertical spines run along the top ridge, set to deter and impale any would-be predators

body whorl, where the body of the snail resides

long siphonal canal

apex

core shadow

outer lip of shell opening

spines on the base point downwards, lifting the body of the shell and preventing it from sinking in soft mud

6 *Create the illusion that the spines hold the body of the shell off the ground by placing in the cast shadow. Finally, using a combination of a fine brush and a sharp watercolour pencil, add in the details. Look carefully at the shell and draw and paint along the growth ridges. Create undulating rhythmic marks that follow the structure and add the detail of the ochre colour bands help to suggest volume. Use White Gouache to add additional highlights, where the light hits the growth ridges of the whorls.*

Coral Reefs

Corals first appeared in the Cambrian period, some 535 million years ago. Just like plants, they root themselves to the ocean floor; however, they are not plants – corals are invertebrate animals, belonging to a large group of colourful and fascinating animals called cnidarians. The name cnidaria comes from the Greek word 'cnidos', which means stinging nettle. Animals in this group, which includes anemones and jellyfish, share similar stinging tentacles.

From a coral larva that initially floats in the sea, a new coral reef can be born. First, it finds a suitable spot, and in a few days the larvae can graduate to the state of becoming a polyp. Identical copies bud off from this initial polyp, surrounding itself with a hard exoskeleton of calcium carbonate if it is a hard, or stony, coral (there are around 500 species of soft corals that do not produce a hard skeleton but feed and behave similarly to stony coral).

Hundreds of polyps make up each piece of coral. They live on the outside of the coral, sitting in the limestone cups and waving minute tentacle arms, a bit like a minuscule anemone. They reproduce, grow and die, and endlessly repeat the cycle over time, slowly laying the limestone foundation for coral reefs and giving shape to the familiar different types of corals. Coral branches can grow as much as 6in (15cm) per year. Over thousands of years, this creates an abundant habitat for tropical life. The largest of the coral cities is the Australian Great Barrier Reef, which has taken around 500,000 years to evolve.

Corals eat by catching tiny animals in the nutrient-rich ocean currents, primarily at night, when it is safest to come out. They wave their long, stinging tentacles to capture tiny plankton, which is then drawn into their mouths to be digested in their stomach.

Coral as a habitat

Coral reefs are only found in shallow water because they need sunlight, for living within the coral are algae. Algae are plants and, like them, need photosynthesis to create sugar for energy. This is a mutually beneficial relationship between the algae and corals — it provides algae with a protective home, gives coral reefs their colours, and supplies both organisms with nutrients.

At first appearance, the coral reef may seem like an underwater paradise, but these are also battlegrounds for space and are often referred to as the rainforests of the sea, where each species has to find its unique way of surviving.

While the really big fish dwell in the open waters, coral creates a habitat for small fish that can take advantage of it by darting in and out of the small gaps, where they can hide from predators.

▼ Coral reefs
Coral polyps, the invertebrates responsible for reef formation, come in various shapes and sizes, including vast reef-building colonies, graceful flowing fans and even small, solitary species. Creating buzzing metropolises for a myriad of lifeforms all dependent on each other.

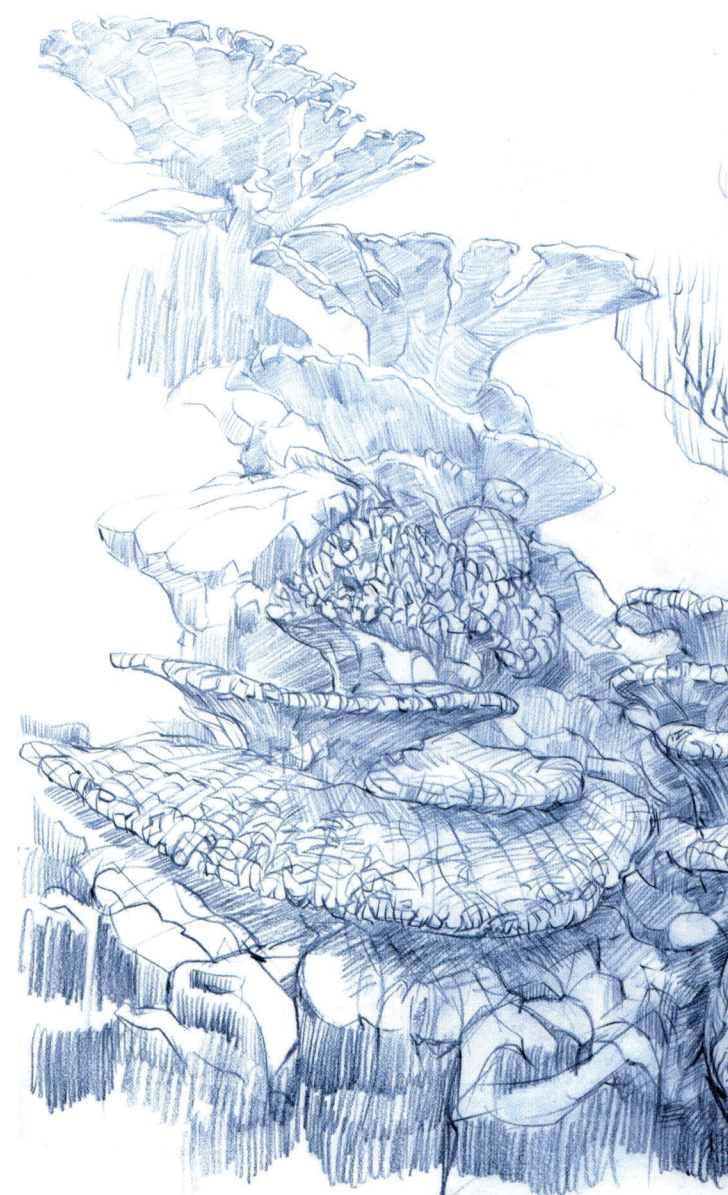

Coral itself creates a variety of habitats for both the small and larger animals in a myriad of fantastic adaptations. Anemones, sponges and filter feeders attach themselves to the coral and Christmas tree worms live inside it. Shrimps and a myriad of creatures use the corridors created by the reef for protection, and confusing shoals of shimmering fish dart through.

None of our tropical fish would be here if it were not for the coral. Some of these adapted to being tiny enough to squeeze through small gaps and take safety in the reef. Others have evolved long snouts to probe into the nooks and crannies of coral. Some fish, such as parrotfish, have evolved specialist coral-crunching beaks; grinding teeth then pulverize the coral to get to the algae-filled polyps inside. Much of the sand in the parrotfish's range is the ground-up, undigested coral they excrete.

A host of sophisticated symbiotic relationships between a myriad of species underpin these fantastic multi-coloured rainbow worlds in this spectacular, interconnected ecosystem.

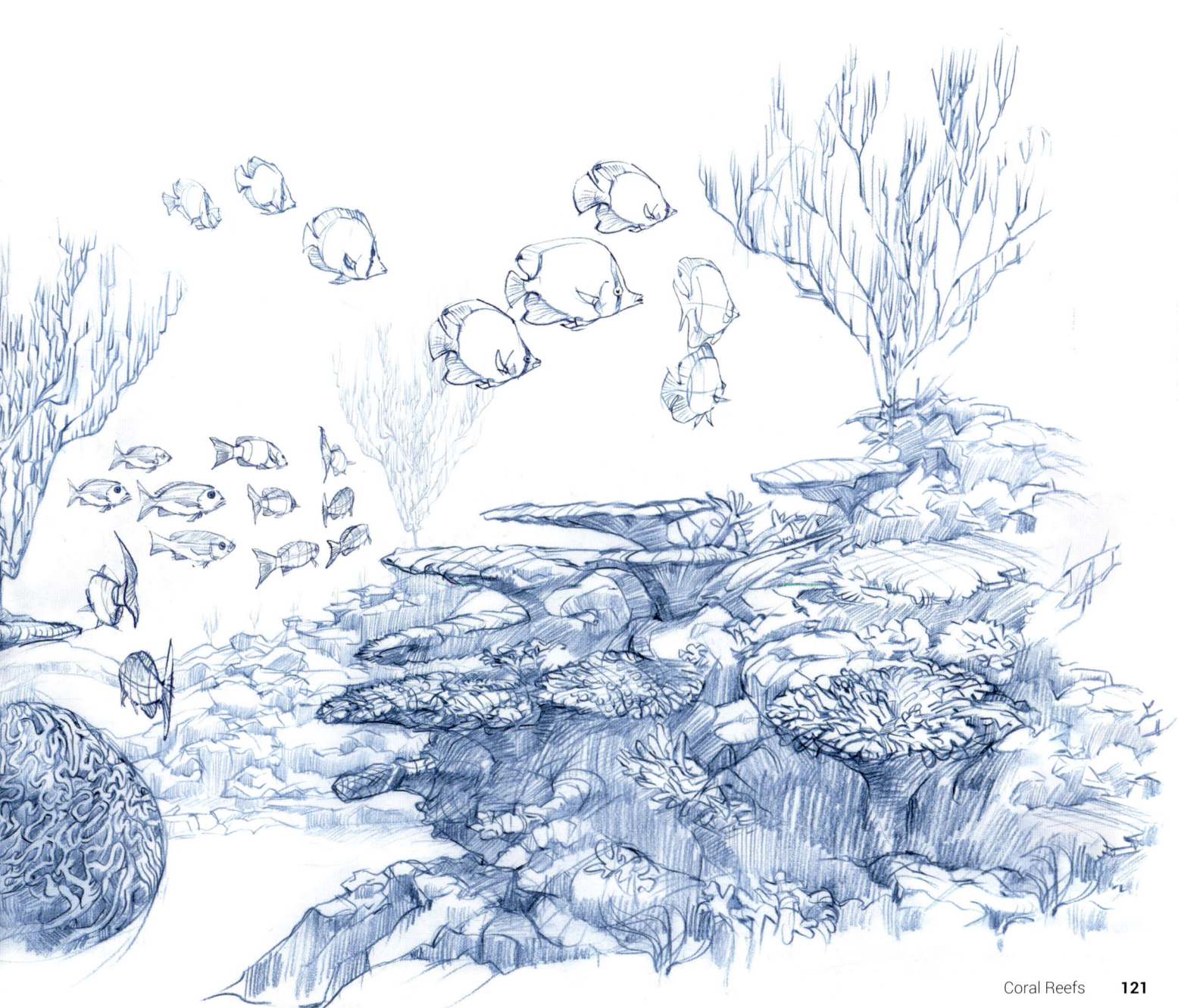

Tutorial: *Seahorse*

This curious class of 54 different species of fish that can be found around the globe are so named because they resemble a horse. In Ancient Greek, Hippocampus means Horse Sea Monster. Seahorses are mainly found in shallow, tropical waters. Seahorses prefer sheltered coastal areas with seagrass, coral reefs or mangroves and don't do well in choppy waters, often fleeing to deeper waters when a storm approaches.

The smallest seahorse is Denise's pygmy seahorse, which measures ⅔in (16mm) from nose tip to tail. This tiny fish inhabits coral reefs that surround eastern Indonesian islands.

Besides being the smallest seahorse, it also ranks as one of the smallest vertebrates. Being so tiny can be an advantage, as the seahorse can dive between gaps in the coral reef when predators attack.

The Australian big-belly seahorse featured in this tutorial is one of the largest seahorse species in the world, with a length of up to 13¾in (35cm). Whatever their size, all seahorses share the same pony-like features that make them such a delight to sketch, from their horse-shaped snout to their spiralling tail. They also have thin gossamer ray fins that create movement, which can be hard to see on your first encounter, but look closer!

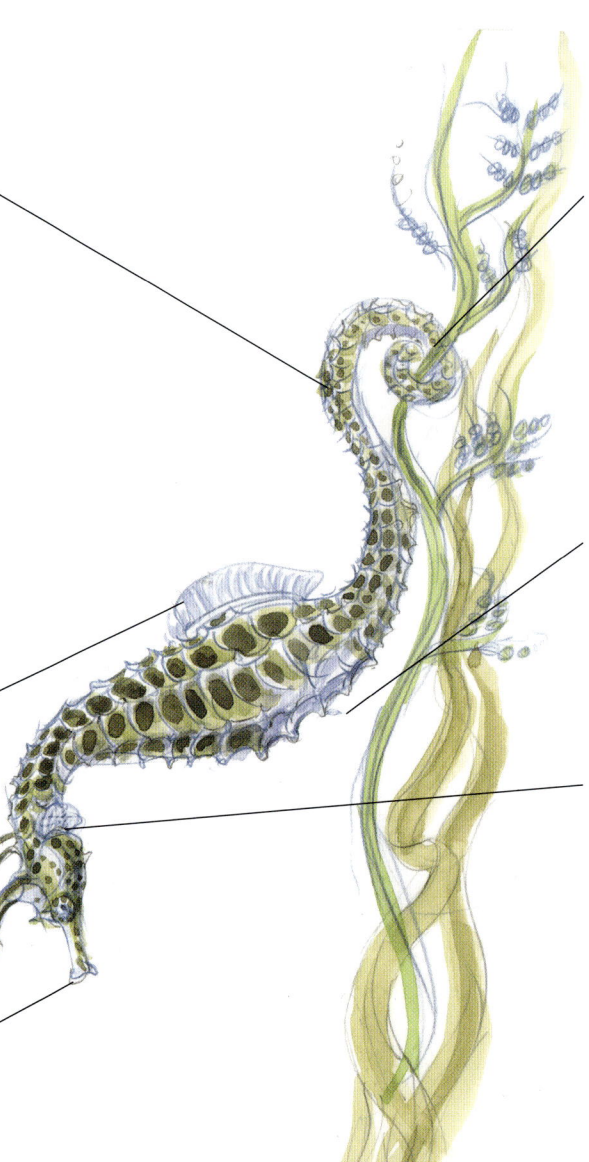

Trunk ring and ridge shapes
Try to capture the concave shapes of the carapace that wrap around an oval body form. Seahorses have a spine, so they are classed as a vertebrate. Unlike most other fish, seahorses also have an exoskeleton. Their bodies are made up of hard, external, bony plates fused together with a fleshy covering. Unlike most fish, seahorses do not have scales. I start to sketch seahorses by creating marks that capture these trunk rings and ridges.

Dorsal fin
The dorsal fin flutters 35 times a second and creates motion.

Fused snout
Seahorses' snouts enable them to probe into nooks and crannies for food. This snout is fused and functions something similar to a vacuum cleaner, which they use to suck up small crustaceans.

Gripping tail
Seahorses are vulnerable in tidal waters and can die of exhaustion in choppy currents. Their tail provides the seahorse with fantastic equipment for gripping and anchoring themselves to seagrass and coral.

Anal fin
On males, this is situated just above the brood pouch.

Pectoral fin
The pectoral fin, which can be hard to see on some species, is usedto steer the Seahorse.

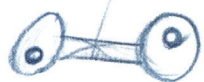

▲ Eye sight
Seahorses are able to move their eyes independently, meaning they can look forwards and backwards at the same time. This is particularly useful as they hunt for food by sight.

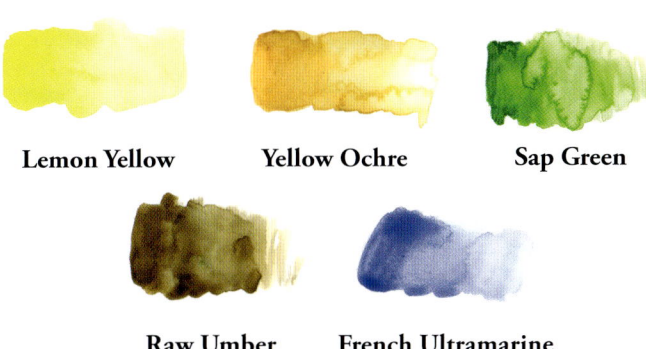

Lemon Yellow **Yellow Ochre** **Sap Green**

Raw Umber **French Ultramarine**

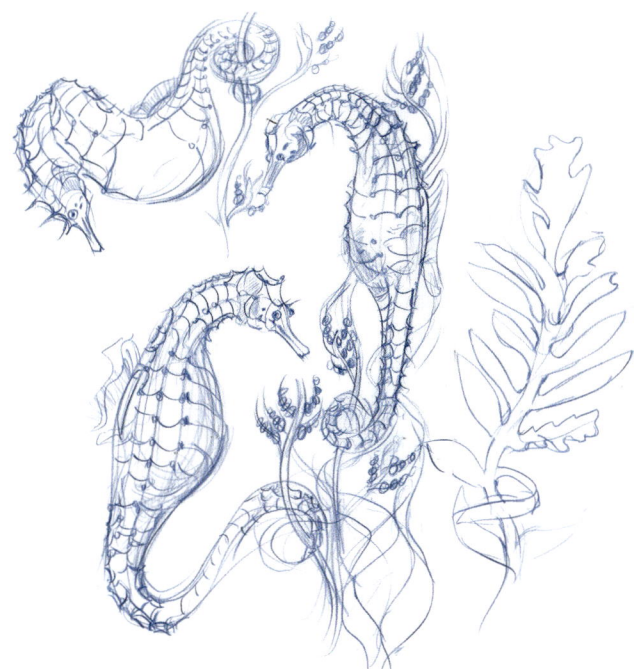

1 *Begin by creating on the spot sketches in the aquarium in a dark blue Polychromos pencil. I start with rhythmic shapes from my wrist to capture the concave arcs of the trunk rings. Take photos for reference so you can finish the painting at home.*

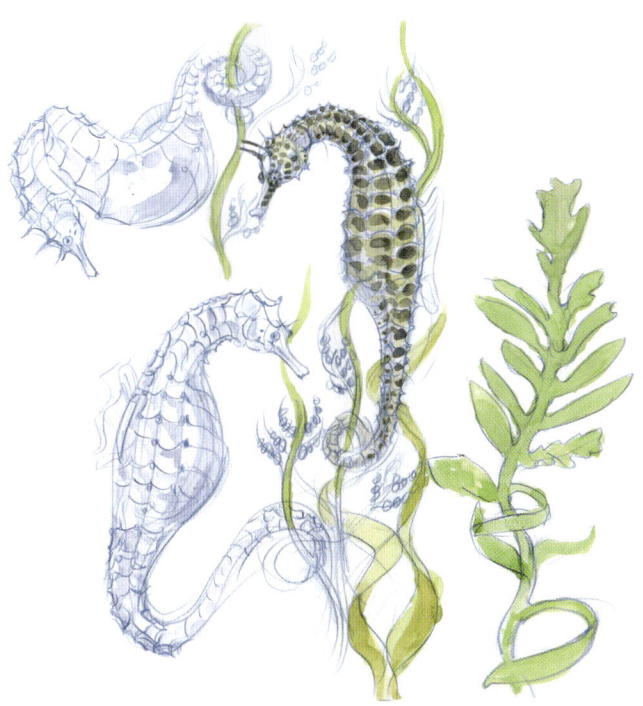

2 *Working from the photos, start by painting a tonal underpainting in French Ultramarine, ensuring that all the seahorses are affected by the same light source. Then start laying in a wash of Lemon Yellow, Yellow Ochre, Sap Green and Raw Umber mix, working from the most delicate and brightest colours covering the entirety of the seahorse, leaving flecks of white highlights.*

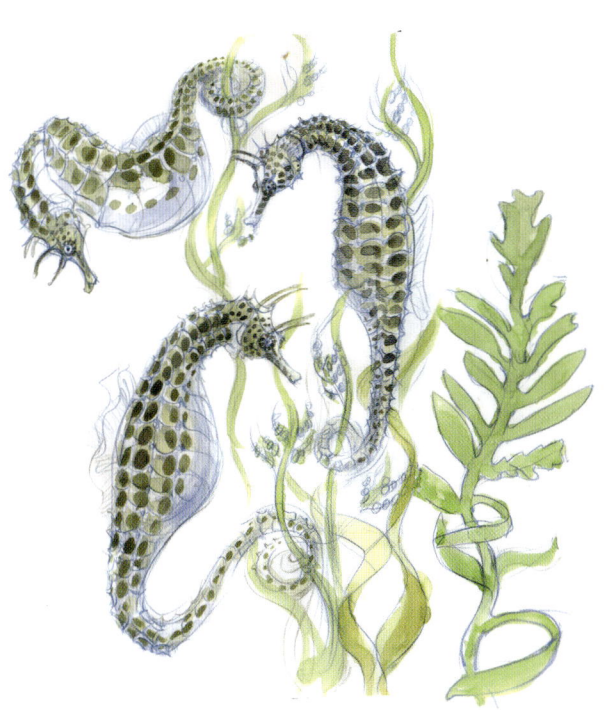

3 *Finally, I add the spotty disruptive colouration with a mixture of Raw Umber, Sap Green and French Ultramarine, gradually working towards the darker notes and using thinner brushes to refine the detail.*

Tutorial: *Spotfin Lionfish*

Lionfish have a dazzling beauty with fantastical colouration and fins, but even the most intricate and daunting subject, such as this show-stopping lionfish, can be tackled by breaking the illustration process down into simple stages.

There are 12 different, recognized species of lionfish. They are slow-moving and rely on a variety of defence mechanisms against would-be predators: their fins, colouration and warning stripes all act as camouflage, breaking up the outline of the fish's body to blend with its surroundings, and they have venomous spines.

Lionfish originate from the Indo-Pacific, where their presence is not considered a problem. However, they have migrated, and in the Atlantic Ocean they are seen as an invasive species. An invasive species is 'non-native' and can create ecological disruption in their new habitat. Lionfish are now one of the top predators in many coral reef environments of the Atlantic. Lionfish consume a vast number of fish species, including some ecologically important species, dramatically damaging reef biomes.

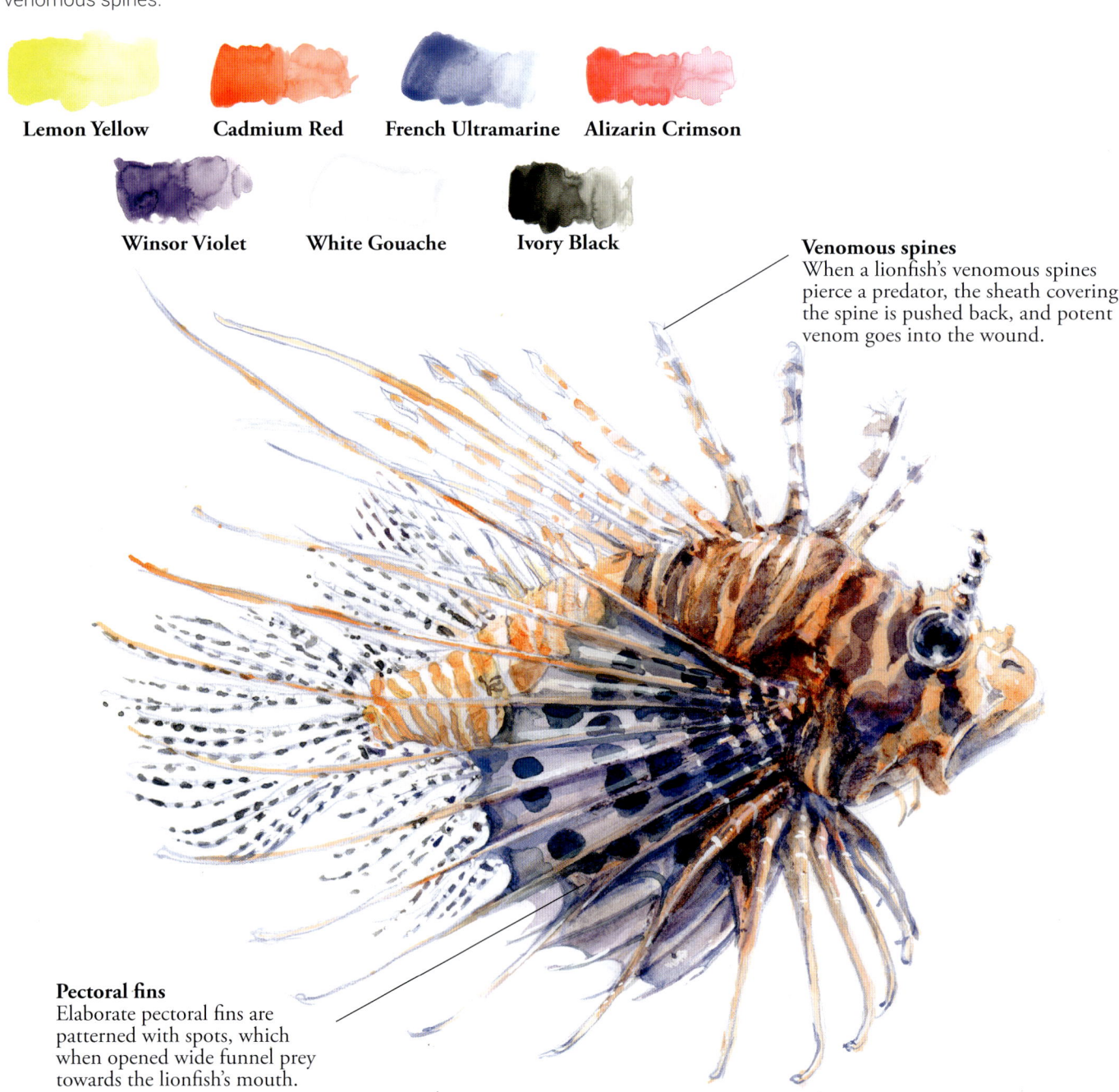

Lemon Yellow

Cadmium Red

French Ultramarine

Alizarin Crimson

Winsor Violet

White Gouache

Ivory Black

Venomous spines
When a lionfish's venomous spines pierce a predator, the sheath covering the spine is pushed back, and potent venom goes into the wound.

Pectoral fins
Elaborate pectoral fins are patterned with spots, which when opened wide funnel prey towards the lionfish's mouth.

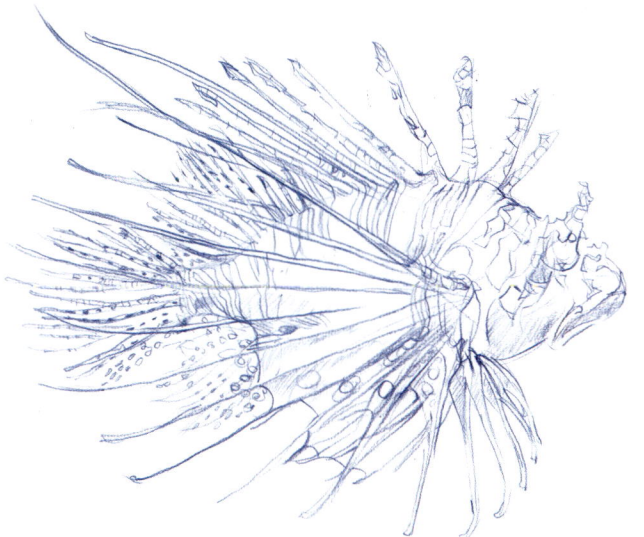

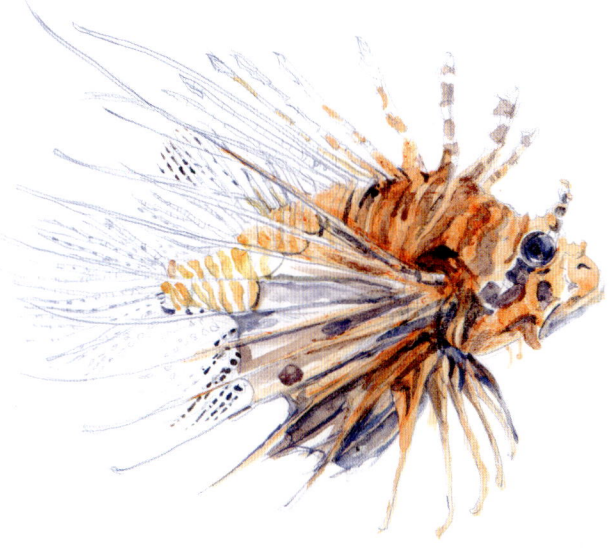

1 As accurately as you can, create an initial sketch; there is no need for shading. I use a high-quality blue pencil because the blue line disappears into the background when watercolour is applied.

2 Lay in the lightest and brightest colours first. Use a high-quality watercolour and ensure that your water is clear and your brush is spotless to achieve the bright, glowing pigment stains on your paper. Draw with the brush rather than filling in the shapes. Allow wet into wet bleeds (see page 27) for interesting naturalistic effects.

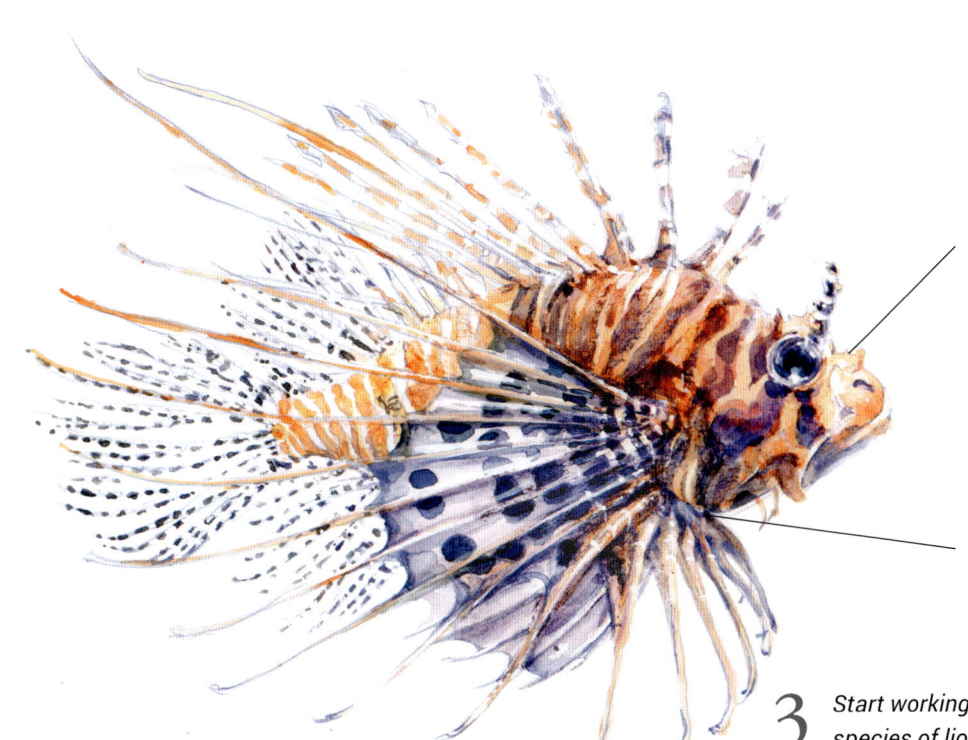

create highlights with flecks of White Gouache

Alizarin Crimson is mixed with French Ultramarine to create purple stripes

3 Start working up the dark notes. Colouration in different species of lionfish varies widely. This illustration is of a spotfin lionfish, a small species of lionfish that has big bluish-black spots on the pectoral fins; mix this colour with a combination of French Ultramarine and Ivory Black.

Open Ocean

The Earth is often called the 'Blue Planet' because water covers almost three-quarters of its surface, and the ocean is by far the largest of all the biomes. Out at sea, it feels fearsome in scale and boundless in expanse, a timeless world away from our modern cities, still moving at the pace of evolution.

Beneath the surface lurk ancient creatures and swift predator species, such as sharks, marlin and dolphins. The largest of them all, the blue whale, sustains its massive body almost exclusively on one of the most miniature animals, krill. Krill are tiny, shrimp-like crustaceans that are a critical part of the food web for many animals, from seals to penguins. Krill also acts as a carbon sink by feeding on carbon-rich algae on the surface then taking it to the seabed in their excrement or, if they get eaten, the carbon is stored in the animal until it dies. In effect, krill act as a carbon conveyor belt, taking it to the bottom of the ocean and helping prevent climate change.

For many creatures, life in the open ocean is nomadic, constantly on the move for their survival.

Vast current systems like rivers move nutrients and plankton around, so parts of the ocean become rich in food, attracting vast schools of fish. They come in their millions to sieve out the plankton, taking in water through their mouths and expelling it through their gills.

These fluctuating currents change like weather patterns and create a movable feast that draws in large predators – pods of dolphins use sonar to track their prey, a sailfish can sense their vibrations, and sharks can even detect electrical currents given off by the school. For the smaller fish, it is essential to be part of the shoal. Alone in these featureless waters, they would soon be picked off.

The defence-mechanisms of fish

In the circle of life, fish are easy prey. They have evolved different adaptations to help deal with this situation. Small fish may dart away to hide in nooks and crannies on the ocean floor to escape from bigger predator fish, such as seals and dolphins. But speed alone is not the only strategy used by fish to survive. Many use schooling, which is disruptive and confuses the predator, not knowing which individual fish to chase for a meal. Others have evolved incredible camouflage, which blends them into their environment. The pufferfish makes itself significantly large by ingesting water, and some have spines so they become a ball that is protected from every angle by projecting spikes, like an orange covered in toothpicks. However, some fishes have evolved other venomous strategies, such as the lionfish, which has venomous spines to pierce its attackers.

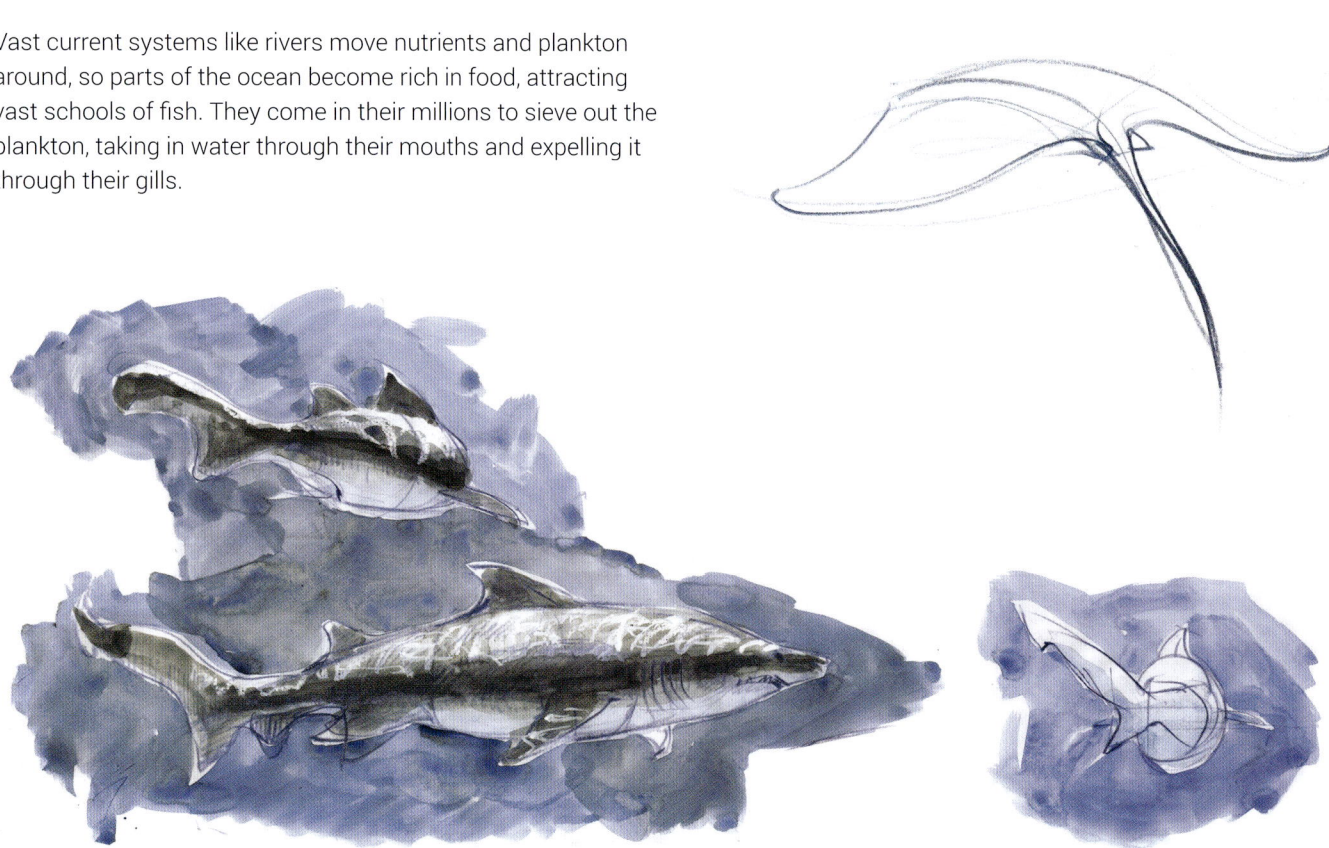

Tutorial: *Green Turtle*

This tutorial aims to demonstrate how to create a natural-history style of illustration, like those that are found in identification field guides. Here, accuracy is key. You can work directly from my painting as a guide, or you can create your own image by using a variety of reference materials and applying them to a single study.

The green turtle is one of the largest sea turtles and unlike most other sea turtles, it is predominantly herbivorous. Green turtles are named for the greenish colour of their cartilage and fat, not their shells or carapace, which can blend different colours and vary widely between individuals. The underside, or plastron, is a yellowish-white colour. They are found mainly in tropical and subtropical waters. Like other sea turtles, they migrate long distances across the open ocean between feeding grounds and the sandy beaches where the females lay their eggs.

Centres and symmetry

The shortest way to find the centre of a square or rectangle is to draw a cross from corner to corner. This also has the fantastic effect of still locating the centre even when the box is placed in perspective. Notice the half nearest the viewer is now broader. This technique is useful if we want to establish the bilateral line of symmetry in forms. Most animals and plants have some symmetry about them, and this is particularly evident in 'box-like' creatures such as turtles, so it's a perfect technique to apply to this drawing.

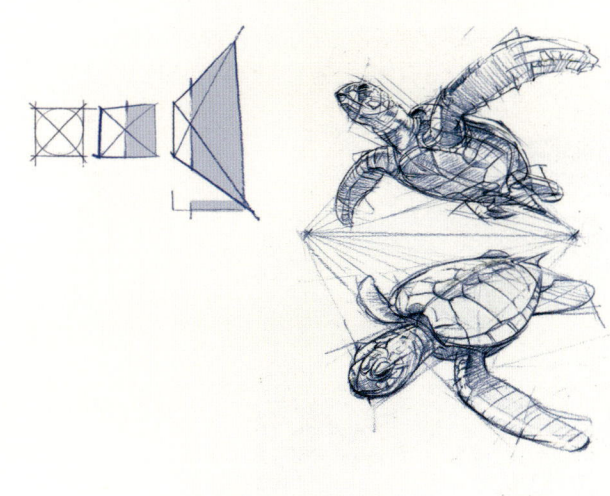

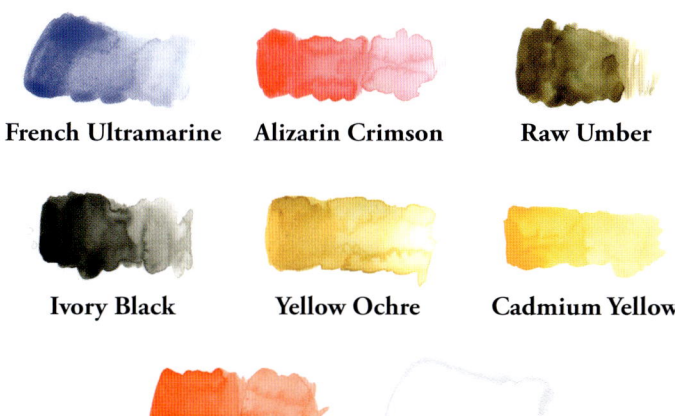

French Ultramarine

Alizarin Crimson

Raw Umber

Ivory Black

Yellow Ochre

Cadmium Yellow

Cadmium Red

White Gouache

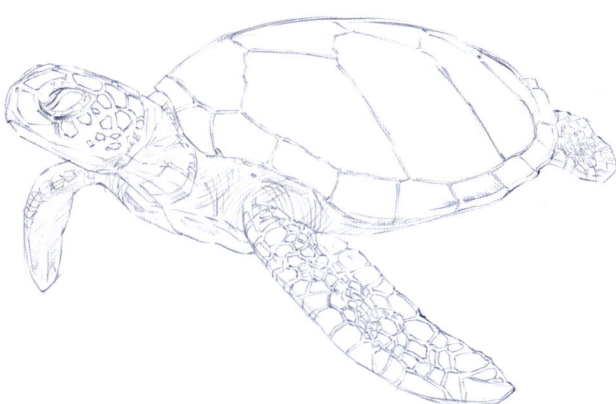

1 Using your reference material or the image shown here, get down as much detail as you can in pencil. I used a dark blue Polychromos pencil. Apply the technique explained in the box for finding symmetry and getting the perspective right.

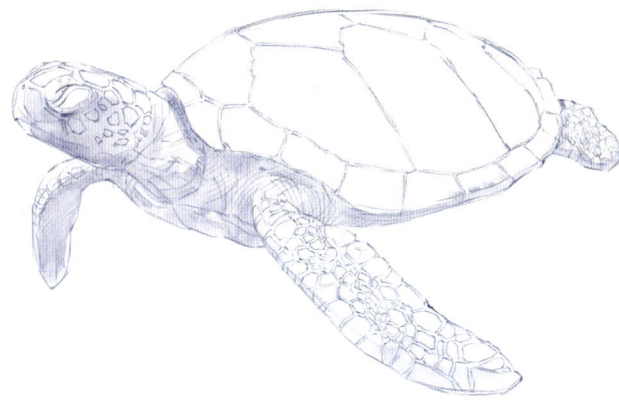

2 Next, create an underpainting in a light wash of French Ultramarine.

► *continued overleaf*

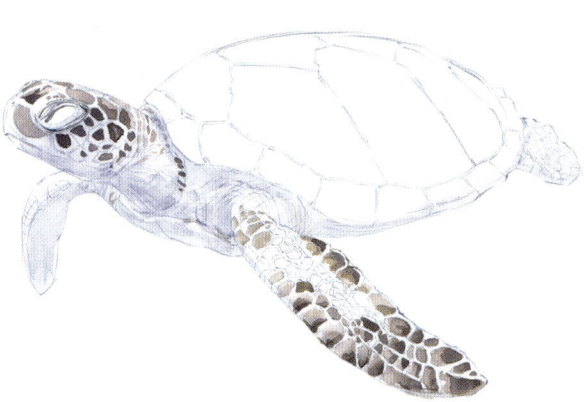

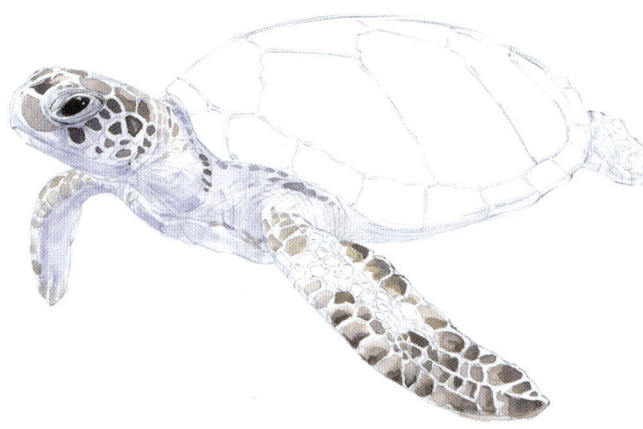

3 *Start painting the purplish-brown crazy paving arrangement of scutes with a mixture of Alizarin Crimson, French Ultramarine and Raw Umber, graduating the tone by adding pure water.*

4 *Paint the pupil with a mixture of Ivory Black and French Ultramarine, leaving a couple of small gaps as highlights to help make the turtle look alive.*

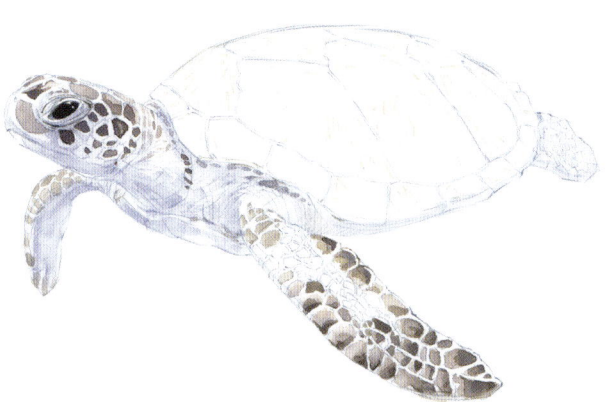

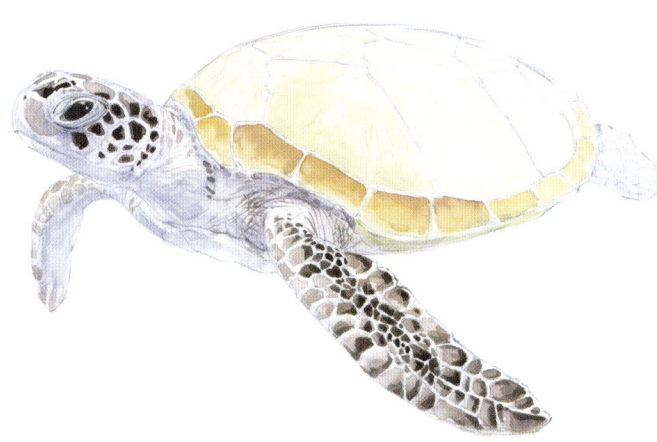

5 *Continue sketching in the shapes of the explosive starburst pattern of disruptive colouration in a Polychromos pencil.*

6 *Paint the shell's lightest and brightest colours with a mixture of Yellow Ochre, Alizarin Crimson and French Ultramarine.*

Nostrils
Although turtles can hold their breath for hours underwater, they regularly come to the surface to fill their lungs with air. This is because they have evolved from land lizards.

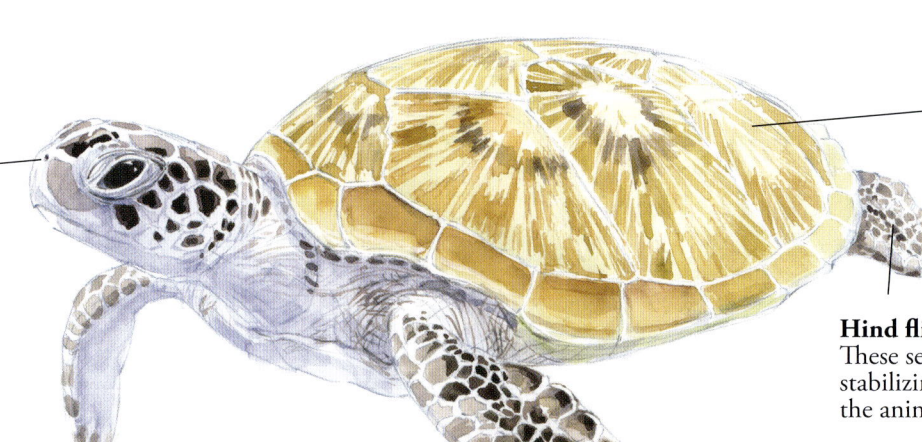

Slimmer shells
All turtle shells are slimmer than tortoises to make them streamlined in the water.

Hind flippers
These serve as rudders, stabilizing and directing the animal as it swims.

Paddling flippers
Sea turtles have long paddle flippers that enclose five bony fingers to propel them over huge distances on migratory routes.

7 *When dry, try to capture the intricate pattern on the central and dorsal scutes by varying combinations of Cadmium Yellow, Yellow Ochre, Cadmium Red and Raw Umber with your thinnest brushes. Finally, embolden any colours that require it and use White Gouache and a thin rigger brush to enhance the white contrasts.*

Estuaries and Wetlands

Wetland habitats perform essential tasks in an ecosystem, such as filtering water, preventing flooding and erosion and providing food and shelter for fish and wildlife. The unique flora of aquatic plants is the key component that separates wetlands from terrestrial land formations or fully submersible water bodies. Except for Antarctica, wetland ecosystems can be found on every continent. Wetlands contain freshwater, brackish water or even saltwater as with mangrove swamps.

Wetlands

Wetlands are found worldwide, ranging from giant deltas, mighty estuaries and mudflats to floodplains and peat bogs. Others are as humble as a marshy bog or garden pond. All play a crucial role in protecting the health of our planet and serve as a lifeline for freshwater species.

Wetlands are one of the world's most biodiverse habitats. The London Wetland Centre, where I created these sketches, is home to lots of endangered species and acts as vital 'service stations' for millions of migratory birds to rest and refuel. Many endemic species are found only in specific wetland areas.

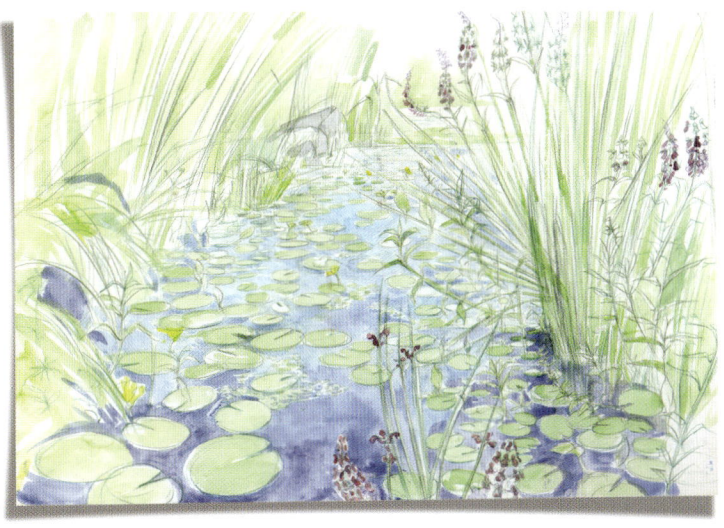

▲ **Pond**
London Wetland Centre, UK.

Estuaries

An estuary is a partially enclosed coastal body of brackish water with one or more rivers or streams flowing into it and connecting to the open sea. Estuaries form a transition zone between freshwater and maritime environments and create a rich habitat for a diverse range of species, with many more than the eye initially sees.

There is much life going on beneath the mud in the form of tiny shellfish and worms, making estuaries popular with birds and an airport for migrating wildfowl. They are great places for sketching birds, and many have hides you can paint from, looking through a pair of binoculars for a closer view.

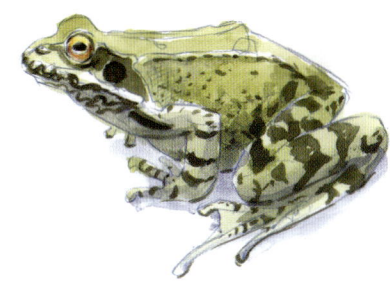

▲ **Common frog**
Barnes Wetland Centre, UK

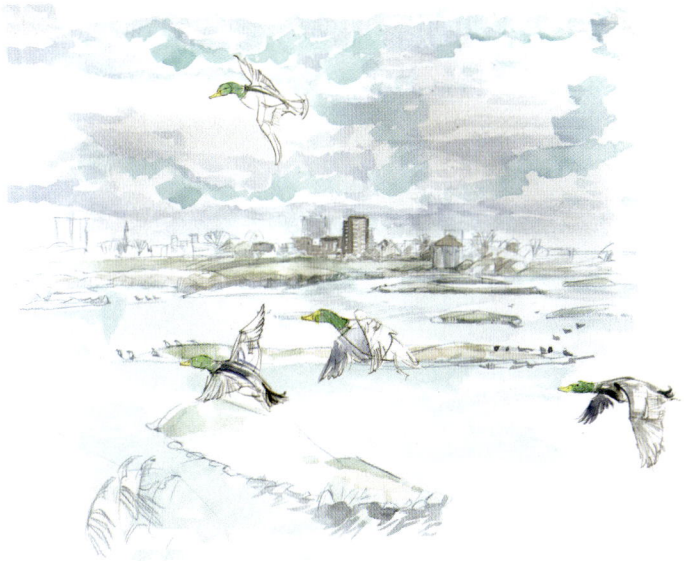

▶ **Splashdown**
London Wetland Centre, UK.

Study Sheet: *Goose*

Geese are divided into two main groups: the 'grey' geese (which can be confusing as it includes white or brown species) with around seven species and the 'black' geese, with around six to eight species. The black geese derive their name from the prominent black colouration areas, sometimes around the neck, like a Canada goose.

In general, most geese are gregarious birds that form flocks during migration and outside of the breeding season. When they are together, they can cause quite a commotion with their honking calls, hence their collective noun 'a gaggle of geese'. When geese migrate, they often fly in a tight 'V' formation; this is known as a wedge, as it looks like a wedge that you'd put under a door to keep it open. Flying in V formation is more efficient for the geese when they are travelling thousands of miles. The goose in front creates an updraft current of air from the downbeat of its wings, which the goose behind it flaps its wings on to create a more significant lift. A male goose is a gander, and a female goose is sometimes referred to as a dame. Baby geese are called goslings.

Anatomy

Head and neck

Ducks have a very pronounced cheek. It is less so on geese. I tend to sit the eye on an eclipse and intersect this with a line for the beak.

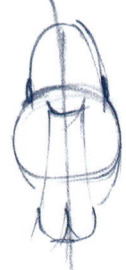 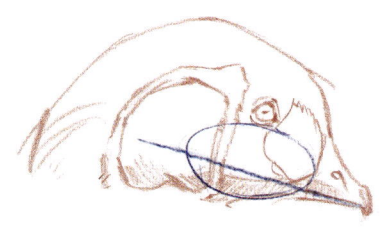

▲ Geese have a long 'S' shaped neck with many vertebrae.

Feathers

Feathers evolved from scales. Now all flying birds share a similar body plan with a variety of exaggerations. Understanding the groups of feathers will help you create accurate bird sketches.

Primary feathers

Primary flight feathers are rigid and provide thrust. These feathers are asymmetrical, with the leading edge of the blade being narrower to aid lift. The vanes of all flight feathers have tiny hooks called barbules that zip together, giving the feathers the strength needed to form an airfoil.

Secondary feathers

Secondary flight feathers are shaped to aid gliding. The number of secondaries is highly variable among all birds (typically 9 to 12, although some, such as albatrosses, have as many as 32) and are related to wing length.

Tertial feathers

The innermost flight feathers of the wing. There are usually three to four tertials. On geese, these are large.

Coverts

Wing coverts are softer than flight feathers and create a smooth surface for the air to flow over the wing.

Scapular feathers

The front part of the folded wing is entirely hidden by scapular feathers that cover the top of the wing when the bird is at rest. They cover the bend of the wing and blend it with the body.

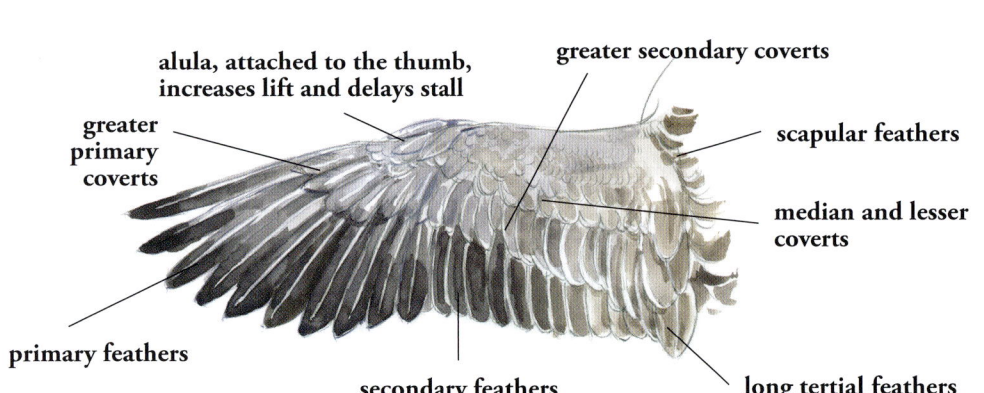

alula, attached to the thumb, increases lift and delays stall

greater secondary coverts

greater primary coverts

scapular feathers

median and lesser coverts

primary feathers

secondary feathers

long tertial feathers

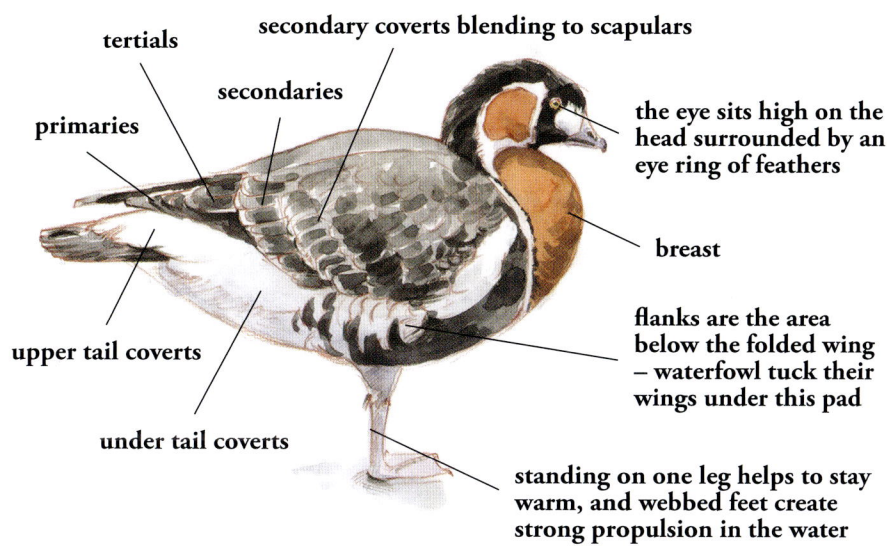

tertials

secondary coverts blending to scapulars

secondaries

primaries

the eye sits high on the head surrounded by an eye ring of feathers

breast

flanks are the area below the folded wing – waterfowl tuck their wings under this pad

upper tail coverts

under tail coverts

standing on one leg helps to stay warm, and webbed feet create strong propulsion in the water

Contour feathers

The contour feathers of a bird are the outer feathers – the ones that you can see. They provide the colour and the shape of the bird. The contour feathers tend to overlap each other, much like tiles on a roof. The feathers tend to shed rain, keeping the body dry and well insulated. The contour feathers used for flight are known as remiges and the tail feathers rectrices.

Tail flight feathers

The tail flight feathers are used as a rudder in the water and in the air, steer, balance and act as a brake for landing.

Bones of the wing

Primaries are the outer wing feathers attached to the bird's small, fused 'hand' bones. Notice that they radiate whereas secondaries run perpendicular to the bone. The tertial feathers are attached to the humerus bone in the bird's upper arm.

Straight wing

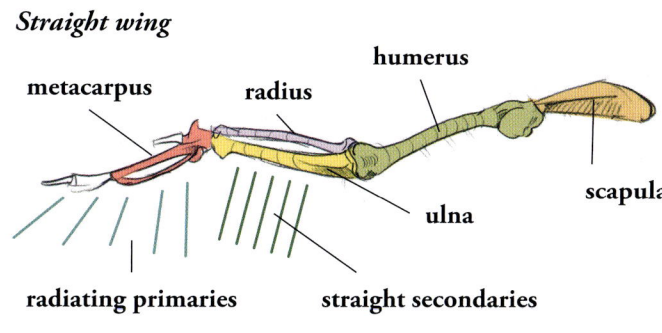

metacarpus

radius

humerus

ulna

scapula

radiating primaries

straight secondaries

Underside view

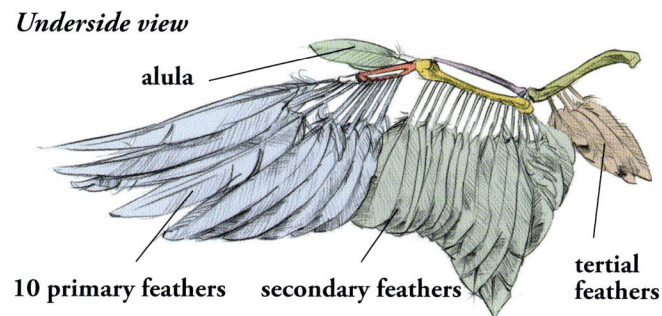

alula

10 primary feathers

secondary feathers

tertial feathers

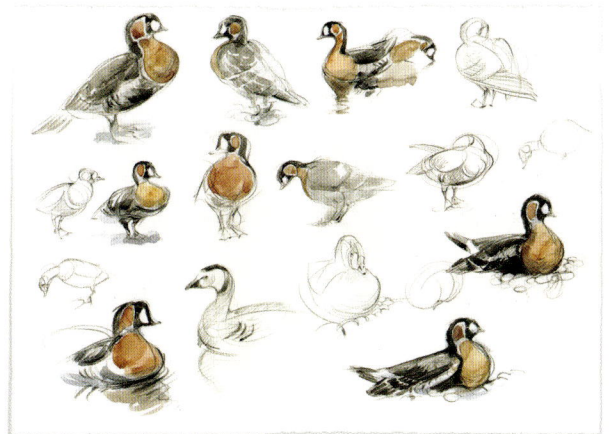

▲ Red-breasted geese study sheet

Sitting on a sketching stool on a sunny afternoon, I began this study sheet with light looping lines. I leave my paintbox on the grass and lean over to mix and load the brush with paint after I have created an initial sketch for guidance. I try to let my understanding of feather tracks show through. I find the line of secondaries a helpful reference point and paint from beak to tail, going from one colour patch to another.

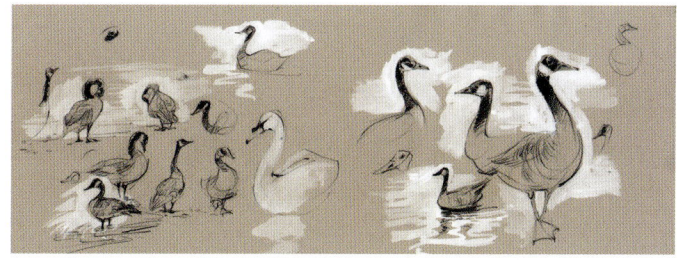

▲ Canada geese on mid-tone paper

Geese are not timid animals and allow you to get quite close. Sunlight danced brilliantly behind the Canada geese, placing them in a halftone silhouette. I allowed the mid-tone of the pastel paper to do the work for me and used White Gouache to create a striking silhouette. I tried to capture whatever they were up to, from meticulous preening of their waterproof feathers with preen oil to courtship displays.

Islands

The boundary of water separating islands keeps both plant and animal species isolated from the rest of the world and potential competition; this can lead to unique evolutionary adaptations. Some islands that are particularly remote, such as the volcanic islands of Hawaii, Papua New Guinea and New Zealand, have evolved their own set of remarkable animals and plants. Islands become testing grounds for the theory of evolution; they are full of evolutionary wonders.

Sometimes it is easy to understand how the ancestors arrived at these new lands: a coconut has a floating husk and can drift in the ocean's currents, a turtle can swim and sea birds can fly there. How other animals made it is more of a game of chance. Once an animal arrives at an island and colonizes it over millions of years, its descendants can adapt to different habitats and take on a different appearance. Indeed, the offspring many generations down the line can become so different both genetically and in appearance that they can be classified as a new species, unable to reproduce with their earlier ancestor.

Island gigantism occurs when animals isolated to an island area grow drastically larger than their relatives on the mainland because there is no significant pressure from predators. The opposite of island gigantism is island dwarfism, where large animals in isolation decrease in size because food and space are limited.

However, islands can be a place of extinction as well as creation. Having evolved from an isolated ancestor and adapted over millennia to their habitat conditions and threats, native species can be vulnerable to any influx of foreign competitors. For example, humans brought pigs, dogs and rats to the island of Mauritius; these animals developed a taste for dodo eggs, which, along with the sailors hunting them, resulted in the eventual extinction of the dodo.

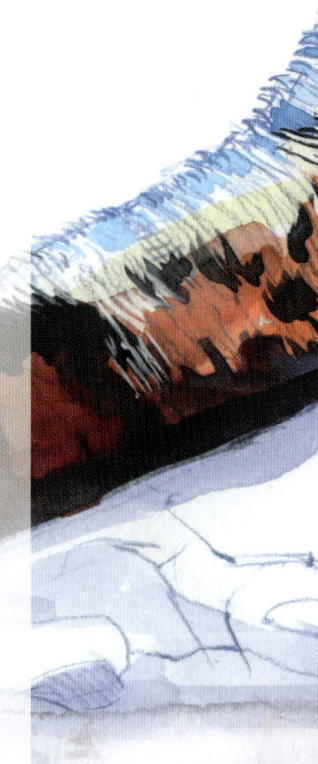

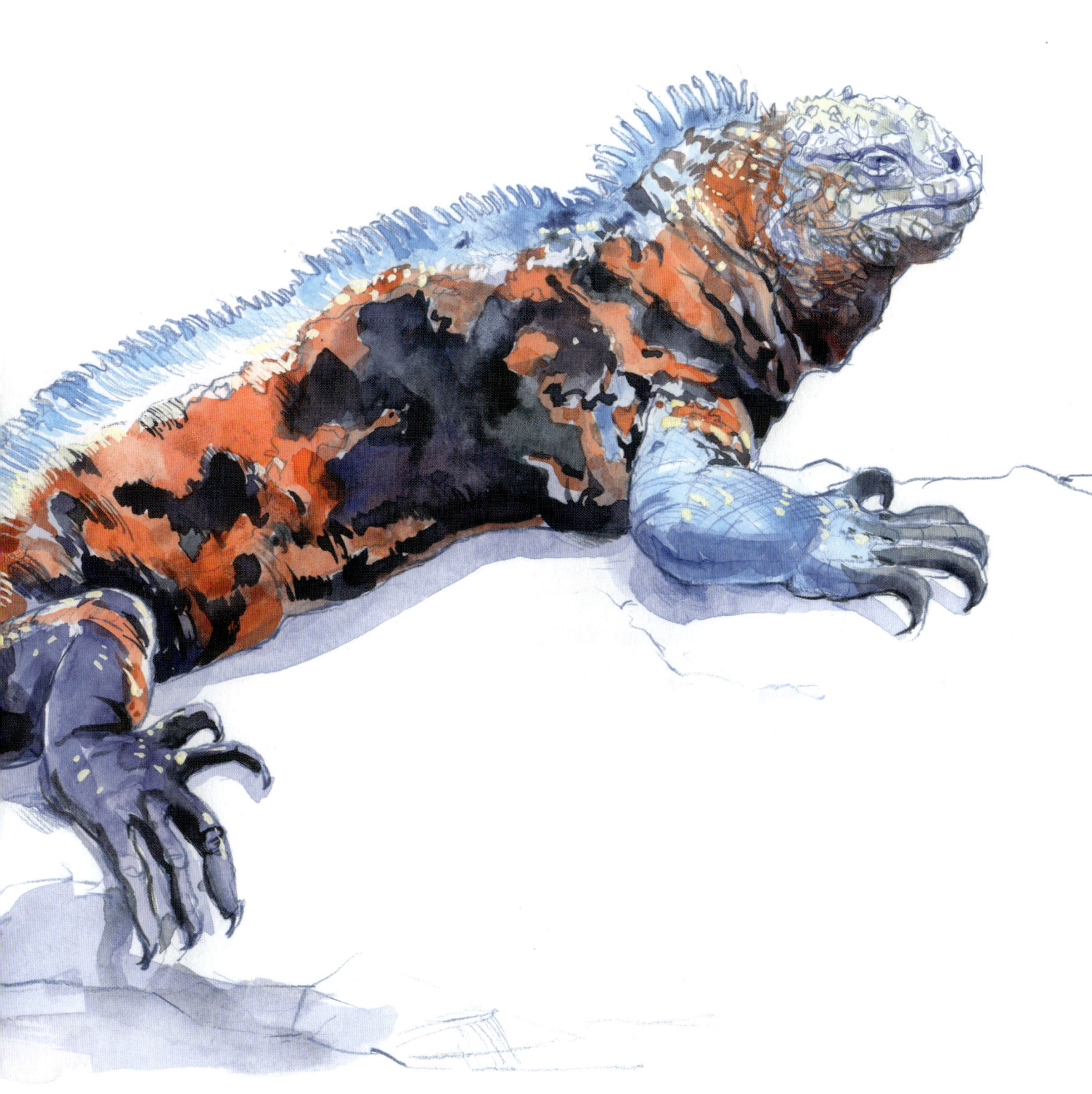

Study Sheet: Domed Giant Tortoise

In the absence of mammal competitors for plant food, several kinds of giant tortoises evolved on the Seychelles, Mascarene and Galápagos islands. 'Galápago' is an old Spanish word for tortoise. When sailors first made it to the Galápagos in the seventeenth century, there were hundreds of thousands of tortoises of around 15 different species, hence the naming of the island after them.

The variety of shapes and sizes of the tortoises' shells helped Charles Darwin, who reached the islands in 1835 aged 22, to solve the riddle of evolution. Each island had a slightly different climate. Darwin noted that tortoises on the more arid islands were smaller with a saddleback shell and a longer neck to reach the nutritious leaves overhead.

Scientists speculate that the giant Galápagos tortoises became established after a breeding pair made a long-distance swim, or floated on vegetation such as a fallen tree, from South America to the islands around two million years ago. The 13 extant species found on the Galápagos islands can be divided into two loose categories: the largest, with big, round shells are called 'domes'; the smaller tortoises which have shells that curl up in front like a saddle are called 'saddle-backs'.

Sadly, the sailors discovered that the tortoises made a tasty meal; so much so, the reason that the giant tortoise wasn't correctly classified by scientists for so long appears to be because they were delicious and no specimens ever made it back to Europe without being eaten on the voyage.

Anatomy

Knowing a little about the anatomy can help you understand what you are looking at and inform your painting.

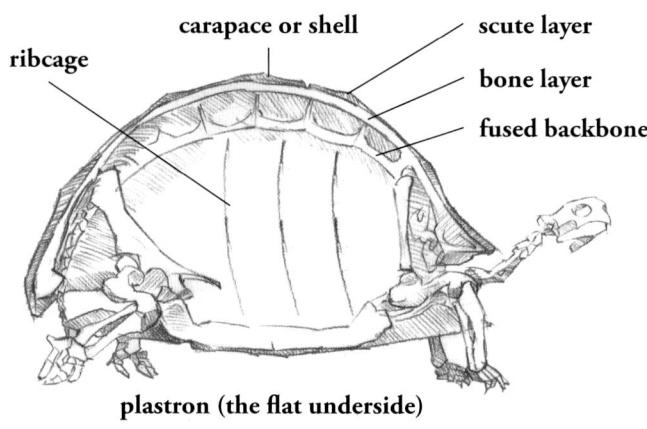

ribcage

carapace or shell

scute layer

bone layer

fused backbone

plastron (the flat underside)

The shell

Tortoises and turtles are unique in the animal kingdom in having a sort of mobile home created of fused scutes, which are bony, rigid plates. Scutes, which provide protection from predators, are also found on reptiles such as crocodiles and on birds' feet. But tortoises and turtles have gone one stage further – their ribs have widened and fused together to create a bulged shell on which the horny scutes wrap around to make up the carapace and plastron underneath. When threatened or resting they retract the soft parts of their body into this keratin shield keeping them out of harm's way.

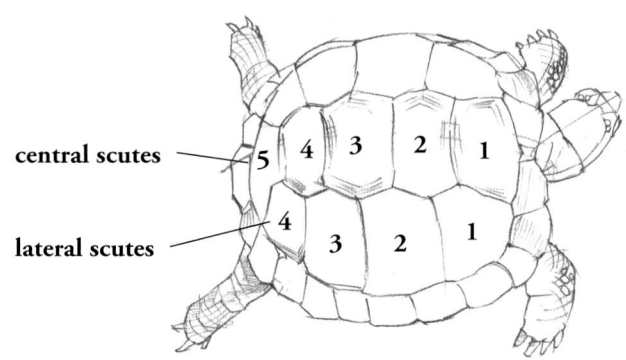

central scutes

5 4 3 2 1

lateral scutes

4 3 2 1

The keel

The keel is made up of central scutes, which commonly amount to five in a single row. However, this can vary in other species and there can be more than a single row.

Claws

Depending on the species, a tortoise can have between three and five claws on each foot.

Beak

Tortoises don't have teeth but a horny beak to snip off vegetation.

Front arms

The front arms are noticeably longer than the back arms so that they can rear up.

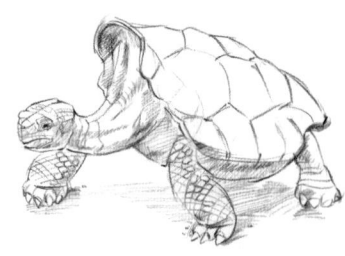

Cerulean Blue

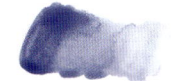

French Ultramarine

Lemon Yellow

Raw Umber

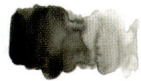

Ivory Black

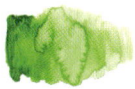

Sap Green

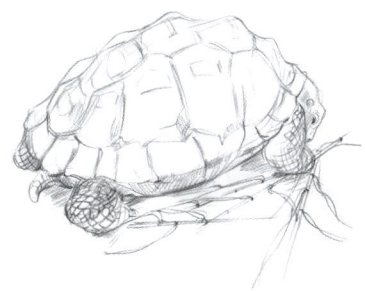

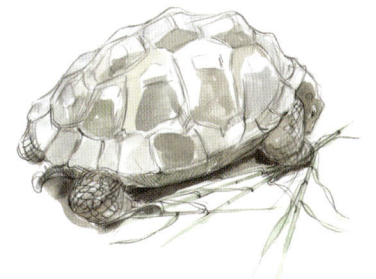

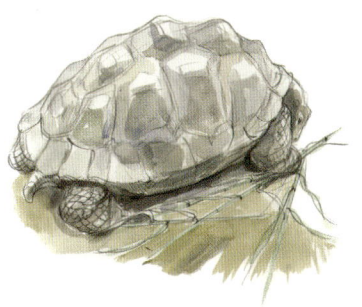

1 *The slower pace of the tortoise means you can relax, take your time and get involved in an on-the-spot study. Sitting so close to the subject enabled me to really get into trying to suggest the pyramiding or raised peaks of the nobbly individual scutes.*

Tip
When I go sketching, I always take a lightweight stool with me as sometimes there is no convenient place to rest a sketchbook.

2 *Next, mix the paints to make the muted olives and smoky greys that camouflage the tortoise with the earth colours. The olive tinge was created with varying combinations of Cerulean Blue, French Ultramarine, Lemon Yellow, Raw Umber and Ivory Black. I included a plant to give a sense of scale, which I captured with a mixture of Lemon Yellow with Sap Green, and used Raw Umber for the dusty ground.*

3 *Finally, accentuate the light source and try to empathize the physicality of the sculptural bulk of the tortoise by developing the shading. Use a French Ultramarine degraded with Raw Umber and a touch of Ivory Black.*

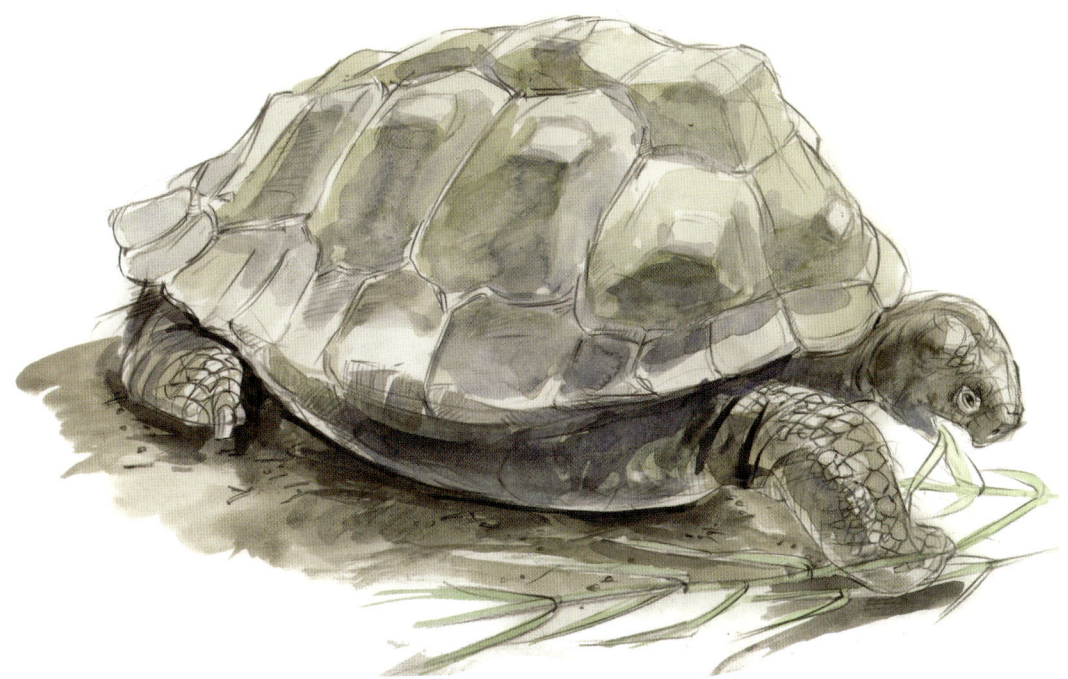

▲ **Galápagos domed giant tortoise**
Zoological Society of London,
London Zoo, UK.

Study Sheet: *Lemur*

Somewhere between 35 and 55 million years ago, a handful of lemur ancestors made their way to the island of Madagascar, perhaps on a fallen tree or floating vegetation with leaves for food. Those that survived this perilous voyage arrived on the beach and made their way inland.

Their descendants diversified as they adapted to their new habitat. From generation to generation, the lemurs evolved different-coloured pelts, perhaps so that they were able to recognize each other. Gradually, the descendants became so unique that they could no longer breed with their earlier, or basal, ancestor and became classed as a new species. With few mammalian predators on the islands (they arrived later) or competitors, lemurs could adapt and occupy a myriad of niches. They have now evolved into some 100 different species. Diet varies between the different lemur species, but each plays a role in Madagascar's rich and varied ecosystems.

Lemurs are primates; their hands and limbs show that they are related to monkeys, apes and us. With their dog-like glistening noses, they are close cousins of bushbabies and lorises, which branched off from the primate's lineage some 60 million years ago. These animals place a greater emphasis on the sense of smell, whereas for apes, monkeys and us, it is sight that plays a more critical role.

Anatomy
Knowing a little about the anatomy can help you understand what you are looking at and inform your painting.

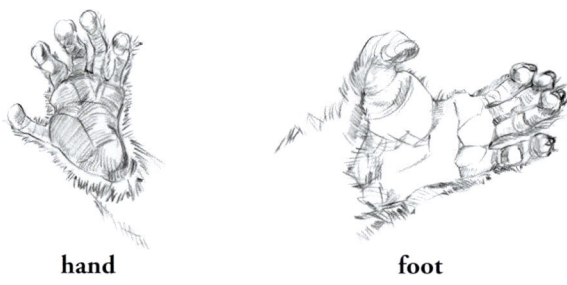

hand   foot

Hands and feet
A lemur's hands and feet have evolved to grasp branches.

Scent brushes
The long tails help balance and also act as scent brushes. Male ring-tailed lemurs wipe scents from glands on their tail and wave it at rivals, known as a 'stink war'.

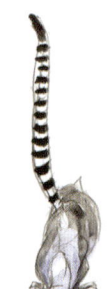

Eyes
All lemurs have forward-facing eyes creating binocular vision to help them navigate their arboreal habitats.

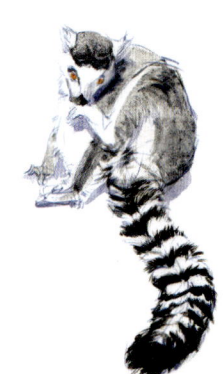

Legs
Long hind legs are perfect for creating long leaps between the trees.

Bones
Knowing the bones can give your drawing structure and the feeling that the legs are supporting weight.

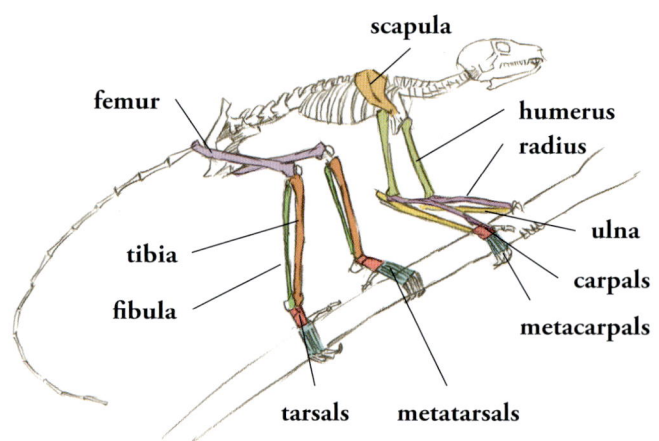

French Ultramarine

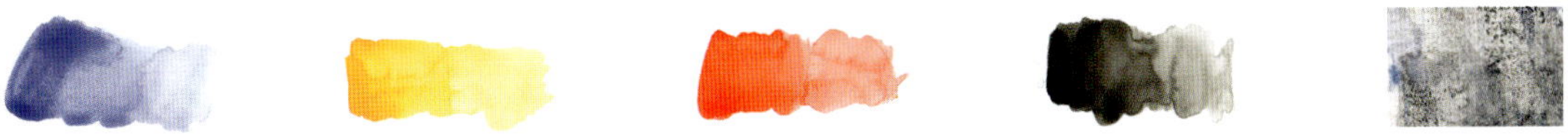

Cadmium Yellow

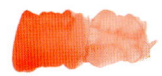
Cadmium Red

Ivory Black

Granulation medium

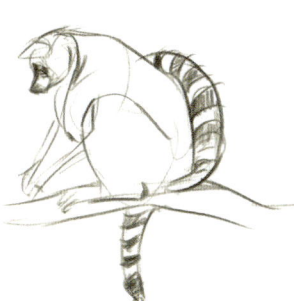

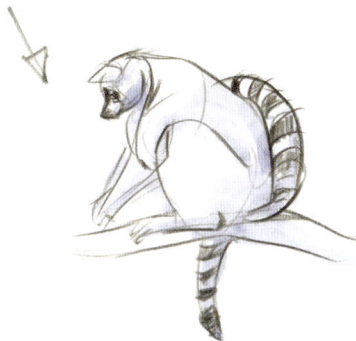

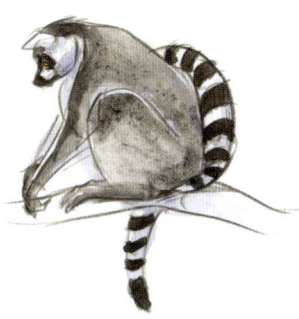

1 I started by creating a series of lively sketches in a ring-tailed lemur enclosure at London Zoo in the UK, attempting to capture many different body positions and gestures. The early drawings help me familiarize myself with their characteristics, including a projecting muzzle, tufty white ears and long hind legs. Take photographs too, so that you can work back at home.

2 Working from the photographs, use a light wash of French Ultramarine to capture areas of the pelt in the shade, and Cadmium Yellow and Cadmium Red for the orange egg yolk-coloured eyes.

3 Ring-tailed lemur pelts are grey to rosy-brown on the shoulders (although the troop I sketched were all grey) with a darker skull cap and arms. Their face and underbelly are white with dark triangular eye patches and a black nose. Ring-tailed lemurs' tails are ringed with 13 alternating black-and-white bands, which I don't count but just create an impression of. I find a granulation medium (see page 27) is particularly helpful in capturing the pelt's texture.

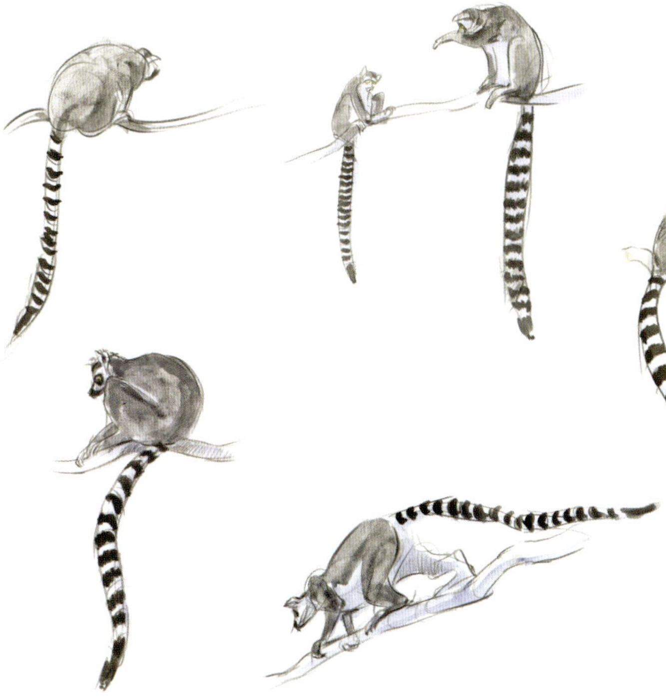

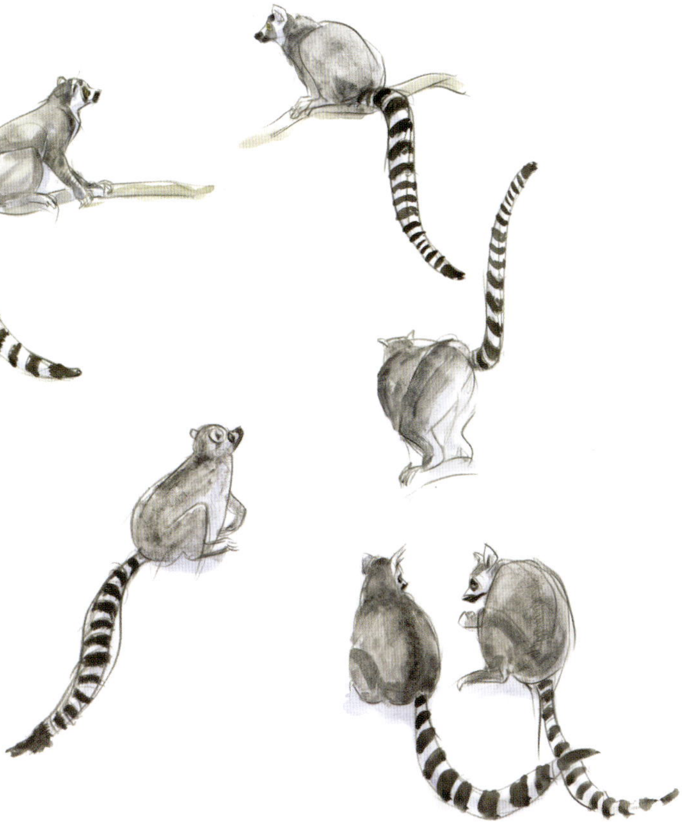

▶ **Lemur study sheet**
Ring-tailed lemurs live in intimate groups called troops of between 6 and 30 individuals with a dominant female who presides overall. Unlike most lemur species, ring-tails spend a lot of time on the ground, where they forage for fallen fruit, leaves, flowers, insects and small vertebrates.

Study Sheet: *Kakapo*

For me, the kakapo is the most endearing parrot of them all, and it is the only flightless one. Evolving on the isolated island of New Zealand, where there were few natural terrestrial predators, nature has conjured a unique set of adaptations. On islands, we can often see evolution at its most creative, and the kakapo combines characteristics seen in a woodpecker's feet and an owl's face.

Before the arrival of humans in pre-Polynesian times, the kakapo was New Zealand's third most common bird and thrived throughout the three main islands. However, when the first settlers arrived, they brought cats, weasels and rats, devastating the populations of the slow, flightless birds. By the 1970s, the general population consisted of around just 18 individuals. However, in the 1980s, the New Zealand Department of Conservation implemented a Kakapo Recovery Plan, and there are now thought to be about 200 in the wild on four remote islands, which still makes them critically endangered.

Kakapos are herbivores, meaning they eat plants, and they are nocturnal, roosting during the day and only becoming active at night. The kakapo's powerful legs make it an excellent hiker, and they move around with a jog-like gait, albeit slowly. They are also excellent climbers and use their wings to 'parachute' to the forest floor. Kakapos, like owls, from which its scientific name derives, have a facial disc that funnels sound to the ears. This helps them to make sense of a very dark world.

The kakapo's anatomy has evolved in the absence of many serious predators. This means it can afford to be big and easier to see, giving it the benefit of being able to travel further and last longer without food and water. Mature adults can grow to over 1½ft (0.5 m) in length and weigh up to 9lb (4 kg).

On adopting a ground-based lifestyle, the flying wings of the parrot ancestor, which became isolated when New Zealand broke off from Gondwana around 82 million years ago, did not evolve large enough to support its weight.

The kakapo has an acute sense of smell to help navigate at night, and they also have a musty-sweet odour to find each other. Unfortunately, this trait helps mammalian predators find them too.

Anatomy

Knowing a little about the anatomy can help you understand what you are looking at and inform your painting.

Wings and feathers

The forest-dwelling parrot's feathers are a moss green mottled with yellow and black specks to help them blend in with the undergrowth. This kept the kakapo hidden from the carnivorous birds which were its original predators.

Small wings

Although the kakapo has lost the ability to fly it still uses its wing to balance when climbing along branches. It can also make a controlled fall from up to 17ft (5m) high with outstretched wings.

Primary feathers

As with most flying birds, the primaries stay in a triangular shape behind a row of secondaries when the bird is stationary.

Scapula feathers

Scapula feathers cascade over where the wing joins to the body almost obscuring the entire wing.

Posture

The typical posture of a kakapo is a horizontal position with its bill nearly touching the ground scanning for food.

Head

The bowl-like facial disc, similar to an owl's or a satellite disc, focuses sound to the ears.

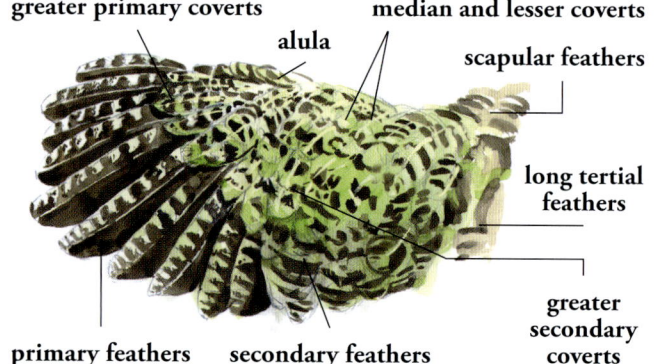

greater primary coverts
alula
median and lesser coverts
scapular feathers
long tertial feathers
greater secondary coverts
primary feathers
secondary feathers

Stout beak

The large, stout beak has a sharp, ridged lower bill with an underbite that can cut through tough plant material. Bristle-like feathers at the base of the beak help the kakapo feel its environment in low light.

Feet

Kakapo have four-toed feet, similar to a woodpecker's, with two toes facing forwards and two facing backwards; they are great for climbing branches and tree trunks.

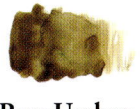

Sap Green

Lemon Yellow

Yellow Ochre

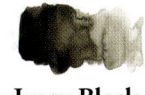

Cadmium Red

French Ultramarine

White Gauache

Raw Umber

Ivory Black

Bones

Knowing the bones can give your drawing structure and the feeling that the legs are supporting weight.

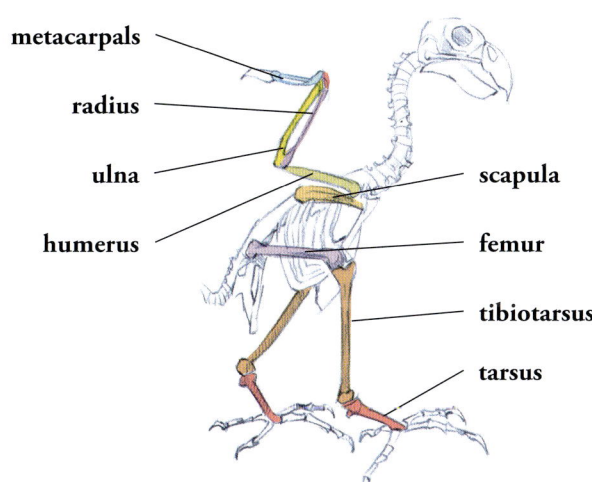

metacarpals

radius

ulna

humerus

scapula

femur

tibiotarsus

tarsus

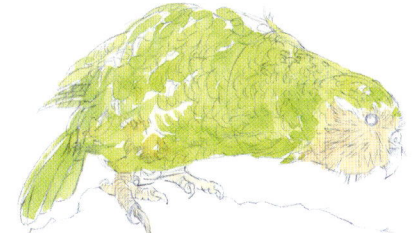

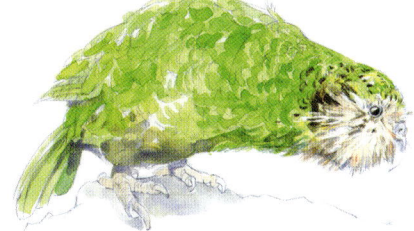

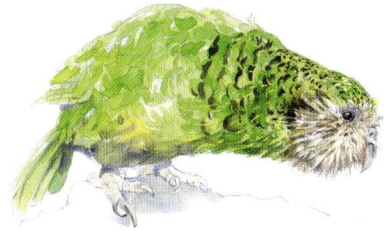

1 *Working from a photograph, begin by creating an initial sketch. I use a dark blue Polychromos pencil. Lay in the lightest and brightest colours – a Sap Green modulated with a Lemon Yellow for the body and a mixture of Yellow Ochre and Cadmium Red for the facial disc.*

2 *Next, embolden the colours with a more saturated wash. Model the form with a French Ultramarine and place in the cast shadow at the feet. Start adding detail with smaller brushes.*

3 *Next, try to capture the feather's rachis with a fine brush and a mixture of Lemon Yellow with White Gouache. Mix Raw Umber with Ivory Black to capture the mottled pattern.*

4 *Continue to add in the fine detail on the feathers and the feet until the painting is complete.*

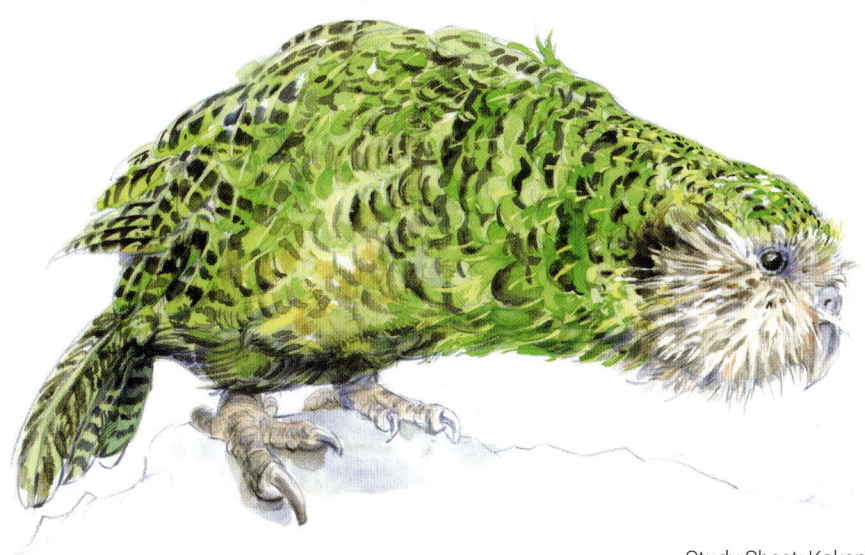

Index

First published 2022 by
Guild of Master Craftsman Publications Ltd
Castle Place, 166 High Street, Lewes,
East Sussex BN7 1XU

ISBN 978 1 78494 639 5

A catalogue record for this book is available from the British Library.

Publisher Jonathan Bailey
Production Director Jim Bulley
Senior Project Editor Dominique Page
Managing Art Editor Robin Shields

Colour origination by GMC Reprographics
Printed and bound in China

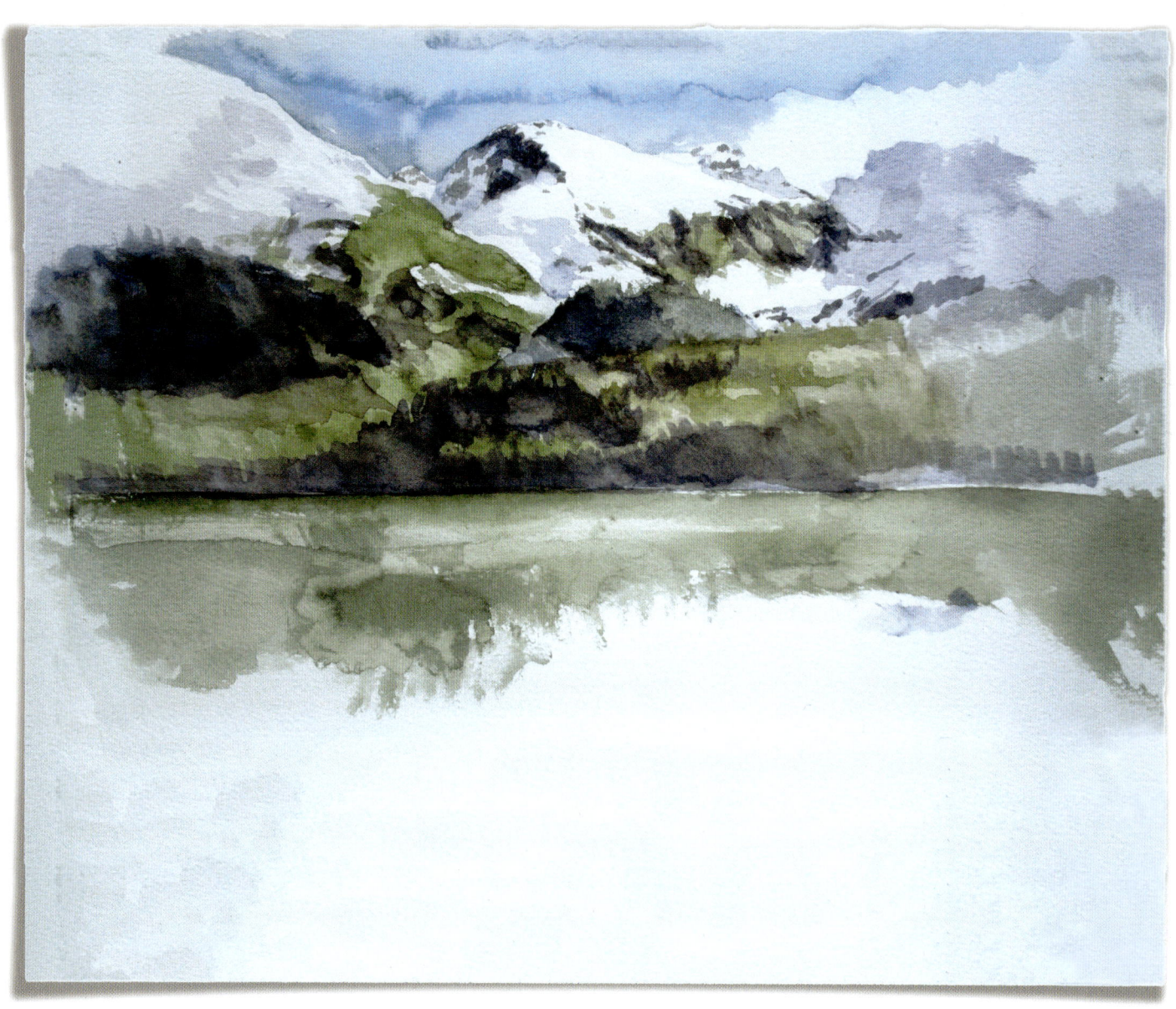

To place an order, contact:

GMC Publications Ltd
Castle Place, 166 High Street,
Lewes, East Sussex,
BN7 1XU
United Kingdom
Tel: +44 (0)1273 488005
www.gmcbooks.com